BRACE FOR IMPACT

BRACE
FOR
IMPACT

A MEMOIR

GABE
MONTESANTI

THE DIAL PRESS / NEW YORK

Brace for Impact is a work of memoir. It is a true story faithfully based on the author's best recollections of various events in her life. In some instances, events and time periods have been compressed or reordered in service of the narrative and dialogue approximated to match the author's best recollections of those exchanges. Some names and identifying details of certain people mentioned in the book have been changed. Pronouns used are each individual's confirmed pronouns at the time of writing and otherwise default to they/them/theirs.

Copyright © 2022 by Gabrielle Montesanti

Published in the United States by The Dial Press, an imprint of Random House, a division of Penguin Random House LLC, New York.

THE DIAL PRESS is a registered trademark and the colophon is a trademark of Penguin Random House LLC.

Portions of this work, sometimes in different form, were published in *Boulevard Magazine, Brevity: A Journal of Concise Literary Nonfiction, Hobart,* and *Just Femme & Dandy.*

Library of Congress Cataloging-in-Publication Data

Names: Montesanti, Gabe, author.
Title: Brace for impact: a memoir / Gabe Montesanti.
Description: First edition. | New York: The Dial Press, 2022.
Identifiers: LCCN 2021016592 (print) |
LCCN 2021016593 (ebook) | ISBN 9780593241370 (hardcover) |
ISBN 9780593241387 (ebook)
Subjects: LCSH: Montesanti, Gabe. | Women roller skaters—
United States—Biography. | Lesbians—United States—
Biography. | Psychologically abused children—United
States—Biography. | Sports injuries—Patients—United States—
Biography. | Roller derby—Social aspects—United States.
Classification: LCC GV858.22.M66 A3 2022 (print) |
LCC GV858.22.M66 (ebook) | DDC 796.21092 [B]—dc23
LC record available at lccn.loc.gov/2021016592
LC ebook record available at lccn.loc.gov/2021016593

Printed in Canada on acid-free paper

randomhousebooks.com

9 8 7 6 5 4 3 2 1

First Edition

TO KELLY

CONTENTS

PART I

1 / RECRUIT NIGHT   3

2 / RITUAL   21

3 / ATTENTION   35

4 / PELVIS BREASTLY   51

5 / FRESH MEAT   65

6 / DERBY MOM   79

7 / HITTING ZONE   95

8 / THE ROOKIE RUMBLE   112

9 / BAD BLOOD   121

10 / THE HAPPIEST SEASON   137

11 / OLD HABITS   152

PART II

12 / ABOUT A MILLION JOANS   167

13 / DRAFT NIGHT   181

14 / DEDICATED AS FUCK   206

15 / THE ENEMY   218

16 / BREAK   238

PART III

17 / LITTLE MOVEMENTS   265

18 / BAGGAGE   283

19 / ONE OF US   298

20 / TEST OF TOUGHNESS   308

21 / DEPARTURES   322

22 / SPLITTING   329

23 / RED TENT   339

24 / BABY STEPS   348

25 / THE WORLDWIDE ROLLER DERBY CONVENTION   366

26 / JOAN OF SPARK   388

ACKNOWLEDGMENTS   403

PART I

1/
RECRUIT NIGHT

From the outside, the St. Louis Skatium seemed just as abandoned as the surrounding buildings. The strip looked like a stage set, all peeling paint and muted colors. There was a FOR LEASE sign hanging crookedly in the window of Kleb Clothing and Shoe Company; both the neighboring storefronts were boarded up. The BUSCH BEER sign hanging from an empty bar was coated in rust and cobwebs. Beside Tucker's Bar & Grill, two old men wearing overalls and yellow gloves were rooting through a dumpster.

Kelly and I surveyed the roller rink from our old Corolla. We had never been to South City before and had no idea what to expect. The building's exterior, a flat, white façade with dull red accents, held no indication we had come to the right place. I'm not sure what I was expecting: something that looked more like the roller rinks of my childhood, perhaps. Kid-friendly graphics painted in bright colors on the walls. A tall roller skate with wings displayed on the roof. A sign would've helped me feel less intimidated—ROLLER DERBY RECRUIT NIGHT or FUTURE SKATERS ENTER HERE. Even HOME OF ARCH RIVAL ROLLER DERBY would have put me at ease; instead, there was only HAP Y BIR HD Y JULIA 7, the missing letters all resting upside down at the bottom of the plastic showcase.

"Are you nervous?" Kelly asked. "Because I'm not even interested in derby and I'm nervous for you."

"Nah," I lied. Then I said, "We should probably go in." But neither of us made a move.

When I was fifteen, my dad took me and my sister, Cam, on a tour of all the places he and my mother used to frequent in the early days of their relationship. We were in Denver visiting my dad's parents; perhaps the absence of my mother, who had stayed home in Michigan, allowed us to experience a rare collective feeling of missing, even romanticizing, her presence. First, we drove past the Grease Monkey, where my parents had first met. Mom came in for an oil change and Dad was her mechanic; we don't know exactly what happened after that, but my sister and I loved to speculate about the initial attraction. Was it her dark eyes? His crooked smile? It was hard to imagine a time when they might have been passionate with each other. Although they stayed married, the sole affection we saw between them was a quick kiss in church before Communion. The only detail I know for certain about that time is that my dad couldn't drive my mom on dates because his license had been revoked for drag racing. This was a particularly juicy piece of intel: his youthful recklessness, his passion. I was proud of him, in a twisted kind of way, for getting in trouble, since it was so uncharacteristic of the quiet, pious man I knew him to be.

When we pulled up to the house they lived in when I was born, we didn't get out of the car. I wondered if I'd have an emotional connection to the house, but when I looked at it, I felt nothing at all. The roof was flat as a ballroom; it was essentially a small box on a shady corner of two unremarkable streets.

"That's it?" Cam asked. Even at ten, she was hard to impress.

Dad tapped on the steering wheel absentmindedly. I could tell he was toying with the idea of knocking on the door and asking the current occupants if we could take a look around.

"It'd be nice to show you your old room," he said. There was a pause; the car was still running.

I understood my dad's apprehension. If we knocked, we might be able to go in—but we'd also face the possibility of rejection; whoever opened the door would have all the power. My dad pushed open the glove compartment, removed a yellow cloth, and began wiping down the dashboard, which he always did when he was nervous. Maybe the thought of being inside our old home was frightening to him, I remember thinking. What if it looked completely different? What if it looked the same, and flooded him with memories of a time when our family hadn't yet done so much damage to each other?

"Are we going in or what?" Cam asked. I cringed, wishing she had let my dad linger in the possibility a bit longer. Her question seemed to snap him out of his reverie. We sat for a moment longer, then drove off. We never spoke about it again.

"LET'S GO," I told Kelly, and got out of the car.

The walk up to the Skatium was flanked by a black chain-link fence blocking off a neighboring bus station. In places, the chain had broken away from the poles anchoring it to the ground, and it had twisted up toward the sky. Several men in navy blue jumpsuits on the other side of the fence were smoking cigarettes and laughing.

The air was thick and wet inside the Skatium. We had to push through a cloud of pot smoke to fully enter; the stink of weed tangled with that of body odor. On the track were purple benches arranged campfire-style around a cooler of beer. About a dozen people, who I presumed to be other recruits, were already perched there chatting. They ran the gamut in terms of age and appearance; I felt curious about what had brought everyone here.

Stepping onto the track to join them was daunting; the surface was white, and for a brief instant I mistook it for ice. In some places, the wood had been stripped. In others, the track was warped and uneven. Small beams of light were shining onto the Skatium floor, reminding me of mornings in my childhood parish when the crucifix was perfectly il-luminated. But unlike at church, where big windows were the source of light, the light flooding the Skatium was the result of holes in the roof. The ceiling was skeletal—barnlike, with crisscrossing wooden beams. Buckets, half-filled with rainwater, dangled from the rafters, and a disco ball hung in the center.

On the sidelines, an elderly woman was vacuuming. Her hair was long and stringy, her body shaped like a question mark. After a few seconds of observation, I realized she was running the vacuum over the same strip of carpet again and again. She must have been gripping tightly, because her knuckles were white; the hand not occupied with vacuum-ing was clenching a fistful of her baggy T-shirt as if to wring it dry.

"That's slightly eerie," I whispered to Kelly. She nodded emphatically.

We took our seat on the purple benches beside another recruit, a butch woman who introduced herself as Alice. She noticed us staring at the vacuuming lady and said, "This place is fucking crazy, isn't it?" Encouraged by our nodding, Alice leaned closer so the other recruits couldn't hear. "I used to come skate here as a kid. Been here a lot over the years. I've sometimes wondered if it's a drug den. My guess is meth."

"Are you fucking serious?" I said.

"How do you know?" Kelly asked. As usual, she wanted facts.

Alice simply gestured to the woman, who was done vacuuming her swatch of carpet and had moved on to wiping down the Coke machine and old arcade games. She wiped the surface of the pinball machine but didn't touch the handles. The sea of stuffed animals and rubber balls underneath the dangling metal claw was covered with a fine layer of dust, but the woman either didn't notice or didn't care. She had a way of walking that looked more like hovering; she disappeared and reappeared with such regularity I became convinced she could float through the walls.

We continued watching the woman for a few minutes as the other recruits trickled in. Alice stuck her arm into the cooler of beer and offered one to Kelly and me.

"You all need to drink more shitty beer!" an approaching woman shouted. "And I'm the one in charge so you have to do what I say!"

The woman was breathtaking. She had a tuft of blue hair and was wearing an exorbitant amount of makeup. Her eyelids were coated in gold glitter, and each eye was framed by a perfect wing. Her lips matched her hair and the blush of her cheeks. On her left arm was a large, unfinished tattoo of a wolf woman. Her right leg bore a hand-sized heart pierced by a dagger and the words KEEP ROLLIN. Though I loved all her ink, what I admired most about the woman was her clothing: she had hacked her jersey into a crop top and wore cheetah-print hot pants that more closely resembled under-wear than shorts. My mother, who surely would have tried to recruit this woman to her Weight Watchers class, always emphasized that women bigger than a size six should cover up, hide themselves, and work hard to get thin, but clearly this woman didn't subscribe to that philosophy.

I recognized the name on the back of the woman's jersey: Soup Beans. We had traded emails; I had asked questions about Recruit Night and offered more information than was probably necessary about my background. Seeing Soup Beans in person made me feel embarrassed and shy about everything I had disclosed. ("I was a competitive swimmer from fourth grade through college, and I really just miss being part of a team.") She had responded that roller derby could probably fill that hole.

"Listen up, sweet baby angels," Soup Beans said, clapping her hands. "Tonight we'll low-key get to know each other and casually ask some questions while we watch derby. The main purpose is for you to experience the action! Who here has seen roller derby live before?"

A smattering of hands went up, including mine. I had gone with a friend in college to see the Killamazoo Derby Darlins. We had no idea what we were watching; to us, it just looked like a street brawl. Still, I was captivated. I couldn't imagine coming to a Recruit Night if I had never seen a live bout before. Kelly's was one of the hands that stayed down, but I made an exception for her since she didn't want to play and was only here to support me. It was surprising, though, that I had experienced something she hadn't. Kelly was four years older than me and had witnessed a lot in her twenty-six years: drag shows at LaCage in downtown Milwaukee, the New York Philharmonic at Carnegie Hall, bullfighting in Madrid. I felt proud that I had seen one small part of the world she hadn't.

Soup Beans reached into the rainbow tote bag draped over her shoulder. It said BE A SLUT. DO WHATEVER YOU WANT. Grinning, I poked Kelly in the ribs to draw her attention to the bag. From the tote, Soup Beans removed a stack of bumper stickers and fanned them out before all the new recruits.

"Here," she said. "Take one. We need to get rid of these."

Kelly and I examined our stickers. It was just the Arch Rival logo I had seen online: the Gateway Arch with Harley-Davidson-like wings and a single wheel underneath.

"We're rebranding," Soup Beans said. "We're not Arch Rival Roller Girls anymore. We're Arch Rival Roller *Derby*. More inclusive. You know, for the skaters who aren't boys or girls." Several people on the bench next to me started clapping, and Soup Beans took a bow. Kelly whispered into my ear, "Toto, I don't think we're in Kansas anymore." And she was right. I had never been part of an organization that acknowledged or prioritized LGBTQ rights. It made me want to plaster my car with Arch Rival bumper stickers.

Soup Beans directed our attention to the track, where a horde of skaters were just starting warm-ups. "As I mentioned, we'll be watching some scrimmages tonight!" Soup Beans said. "Love me some scrim scram. Pay attention to what they're doing out there while I go get some more benches."

There were close to fifty skaters on the track. Some swung their arms in circles. Others balanced on one skate and shook out their other leg. One was wearing anatomical leggings that made her look like a cadaver from the waist down. All of the wheels made the floor vibrate, and their stopping caused long, screeching noises like hawks. To Kelly's delight, lots of skaters had their names on the side of their helmets. Every time she found one particularly amusing, she would nudge me discreetly and point. "Her name is Snotface," she whispered. "Oh my god—Jamheiser Bush."

Although I felt incredibly awkward about meeting all these new people and unsure if I should make small talk with the other recruits during warm-up, I was glad Kelly seemed to be having such a good time. Her stack of crosswords— a permanent artifact in her purse—sat untouched in her lap. On the way to the Skatium, she told me she had filled out ten new job applications that day and this was her reward. Even though we both identified as introverts, I could tell the social isolation of job searching was getting to Kelly. Her only interaction with people besides me was her Saturday night volunteer ushering gig at the Fox Theater, which she had found soon after we'd moved to St. Louis four months earlier, at the end of May. She didn't even care that she was the youngest usher by nearly forty years.

Occasionally, someone would break away from the track and barrel over to where we were sitting. The skaters we met this way kept their introductions brief. "Ginger Assassin. I play for the M80s," one said, extending her knuckles for a fist bump. A woman with a long blue braid dropped to her knees, plastic pads clapping like hooves on the wood, and slid to a stop in front of me. "Rock Slobster. Smashinistas' captain. Happy you're here." There was something military in the way she spoke—clipped, not in full sentences, anything nonessential boiled away—but there was an unmistakable warmth in her eyes and the way she smiled, a mouth guard blocking all her teeth like an orange slice.

Soup Beans eventually shooed the skaters away and asked for our attention. "While they're warming up, I want to hear from you," she said. "Just your name, pronouns, and how you found out about roller derby."

The first woman to introduce herself, Birdsong, was a transfer. She was blond and tattooed and looked to be in her mid-twenties. "I just moved back home from South America and I'm looking forward to learning the rules in English," she explained. "My league in Chile was pretty lax; we just kind of hit however we wanted."

I began to worry that I would be the only true beginner, but the woman who went next said she hadn't skated in thirty years. She'd seen a van on the highway with information about Recruit Night painted on the windows. Soup Beans clapped and began jumping up and down. She turned and called to one of the skaters warming up. "Dad Bod! Dad Bod! Our windows worked!" She pointed a perfectly manicured nail back at the recruit. "This dreamboat is here 'cause she saw our windows!"

Two other recruits confirmed that they too had seen the van on the freeway, which only heightened Soup Beans's excitement. She didn't fully calm down until Alice stated that the movie *Whip It* was the reason she had come to Roller Derby Recruit Night.

"I need you all to know that modern roller derby is nothing like *Whip It*," Soup Beans said. "Well, it's a little bit like *Whip It*. I mean, I joined a million years ago because I wanted to drink and wear hot pants. But the rules are nothing like in that movie. And you can't just punch a bitch in the face any-more."

Alice was visibly disappointed. "But it's still full contact, right?" she asked. "Like, what if I punch a bitch in the face by accident?"

Soup Beans pursed her lips. "Look, if any of you are here because you want to punch somebody in the face, leave now." She paused dramatically to see if anyone would get up; I averted my eyes. "Good," Soup Beans finally said. "And besides, in the first six months, none of you will be able to control your bodies enough to throw punches anyway. You're all gonna be flappy-armed loose cannons, and nobody is going to want to skate within arm's reach of you."

None of the remaining six recruits mentioned *Whip It,* but the woman sitting on the track below Alice said she had come because she had the perfect roller derby name, which also irritated Soup Beans. "So like, I'm a cosmetologist right," she said, smacking her bubble gum. "And suddenly it just came to me. *Blades of Glory.* Wouldn't that just be the best roller derby name? Blades for short? Do you get it? Cause I'm a hairdresser?"

Some of the other recruits laughed, but when Blades wasn't looking, I saw Soup Beans roll her eyes, fluttering her eyelids for dramatic effect.

Kelly didn't even offer her name when it was her turn. "I'm just here for moral support," she said, nodding at me. "I don't want to skate or anything."

Then all eyes were on me. I felt suddenly nauseous—unsure how much information to give. I said my name and repeated what I had written in my email exchange with Soup Beans. It seemed important to justify my presence with my decade-long sports history, even though I knew the skill set I developed as a competitive swimmer probably wouldn't translate at all to this game. What I didn't say was that I couldn't stand to look at the water anymore, not after my disastrous last college season. That I'd only played individual sports and worried I wouldn't know how to fit into a team. That I needed a physical activity I wouldn't turn into a weight loss regimen. What I didn't say was that I had just moved to St. Louis and was desperately lonely for a community, queer friendship, and something fun that felt as far away from my hometown as possible.

"And how did you find out about derby?" Soup Beans asked, eyebrows raised.

The truth was a derby player had approached me shortly after I had left home in a hurry (hoping Kelly would let me stay). Kelly was studying math at Bowling Green State University, and I arrived one day with everything I owned. "How long will you stay here?" Kelly had asked me. I knew she wasn't being rude—she was a pragmatist, always blunt in assessments and questioning. I told her I didn't know, but I knew I would not be moving back home. While Kelly was at class, I'd go to the coffee shop around the corner, and I was in line one morning when a woman who was visibly queer—something I was not yet used to seeing, and which gave me a jolt of admiration and envy—struck up a conversation with me. It turned out she was on the Glass City Rollers, a roller league based in Toledo. She said I looked like the kind of gal who could be a big threat on the track; I wished I knew what it was about me that gave her that impression. Still, our encounter had the effect of making me immediately enamored with the sport and those who played it.

That was way too much, I knew, to convey to a group of strangers. The long pause I had taken was already bloated and uncomfortable; I felt a familiar nervous tingling in my stomach. Was I being questioned more than the others? Could they sense how badly I wanted this Recruit Night to go well? Was this just a friendly way of trying to get to know me?

"I don't really know how I found derby," I lied. "Kelly and I just moved to St. Louis. I guess I've been thinking about joining a team for a while."

"Did you move here for work?" Alice asked.

"Graduate school," I said, shyly. "I'm in the writing program at Washington University." I thought about adding that my undergrad degree was in mathematics and art, but it seemed unnecessary and slightly pompous. They didn't need to know that I chose math only because I thought a STEM major was a guaranteed career. Plus, Kelly worked in the math center: an easy way to get close to her when we were still building our relationship. Art was where I really excelled. I made huge pieces with pressed flowers and leaves, cyanotypes and old-fashioned medium-format Holga prints: once I even ditched my canvas and painted Kelly's body instead.

Soup Beans pointed to an older woman, maybe fifty, who was skating by herself on the side of the track. On the back of her helmet, purple stickers spelled out her name: NANNY MCWHEE.

"Nanny's a professor," Soup Beans said. "I forget what she teaches. I know she's fluent in at least one other language. She has a fucking PhD! You should go ask her about it and talk about smart-people shit."

I smiled meekly, and Kelly reached for my hand. I was always uncomfortable with labels associated with my education. One of my mother's greatest achievements had been the day she called in to an NPR segment on "surviving in

America without a college education." I was too young to remember it, but she spoke of it often, and I always felt a sense of pride on her and my dad's behalf. After I graduated from college, my mother once approached me while I was trying to grind coffee beans for my dad and reprimanded me for not knowing how to use the machine. "You're college educated now!" she said. "There's no reason you shouldn't know how to do this." In her mind, college inevitably led to wealth, which she resented in any form. She once rearranged the Nativity scene I had set up at Christmastime, shifting the Three Kings out of the barn with Mary and Jesus to make room for the livestock. "These rich men don't deserve a front-row seat," she said. My diploma and the status it represented made me feel like one of those tiny kings, looking in on a family in which I felt I'd never really belong.

I checked my watch. I knew the agenda for Recruit Night was to watch a full scrimmage, but I had no idea how long that would take, and I only had twenty minutes left before I needed to leave to get back to campus. As though reading my mind, Soup Beans directed our attention back to the track. I was surprised by the presence of officials. On the backs of their jerseys were their own funny names—Ninja Sass'em, Code Adam, and Chopsaw. Before the first whistle, the officials gathered in the middle of the track for a meeting; it appeared they were divvying up their positions.

When there were thirty seconds left before the first whistle, five blue and five red players skated onto the track. One from each team wore a helmet cover with a big star on it and lined up behind all the other players. I knew enough from watching footage online to identify them as the jammers— the only skaters who could score points for their teams. The other eight players on the track were blockers, and their job was to prevent the opposing side's jammer from getting through the pack.

With twenty seconds left, Soup Beans said, "All right, y'all. Your job is to watch carefully. On the jammers' first pass, they don't score any points, but whoever gets through first is the lead jammer, which is a huge advantage because the lead jammer can decide when the jam is over. For every subsequent pass through the pack, they score a point for every person on the opposing team they pass."

Blades of Glory raised her hand. "So there's no ball?"

I cringed at her ignorance. Soup Beans ignored her question entirely.

When one of the officials shouted, "Five seconds!" all the blockers crouched low. I heard them talking to each other. "She's looking in," one said. "Now she's looking middle." I didn't know what that meant, but I guessed it had to do with the jammer's position on the track. They were trying to pinpoint her route through the blockers in order to stop her.

While Kelly was completely engrossed in the action, the recruit standing above me tapped me on the shoulder. I couldn't remember their name, but I recalled that they used to roller skate as a kid and used they/them pronouns.

"Do you want a beer?" I asked, gesturing to the cooler in front of me.

"Nah," they said. "I was just wondering how you and your girlfriend met."

"Oh," I said, tearing my eyes away from the track to return their gaze. "Our college swim team. She was a senior captain when I was a freshman. She likes to say she's a cradle robber."

"Funny," they said, pushing a stray piece of hair behind their ear. "I'm hoping I can meet somebody here."

I glanced quickly at Kelly to see if she had heard what the recruit had just said, but she was preoccupied by the derby scrimmage happening right in front of us.

"Who knows," I said, in what I hoped was an optimistic tone. "You might!"

In an attempt to change the subject, I pointed to the track right as the whistle blew. We watched together as the jammers barreled toward the wall of blockers, and the Skatium filled with the sounds of screeching wheels and screaming skaters. "Out!" they yelled. "Flip! Flip! Here she comes!"

The most effective blocking formation seemed to be three players in a triangle and the fourth—a floater—supporting the other three. Every time the jammer tried to get around them, the blockers in the triangle would rotate; whoever was the top would catch the jammer with her hips and whoever was previously in the corner would become the new top.

After a few minutes, the recruit who had struck up a conversation with me started scrolling on their phone—a dating app?—but I was desperate to watch as much of the action as I could to make up for my lack of knowledge. I was already making mental notes and taking inventory on the type of equipment and apparel the skaters were wearing. I was also imagining how it would feel to slam into another person like that. I knew what it felt like on the receiving end: my mother had once done it to me when I was in elementary school. We had been out on a snowy walk with my sister, and Cam and I had been fighting. She kept running up to me and prodding me in the back and giggling as I stumbled forward. Finally, I turned around and shoved her.

"You seem like you want to know what it's like to get pushed around by someone bigger than you," my mother had said. Then, she wound up and slammed into my body with the full force of her own. I hadn't had time to brace myself. Even if there had been time, I doubt I would've been able to stop her momentum. The hit sent me flying. I landed a few feet away from Cam, who immediately started laughing.

"Don't forget this," my mother had said. Then she continued walking.

I didn't cry, because I thought my mother's hit had been justified. I knew that using my size against Cam was wrong, and I shouldn't have been pushing her in the first place. But I also couldn't pick myself up. I couldn't unfeel my mother's big body hurling into my little one, or the stinging in my ribs and hip bone as I lay sprawled in the snow.

I scanned the track for skaters who looked like me—though it was hard to explain exactly what that meant. I had always been small; when I was swimming, I had been very lean, but over time had developed a thickness that my mother had called "a fat woman trying to get out." Most skaters weren't twigs; in fact, it looked like the heftier skaters were a bit more successful—especially at moving other bodies and creating space on the track. That gave me hope I could find my place in this sport too.

"What do you think?" I asked Kelly, checking my watch again.

"It's very rough," she said. As if on cue, two skaters collided so hard that one fell backward onto her head. Whistles were blown and the action stopped. One of the refs knelt to check on the downed skater. I could see him waving his fingers in front of her eyes: a concussion test. How many concussions happened in this sport, I wondered? More than football? And, more important, why didn't that scare me?

The worst I'd gotten hurt in swimming was a black eye from smacking into another girl right as I pushed off the wall. I had been oddly proud of that injury at school the next day. Would I feel the same way about my derby bruises? What about the potential for even worse injuries? Was I willing to take that risk?

"We should probably head out soon," I said. In our relationship, it always fell to me to find a way to disentangle us from social situations. Even in moments like this when we had a legitimate reason to leave—I had to be back on campus in half an hour—Kelly usually floundered. I never felt especially adept at social interactions, but Kelly's awkwardness forced me into the role and made me realize I was better at it than I thought.

"Wait!" Soup Beans said. "Before you go, let's take a group photo!"

Kelly and I put our bags back down as Soup Beans stood to snap a picture. It was difficult not to imagine what the camera was seeing: me, with my closed-lip smile (self-conscious about my crooked teeth), shaggy bob, and hoop earrings, my flowy pants and jean jacket. Kelly once called my style quasi-hipster—*quasi* probably because of all the athletic apparel. Her style, a fusion of butch and femme, was more cautious. Even her hair, which was dirty blond and curly, seemed more timid than mine.

"Will we see you in a few days for On-Skates Meetup?" Soup Beans asked. "I'll message you about it."

It was a simple enough question, but it still sent me spiraling. I didn't want to make a verbal commitment to roller derby right away, but I also didn't want to let down this bad-ass woman in cheetah-print hot pants and gold glitter eyeshadow. I needed time to think about it—to puzzle out if I was putting too much pressure on a sport I barely knew about to fill the deficits in my life. That struck me as obviously true from the way my heart beat faster when I looked out at the track. I worried that my motives weren't pure; I was looking for a community, but I also wanted to feel pain. I wanted to hit and be hit. The unpredictability and violence of the sport were magnetic in their appeal—it was an arena I already understood.

I settled for a thumbs-up, which felt immediately humiliating. As I was turning, I said, "I think that sounds good. I mean, I might be there," and Kelly and I walked back out into the crisp fall air.

2/
RITUAL

The morning after Recruit Night, I awoke to an email from my mother. *Are you dead? Haven't heard from you in a while.* I put my head into my pillow and groaned, and Kelly stirred beside me. I scrolled through my texts and emails to find our last correspondence. She was right; I hadn't communicated with anyone in my family for over two weeks. We hadn't spoken on the phone in over a month.

It wasn't unusual for us to go long periods of time without speaking, especially since I'd finally left home a year ago. I had graduated from college a year early and spent the summer nannying for a well-known artist couple in New York. I went home for the last time at the end of that September, two weeks that had been filled with accusations and yelling and slamming doors. I left for Kelly's in Ohio when my parents were both at work and Cam was at school, leaving a note on my sister's pillow that said, *I know you won't understand this right now, but you know how bad it is for me here. I can't survive here.*

I wasn't so sure that my sister *did* know the reality of my situation at home. She certainly knew my mother was not happy to find out I was dating a woman, but maybe she thought it had been a somewhat typical parent response. I had tried to shield her from as much of the worst parts as possible, so maybe my exodus came as a complete shock. She never told me. All she said, when she found the note on her bed after swim practice, was "Mom just wrote you out of the will." Her tone was joking, but we both felt the gravity behind her words. I had left her with a shitstorm to deal with, and we both knew it.

I swung my legs out of bed and put my running clothes on in the dark. Our dog, Lady, crawled out from under the covers and shook loudly, which I always feared would wake up Kelly but never did. She followed me into the bathroom while I brushed my teeth, racking my brain for ways to respond to my mother. For years she had said, "Don't you dare talk to me about Kelly," and while some of that tension seemed to have lifted, she still hadn't revoked that initial warning. She didn't seem to like hearing about Lady, who she called a "spindly lizard freak." And I certainly couldn't talk about grad school, which she said I was only pursuing because I couldn't find a job.

In the living room, which doubled as the dining room, I rolled out my yoga mat and held a plank until my arms started to shake. Then I flipped onto my back and did one hundred crunches. Ever since varsity swimming in high school I would do exercises like these before my main workout. It gave me such a rush—a sense of control over my unruly body.

"How long should we run today?" I asked Lady, leashing her up. "Four miles? Five?" My stomach growled and I thought about grabbing a banana, but that was ninety calories I didn't necessarily need. When I was a child, my mother often made us go on long walks before eating, especially on holidays. On Christmas, our route was eight miles, and by the end my hips and feet would ache. "Just think," she would say. "If we work out now, we can stuff our faces later." My mother stuffed her face often, which is probably why she struggled so much to lose weight despite being seemingly obsessed with it. "This is the last Snickers bar I am ever going to consume," she once told me. The way she restricted herself was disciplined and militaristic—until it wasn't. Over the years, I saw her binge on candy and cereal and other sweet things: all the foods that inevitably led me, in the years to come, to purging.

For years, my mother was a Weight Watchers leader. She was a charismatic and impassioned speaker. People loved her; she had a devoted following of women who signed up for her sessions week after week. My sister and I would watch from the back of the room, glowing with pride as my mother mobilized an army of women. One of the skills she developed over years of weighing women was the ability to predict with remarkable accuracy what a stranger weighed. It was a game we played together in public spaces—the grocery store, the park, a crowded restaurant. "She's probably around 165," she would say, scanning the woman at a nearby table. "And over there, by that window? She's around 192." It always awed me even though there was no way of telling if she was right. That was, until she used the technique on me.

My dad wasn't exempt from our family's focus on weight, either. After Denver, we lived in Alaska, where he fell into a deep depression and gained nearly fifty pounds. When we moved to Michigan four years later, my mother made him a list of foods that he could and could not eat. Croutons were a no-go. Diet pop was fine. Dad started weighing himself every morning, naked, and kept a chart on the bathroom wall. He counted his pretzels and packaged his carrot sticks for work in little baggies. He never commented on my weight, but my mother did. "If you just lost ten pounds, you'd have so much less weight to haul from one side of the pool to the other," she would say. This was a constant mantra I heard growing up: weighing less means winning.

I TOOK COMFORT in the slap of my shoes against the pavement as I ran. Lady trotted beside me, black fur barely visible in the darkness. Steadily we moved out of the area filled with duplexes like ours and into wealthier, gated neighborhoods where the houses were mansions with small lion statues flanking the porch steps. Weaving through streets with college-inspired names like Stanford and Princeton, we passed the big city hall building and the public library and popped out onto one of St. Louis's main drags. Even in the early morning it was rich with smells: Chinese noodles and smelly dumpsters and Thai-Mexican fusion. Sundays were farmers markets, and I'd run past vendors propping up petunias and fresh radishes to sell. Today, there was a man sleeping under the statue of rock-and-roll legend Chuck Berry.

When we approached the art studio, I slowed to a walk and paused the running app on my phone. I didn't like to take breaks and usually was very competitive with myself, pushing myself to go farther and faster, but I could never resist peering inside. The art on display changed frequently and reminded me how much I loved studio classes in college. If I passed during business hours, I could watch artists spinning the pottery wheel and pulling up wet vessels from slabs of clay.

In college, much of my art had to do with coming out

and the disastrous effect it had on my family. My pieces were dark in both subject and exposure. I recruited my friends to be models and photographed them underwater pretending to drown in the college pool. We took long walks in the local cemetery, and I shot double exposure portraits that made it look like my subject had died and come back to haunt her living counterpart. In one series, I photographed the act of screaming. When I had no model, I used myself. I took one self-portrait on my dormitory's steps, head in hands, the very picture of desperation, while thinking about the phone call I had made from my freshman dorm room to my mother.

Coming out to my mother had been on my to-do list, wedged between a long series of calculus problems I anticipated would be far more difficult than the call itself. My mother championed gay rights—at least, that's what she'd always claimed—and refused to even buy popcorn from the neighborhood Boy Scouts because of the policy forbidding gay men from being troop leaders. Once, when Cam and I were still prepubescent, my mom mentioned to my father offhandedly how lucky he was that neither of us were lesbians. "You would have a really difficult time with that," she said.

For most of my childhood and adolescence, I only knew one queer person in real life, who was my dad's sister. My mother had always explained my aunt's queerness by telling me she had been abused by a man. Mom never went into details, and later I found out from my aunt that no such thing had ever happened. All my life, my mother speculated that my aunt's relationships with women were rooted in companionship. "I can tell it's not a sexual relationship," she always said. That notion was threatened when my aunt and her partner visited for Christmas one year and my mom caught them showering together. Horrified, she came to me for validation, which I dutifully gave. "Why would you do something that gross in someone else's house?" I asked. Wide-eyed, she nodded as if to say, *Exactly.*

I HADN'T FULLY come out to myself when I decided to call my mother from my freshman dorm room to tell her I was dating a woman. I had known I loved women for most of my life but never thought deeply about the implication other than that I would probably live alone. With Kelly, I thought I was just having fun.

The phone rang several times before she picked up.

"What did you just say?" she asked me. She had been napping; I could hear the sleep in her voice.

"I'm in a relationship," I repeated. "With a woman. Her name is Kelly."

"I was afraid this would happen," my mother whispered. "You're too stupid to be making a decision like this. You don't know yourself well enough." That was a refrain I would hear constantly for the next year: how little I knew myself, how stupid I was. When the call ended, she sent me several emails about how I had made it impossible for her to breathe, to eat. I pictured her curled up on the kitchen floor, withering away.

After my freshman year I told her Kelly and I had broken up, hoping the lie would make things go back to normal. For the most part, she seemed delighted by this news, but every so often, my mother accused me of sneaking off to sleep with Kelly. For two years, the rest of my entire college experience, I hid my relationship with Kelly from my mother.

It took almost three years to work up the nerve to reintroduce Kelly's presence to my mother. When I was a senior, a photograph that had been accepted into an art show at a college about an hour outside my hometown won best of show. Knowing my dad had to work, I invited my mother and sister to come to the awards ceremony. Kelly decided to visit me in college the same weekend as the show. Bringing her to the show—into the same space as my mother—was too terrifying, but I asked if Kelly would drive me. It felt important to show her I was trying—even though I feared it would uncork a momentous and public eruption from my mother—because of a promise I had made. "We won't have to hide forever." That's all Kelly had asked for, even after years of closeting.

I knew the topic of my ride would come up because my mother was bringing my bike from home; she wanted me to have it since my swim season was over and I would no longer be training. It was a thoughtful gesture I appreciated greatly, but one that also suggested, not so subtly, that I needed to continue working out.

Kelly waited in the nearby library while I met up with my mom and sister in the gallery entryway. My mom asked about the bike within the first few seconds of our reunion.

"Let's unload it now, before we go look at the art," she said. "Can you tell whoever drove you here that we're parked out back? I brought Cam to help move it."

My heart was beating fast; if I could, I would've chickened out.

"I'll have to call Kelly and ask her to bring her car around."

"What did you just say?" she asked as we entered the gallery, my fifteen-year-old sister trailing behind. "How could you do this to me? I thought you were past this. I thought you were better than this. Where is she?"

"I asked her to wait in the library," I said.

"She's *here*?" my mother hissed. "She's right down the street?" She gripped my arm tightly the way she did when we were somewhere crowded and she didn't want to lose me.

"Don't you understand?" she asked, pausing for a group of passing people. "Don't you know how badly you've hurt me? Homosexuals are oppressed. They're people you and I need to take care of. We're better than them. And you're better than this behavior."

I heard myself say, "I just really like her."

"I don't care," my mother continued. "Don't you dare bring her near me." Her voice softened ever so slightly as I started crying. My nerves had disappeared and instead I was shaking. "I just keep imagining these protests like I see on the news. People will spit on you, kid. You'll be fired, which can happen in Michigan by the way. You won't ever have a stable relationship because that's not the nature of homosexuality. Those people don't stay together."

She told me she was counting down the minutes until Kelly broke up with me. She told me no man would want to marry a woman like me; I'd damaged myself irreparably. I heard my mother's voice, but I also felt my attention split. While she spoke, I allowed myself to focus on my body. My thighs, struggling to hold my weight. My back, curved. I felt just as on display as the pieces of art hanging on the walls. We were drawing attention. People were staring. I would've done anything to make it stop. Would've promised anything. I had a sudden vision of Kelly crashing through the doors and whisking me away from my mother forever.

My mother continued. "Everything you are is shattered. Everything you were supposed to be is gone." Then, sharper, "*Look at me.*"

I raised my eyes but looked straight through her.

"You won't understand until you have a child," she said. She reached her hand toward me but let it fall before touching me. Her perfect pink nails. Her perfect skin. "You won't understand until you have a mental image of your own child. Please believe me when I say I want to protect you. *I just want to protect you.*"

I believed her because I wanted her protection. I always had. The reality was she was the one I often needed protecting from, a fact I seldom could admit to myself.

We approached my photograph together, blue ribbon hanging from the upper left corner. The black-and-white image depicted me, naked, in a wintery forest facing away from the camera. As I looked at it, I strangely didn't see any of the technical faults or the physical flaws I'd been so quick to identify before. Now, the photo just reminded me of how liberating it had felt to be naked in the snow. I'd traipsed into that forest with my tripod and camera in celebration of the new year. I'd stretched my arms out like I was welcoming the unknown, like I could handle anything, and maybe I had even believed it. The judge said she had selected my piece to win because she loved the way my body mirrored the trees: everything in the frame was stripped bare.

Back in my dorm at school after the show, I made a list of reasons why my mother was a good mother. She got me to college even though it was a world with which she was unfamiliar. She advocated for me when there was a schedule mishap at school. She came to all of my swim meets in high school and cheered the loudest. Growing up, I kept other lists about her generosities and kindnesses too, as proof that she loved me. It seemed like my strongest reaction to the painful memories was to sift through the positive ones. One of the good memories I held on to most tightly was of a time she'd woken me up to catch fireflies in the backyard and bake chocolate chip cookies. I must have been only five or six—young enough that I'd fallen asleep on the couch while the sun was still out. Once it was dark, Mom gently woke me up. She couldn't sleep, she said. She needed my company. Only half awake, that line caught my attention. I felt special. Important.

In the backyard, we ran barefoot through the grass, fingers closing around the little bugs that lit up the cavern of our hands. She let me bake with her in the kitchen, and we ate the cookies while they were still warm. On the couch, I put my head on her belly, imagining myself twisting and turning inside before she gave birth to me. I reached for her hand and held it.

At the time, and for years afterward, I thought it was the best night of my life. She needed me. She adored me. Our hands intertwined; it was impossible to tell where I started and where she stopped. We were one, even though there was something crazed in the way she looked at me that night—a manic, gleeful sort of energy that felt like the opposite of other unexpected moments, like the time she threw my toys out into the rain or put dirty dishes in my bed. On that night, we were the most important people in the world to each other.

Years later, when I was in college, she told me, "I birthed you. You will always belong to me," and in an instant, it was as if I could see the fireflies' winking lights in our backyard, feel the chocolate warm and sticky between our palms.

I FINALLY RIPPED my eyes away from the artwork and turned my running app back on. Past the art studio stood a vintage vinyl music store, a Middle Eastern restaurant, and an Asian grocery store. Like the man I had seen underneath the Chuck Berry statue, most homeless folks were fast asleep on nearby benches and in store entryways. All the hookah equipment had been taken in for the night and the tarot card reader hadn't yet arrived. The flutist who exclusively played "Tomorrow" from *Annie* wasn't yet perched on his corner. Still, running by I felt a surge of gratitude for the city I lived in. We could've ended up anywhere; I had applied to twelve graduate programs all over the country, but of the ones that accepted me, St. Louis had the best faculty, the biggest stipend, and the lowest cost of living. I knew nothing about the city when we visited on Kelly's spring break, but I left feeling at peace with the scrappy energy. The only reference I had to compare it to was New York City, where I lived for a semester in college studying art. It had been the best term of my life—I felt a freedom from swimming and liberation from my family. I came out to the twenty artists I lived with in a townhouse in Chelsea, many of whom were also queer, and toward the end of my stay, Kelly came to visit. In New York, I felt an ownership of my body for the first time. There was too much art to worry about my weight—too much I wanted to see and explore.

While running, though, I didn't feel at home in my body. In the shop windows, I scrutinized my thickness, the way my belly and legs jiggled. After my senior-year swim season, I started running to punish myself and lose weight. I started timing everything. I bought a metronome and developed a reliance on its ticking to fall asleep. I charted my weight on a sheet that hung on my dorm wall and reported it back to my mother. Even when my body failed—a twisted ankle before a half marathon—I pushed through, unable to bear the thought of a missed race.

I put in a tampon the first time for the same reason: my mom said she couldn't stand to imagine me missing a swim meet if I happened to get my period. I was just starting to break club team records when she locked me in my room with a jar of Vaseline. "Don't come out until it's all the way in," she said.

For the first hour, I cried. I didn't know anything about my own anatomy or how tampons were supposed to work. We had just gotten home from a puberty informational session at the local hospital, but I left more confused than I had gone in, even though we played "Puberty Jeopardy!" I knew enough about acne to sweep that category—I had started getting breakouts when I was five—but the one about periods went right over my head. I could hear my mother banging pots and pans in the kitchen. She was clearly irritated at my nonsense. "It's not that hard," she called. "Every woman on earth can do this. Figure it out."

I felt so much fear my vision was going black. It was possible, I thought, that I would never get out. I lay down on my bed and started taking off my clothes. My T-shirt, a former jersey from third-grade basketball. No bra. There was no need. My pink Crocs. My shorts with elastic at the waist. My underwear that said Wednesday even though it was Sunday.

All I remember after that was pain. More crying. When I thought it was in, I stood, legs shaking. It was excruciatingly painful; I couldn't walk right. I cried out to my mom and she said, "That means it's not in all the way." Her tone was exasperated. She couldn't understand the problem. Another tampon came flying through the door. "Do it again."

BY THE TIME Lady and I looped back around to our apartment, my clothing was soaked with sweat. Lady had slowed and was trotting behind me instead of beside me. "You got this, girl," I encouraged. She was still practically a puppy but always burned all her energy in the first thirty minutes, zigzagging excitedly from side to side.

The lights were on in the unit above ours. James, a recently single dad of two daughters, was probably already getting ready for work. He had been the one who suggested calling the cops after our next-door neighbor spotted a Peeping Tom peering into our bedroom window. "I hollered at the guy," he had told Kelly when he saw her letting Lady out the next morning. "And he ran off." Under the window, we found over forty cigarette butts. We also discovered that, at just the right angle, it was possible to peer through the closed blinds for a stage-like view onto our bed.

It was difficult not to imagine what this man had seen. Had he returned multiple nights? The cigarettes suggested so. Had he seen us naked? Having sex? Had he noticed details like our Salvador Dalí poster of a naked woman, dreaming, hung across from our bed?

Yet, in spite of the Peeping Tom, I felt fairly safe in the neighborhood, especially when Lady was with me. Kelly and I fit into the quirky diversity there—the mother and daughter who lived across the street and spoke Spanish on the front porch well into the night, the single, bodybuilder type with a tiny female puppy, the family with five sons who played basketball in the street. I was proud of the life we had built, proud even of my relationship with Kelly given that I didn't think a stable relationship was possible. When I was in elementary school, my mother had sat me on my bed and told me I was going to die alone. It was Mother's Day and I had ruined her day with my complaining. "You think you're the center of the universe," she had said. "You can't see anyone besides yourself and never will be able to. No one will ever love you besides me."

I never dated in high school, even when boys asked me out, not because I knew I was gay but because I thought something else was wrong with me. Kelly was the first person to show me that wasn't true.

SHE WAS STILL sleeping when I crept back in. I stripped naked and adjusted our new curtain, which was thick and made it impossible to see inside. "You're damp," she said when I squeezed her. "But I don't mind." We stayed that way for a long time, and soon I could feel her body twitch back into sleep. I still felt wide awake—lonely even though Kelly was with me. Running always made me feel lonely. Swimming had been isolating too. I craved connection, a kind of intimacy with other athletes that couldn't be achieved by racing in separate lanes. It seemed impossible to believe you were the only person in the world while playing roller derby. There was too much contact, too much yelling. How refreshing that seemed—how tantalizing.

I thought about responding to my mother. Her message was still bothering me, but I was no closer to a decision about how to reply. What was safe to reveal to her and what should I keep to myself? What did I trust her to know? It was all so complicated and painful—I wished someone could just tell me the answer.

Instead of replying, however, I put away my phone. I took down my hair and slid under the covers. As I lay with my eyes closed, I put my mother out of my head and imagined how it would feel to roller skate again after all these years.

3

ATTENTION

A few days later, Kelly and I were sitting on the couch with our feet resting in each other's laps, absorbed in our computer screens. Lady was curled up on the top of the couch like a cat. I had told Kelly I was making a list of every essay I had ever read, my first assignment for graduate school, but I was really browsing Facebook. She told me she was looking for jobs, but her hand covered a smile that her eyes betrayed. I tickled her foot. "What are you *really* doing?" I asked.

She lowered her hand, unplugged her headphones and beamed, spinning her computer to show me a lip-sync performance on *RuPaul's Drag Race* to Blondie's "Call Me." I wasn't surprised. Kelly consumed more queer media than I would've thought possible; it was how she felt connected to other queer people despite us having no queer friends. She was also resisting the job application process, which, for her, was riddled with doubt. Although she had a master's degree in math, she didn't want to teach anymore: that was the only thing she knew for certain. I had to be careful not to put too much pressure on her to find something quick—I knew that would stress her—but I also knew we couldn't survive on my $1,200-per-month stipend for very long. Rent alone was nine hundred, and I had less than a thousand dollars in my savings account—money I'd saved from tutoring in Bowling Green. She didn't have much more.

If Kelly's parents knew how badly we were struggling, they might have sent money. They were both doctors—her dad a psychiatrist and her mom a nephrologist. She had grown up in a big house in a suburb of Milwaukee with three other siblings, including a nearly identical twin sister. Often, I felt resentment about Kelly's upbringing. Our arguments about class sprang from little things, like the fact that she rarely noticed prices at the grocery store and sometimes went weeks without checking her bank account balance. While I had two jobs in high school, shelving books at the public library and lifeguarding at the local pool, Kelly hadn't needed to work. In college, my financial aid was extensive and had included work-study; I was immediately hired as a tech specialist. We also worked together teaching children from disadvantaged homes how to swim. I counted on that money, but she donated it back to the program.

I chose not to say anything about RuPaul and instead picked up my phone, which was vibrating. As promised, Soup Beans had sent me a message saying, "Come out and skate today! Just for funsies! And at a rink that's not as stabby as the Skatium!" A few seconds later, she sent a flashing GIF that said, CASH ONLY.

I started thinking out loud. "It would be really nice to skate once before I commit to a twelve-week Fresh Meat program," I said. "What if I've completely forgotten how? What if I'm horrible?"

"I've got to see this," Kelly said. I knew her main motivation for wanting to come was to further avoid her job applications, but nothing in Soup Beans's message had specified new recruits only. In fact, it was an open skate, so there would probably be at least a few people there unaffiliated with derby. And even though I wouldn't have admitted it, I was glad Kelly wanted to come. It didn't matter that I had met Soup Beans before: the prospect of going alone seemed terrifying.

When we pulled up to the rink a few hours later, Kelly observed, "There are a lot of minivans here." Just inside, an elderly man was sitting behind a square glass window. We traded him five-dollar bills for stamps on the back of our hands, and we pushed open the heavy door leading to the rink. If not for the music, which was a new song I recognized from the radio, I would have been convinced I had traveled back in time. Unlike the run-down Skatium, this rink had all the trappings of the ones I had known in childhood: glow-in-the-dark carpeting, small orange lockers, cubbies housing dozens of tan roller skates with orange laces and toe stops. Big golden balloons shaped like the number nine hovered around the periphery of the track. Round tables heaped with polka-dotted gift bags and cake with frosting roses. Even the pimpled teenager who was fitting all the party guests with skates provoked a deep nostalgia in me.

Soup Beans couldn't have known that my induction into roller derby would double as a nine-year-old's birthday party. She also couldn't have known that the last time I had gone roller skating, I had been the exact same age as today's birthday girl. It was a fourth-grade Halloween field trip, and I had planned my costume to maximize my skating potential. My black turtleneck and eyeliner whiskers, though cliché, were ideal for skating. Even when I grew tired of holding my long tail like a handbag, I felt grateful I hadn't opted for a dress, like the witches and princesses, or a plain white sheet with a couple of eyeholes, which snagged on the ghosts' wheels and sent them careening to the ground.

To my delight, the Halloween free skate that day had been regularly interrupted with short games and competitions. I had no interest in the Hokey Pokey, and I sat out the limbo competition because I knew I wasn't flexible enough to win, but when the speed skating race was announced, I ripped off my tail and lined up. The referee was a teenager wearing in-lines and a striped jersey with the rink logo on the breast pocket. He positioned all of us behind one of the lines painted on the track, and as I waited for his whistle, I realized that my heart had already started racing.

I won the race that day. My prize was three stale Tootsie Rolls and a certificate signed by the teenage referee. I hung the certificate in my locker at school, and while I never pointed it out to anybody, I made sure to always open my locker wide enough for anyone walking by to notice it.

Less than a month later, my mother would take me to swim team tryouts, which would be the start of my twelve-year career in the pool. I had always had a natural affinity for the water, and according to Mom, was too short for basketball. Even from the beginning, the goal was simple: get a scholarship. I hadn't put on skates since.

WE HAD JUST put on our rental skates when Kelly grabbed my arm and pointed. "Look over there," she said. "I think your people are here."

She was referring to a group of about half a dozen women wearing mostly black and carrying customized skate backpacks. They looked disproportionately large, almost godlike, weaving around kids gathered near the presents and all the people sitting on the floor trying on rentals. Kids stared up at them; a toddler in somebody's arms reached out to touch the roller skates slung over their shoulders.

Soup Beans was easy to identify even though she'd changed her hair color from blue to a shade of poppy red. She greeted me and Kelly with excitement. "Sweet baby angels! You came back!"

I felt myself blushing. Internally, I was ecstatic she remembered us. My greatest fear had been showing up at the rink and being overlooked.

I recognized a few other women from Recruit Night, two of them wielding identical pairs of brand-new roller skates. They were black with pink laces, and suddenly I became very aware of the dirty tan ones I had rented, which made me feel like a tourist. The wheels looked like they belonged to a grocery cart; they were caked with grime and barely spun. As we all sank down to the ground to put on our skates, I tried to memorize the various brands the other skaters were wearing. Riedell. Bont. Antik. Soup Beans's were custom designed: the strap on the right skate said soup and the left said beans.

The woman sitting next to me must have noticed me ogling everybody else's skates, because she asked me if I wanted to try hers. She extended them to me like the Host during Holy Communion. They were exactly my size.

"What will you wear?" I asked. I tried to meet her gaze but was too transfixed by the tattoo on her inner arm: a huge lightning bolt framing the St. Louis skyline.

"I haven't worn shitty skates like these in six years," she said, scooping up my rentals. "It'll be fun." She introduced herself as Bolt Action and said that she had moved to St. Louis from Fargo, North Dakota, specifically for derby. "It was my dream to play for a league like Arch Rival," she said. "And I wasn't happy in Fargo anyway. So I just said fuck it, quit my job, and moved down here. No regrets so far."

I wanted to ask her questions, but I couldn't find a way without revealing how little I knew about the world of derby. For some reason, it felt important to play my cards close to my chest so that these skaters would think I belonged. I was desperate for immediate connection.

"What do you mean a league like Arch Rival?" I asked.

"Oh, I just mean such a highly ranked league. There's over four hundred now—so being number nine in the world is a pretty fucking big deal."

Bolt stood up and skated past the other players, laughing and pointing at the rented skates on her feet. I turned to Kelly, stunned. "Did you know that?" I asked. I didn't recall seeing anything about rankings when I had visited the Arch Rival website; all I remembered were several photos of skaters mid-hit and a banner with the words STRONG. AGGRESSIVE. DETERMINED. No one had mentioned rankings at Recruit Night, either.

Kelly and I stood up, clinging to each other for balance. The skates added several inches of height and made falling seem even scarier. I cursed myself for not considering knee pads, which Soup Beans and many of the other skaters were wearing, and for dressing in a baggy college T-shirt and jeans. Even with Bolt's skates, no one would have ever confused me with a derby player. My clothes weren't sleek or athletic or black. My movements weren't fluid or even remotely graceful. I was too afraid to even try skating on the carpet, so I simply picked up my feet and walked.

Kelly and I continued holding on to each other as we stepped through the gate and onto the hardwood. Right away, Kelly almost lost her balance, but she recovered with a motion that made it look a little like she'd been electrocuted. We both laughed once she was sure she had regained her footing.

Skating for the first time since childhood felt magical. Every few seconds, my stomach lurched like I was about to fall, but somehow I remained upright. My hair blew back and my legs quickly found a rhythm. Bolt's skates were smooth as butter: gone was the vibrating that I remembered rattling my feet inside my skates and sending shockwaves up my calves and thighs. On the rink, the extra height from the wheels seemed less dangerous and more powerful.

What scared me were the kids. They weaved in and out around us, slamming into each other and hitting the ground so frequently that the teenager monitoring the rink didn't bother checking on them unless they remained immobile for a few seconds. Swerving around them and observing them from a distance made it hard not to remember how it felt to be that age. A few months after I had won the roller skating race and started swimming, not long after I turned ten, I started having terrible pain in both my feet. The pain worsened until even walking became unbearable, and I had to sit out of recess and gym class. Not long after, I started using a cane. It had been my grandpa's and it was too big for me; I held onto it like Moses holding his staff.

The other kids were relentlessly cruel, mostly without meaning to be. They asked questions that I didn't know how to answer, like "What's wrong with you?" and "Why can't you walk like everyone else?" Even the doctors were stumped, although they postulated that my pain had something to do with my emotional problems. At school, I often had to excuse myself to go to the counselor's office. There, I sobbed or worked myself into a panic that my mother needed me at home—that I was somehow betraying her by being apart from her. At home, I would double- and triple-check the locks on our doors, which my mother often left open at night. I was certain we would all be shot in our sleep. Our neighborhood was very safe; we lived across the street from a large insurance company. There was no reason to think we were in danger, but still, I never felt safe. Sometimes I would crawl into Cam's bed, which made me feel slightly better, even though my mother would mock me for it in the morning. "You better be nice to her, kid," she would say, whenever bickering broke out, "or she's not going to let you sleep in her bed when you're all nervous."

I didn't understand the term *psychosomatic* when the doctors used it for the first time. My mother had to explain. "They don't believe you're in pain," she said. "The doctors think you're faking it for attention." Immediately I felt caught. Was I making the whole thing up? Did I just want attention? Maybe. I felt better when the school counselor's eyes were on me. I felt better when the gym teacher came to check on me reading out in the hallway. Sometimes the attention I received from my mom made me beam on the inside, but most of her attention I would've gladly given up. My mother insisted, again and again, that I was the sloppiest girl on the planet, the rudest, the cruelest to her sister. When her eyes were on me, I felt myself shrinking.

When the pain became debilitating, I started missing school for doctors' appointments. My mother scared me once by saying I'd have to repeat the fifth grade, but the threat didn't ease my pain or my insistence to find a cure. Did this mean she believed me? Was it a test? I couldn't tell.

Eventually the doctors diagnosed me with a cavus foot deformity. Essentially, that meant the shape of my feet weren't suited for walking. My arches were too high, and all the pressure of my weight went on the balls of my feet. We tried everything to avoid surgery: creams, inserts, the cane. The whole academic year was just one experiment after another, and in the early spring it was determined that there was no alternative: they needed to reconfigure the shape of my feet.

On the way to the hospital the morning of the procedures, I imagined telling my mother to turn the car around. *It's all been a lie, just like the doctors thought,* I would say. *I can walk just fine.* Though it wasn't technically true, the shame of my "made-up" ailments was making me feel ill.

The surgeries both went exactly according to plan, and my parents drove me home just as the sun was starting to set. My dad carried me from the car to my bed and placed me gently on top of the sheets. "Do you need anything?" he asked. Groggily, I shook my head no, but when he left, I felt lonely. When would Cam be getting home from our grandparents' house?

On the back porch, I could hear my parents talking. Slowly, I eased myself out of bed and onto the floor and crawled on my hands and knees to the back door, dragging my bandaged feet behind me.

My mother looked unsurprised to see me. "Want a grape?" she asked.

My head was pounding. I couldn't feel anything from the calf down. I shook my head no.

"I was just telling your father I think sunshine is more

important than any drug. Sit out here and the sun will heal you."

I nodded obediently. More than anything, I wanted to please my mother. I would've stayed out until the sun slipped behind the trees. What I didn't realize was they were talking about the drugs I couldn't have. There was a medical reason I couldn't take opioids, but I didn't understand it. Something about my age. Something about adverse effects. Sitting outside on the back porch, I felt the nerve block slowly wearing off, and it was like stepping into a fire pit.

That evening, I sweat so much I soaked the bedsheets. I writhed and cried out for it to stop. My mother fed me ibuprofen and Tylenol in alternating doses every four hours, but neither did much good. Cam, home from spending the day with our grandparents, slept on the couch because I was being too loud. Mom knelt on the floor by my bed. She brushed my hair out of my sweaty face and told me I was the strongest girl in the world. "You don't know this yet," she said. "But you can do anything."

In spite of the pain, I basked in her love. My mom so rarely touched me, so rarely comforted me in difficult moments. I would've done anything to make it last. It felt like she was really seeing me for the first time—her love was worth the excruciating pain.

The next day, though, the sweet mother from the previous night had disappeared. School was still in session, so Cam was gone, and Mom and I spent all day together. "Wash your hair," she ordered. "You stink." When we received a bill in the mail for my hospitalization and surgery-related costs, Mom asked me to sit down at the table. "I want to go over this with you," she said. "You need to have an understanding of how much money operations like this cost. And anesthesia." She pointed to the numbers, which had a trail of zeros following them, and my eyes widened.

"Do we have enough money to pay this?" I was ridden with guilt, shame.

"You're lucky your father and I save our money and don't blow it on frivolous things," she responded. Then she dismissed me.

After two weeks cooped up in the house together, me crawling to get around, my mother declared we were both going crazy. "We need to get the hell out of here," she said. "I need a Diet Coke."

I don't remember being offered a wheelchair post-surgery, and I don't remember any discussion of how I would get around in the aftermath. The doctors had given my parents the choice about whether to do the surgeries on different days, but they had opted for the same day. "Just like piercing your ears," my mom had said. "All the pain at once and that way it's over faster." What I learned years later was that they had been offered a choice in the quality of hardware too— the screws and wedges that would go inside my feet to reconfigure the shape. My dad told me, laughing, that they had opted for the cheapest metal.

"You know your mother," he had said. "Always pinching pennies."

I wish I knew how much the surgeries impacted my family financially. I wonder if they had felt any guilt or shame around not being able to give me the highest quality screws and wedges. Did they feel torn about whether to spread the surgeries out, so that I would be able to hobble around on one foot for a few weeks before the operation on the other?

As far as I knew, the lack of wheelchair was another cost-saving measure; my mother's alternative was to load me into my little sister's wagon, red with round edges, which felt like riding in a miniature bathtub. It was so small that, even sitting with my back pressed against the plastic, I had to either bend my knees or stick my bandaged feet out the sides. The bumpy sidewalk jostled my legs, but I tried not to wince or give any indication of pain in case she decided to turn around.

I was heavy in the wagon and Mom had to switch arms every block or so as she dragged me downtown. Occasionally, she stopped to take a break. "I'm sorry," I offered, but she didn't respond. When we passed a couple walking in the opposite direction, the man averted his eyes, but the woman stared at us.

"Take a picture!" Mom yelled after her. "It'll last longer!"

I felt a swell of pride—my mother, my protector. This woman's gaze had been judgmental, and I had felt my cheeks reddening. I hadn't expected my mother to intervene, but she seemed just as bothered by the woman's staring as I was. Mom was bolder than me, braver than me, I realized. I wondered if that was something that just came with age, or if I would always be too shy to defend myself.

Mom was still irritated when we arrived at the candy shop. The wagon couldn't fit through the doorframe so she asked me what I wanted, and I said, "Can I have anything?"

"Within reason," she answered. "You're having a hard day."

The news that I was having a hard day came as a surprise to me. It didn't seem any harder than all the other days. I told my mother I wanted a roll of candy buttons.

"Sometimes I think you're not my kid at all," she said.

It wasn't easy to eat candy buttons with a big gap between my teeth, and sometimes when I plucked the button off, little bits of paper were still stuck to it. At first, I tried to make sure each button was spotless, but finally I just ate the paper too. Mom watched me, disgusted, sipping a Diet Coke in a slim glass bottle. I expected her to tell me to quit eating the paper, but she didn't, so I started eating more. Sometimes I consumed more paper than candy: big, quarter-sized bits that I placed on my tongue like the body of Christ.

As soon as her pop was gone, Mom stood up to leave. "Let's go," she said.

But I wasn't ready to go. I wished I could tell my mother that I didn't want to leave yet, that I liked being outside. I wanted to point up at the sky and tell her the sun was helping to heal me, but she had already grabbed hold of the wagon handle, and my mouth was too full of paper to speak.

AS I SKATED for the first time as an adult, I looked out at all the kids on the rink and at the tables where I would've been sitting at that age, watching from the sidelines. I could see myself: cane resting on the tabletop, oversized T-shirt and ripped bell-bottom jeans that accentuated my orthopedic shoes. I would be reading something age-inappropriate that I'd plucked out of the adult fiction section of the public library while my roller skating classmates squealed in exhilaration and delight. At twenty-two, I felt no less lost than the child I was then, no less isolated, no less desperate for meaningful friendships. I wanted to connect with people who could understand my past experiences, my pain, the reason I wanted to be included so badly.

On a literal level, the scars on these derby players' bodies attracted me too. Soup Beans had multiple surgical incision marks spouting from her ankle-length socks and crawling up her legs like vines. Bolt had a scar on each calf. It was clear, just from watching these players, that they not only underwent physical pain, but they knew what it was like to be an outsider too. I could tell by their bodies, the way they dressed, their piercings and tattoos, the way they carried themselves. I was attracted to the performance of power and dominance I'd seen at Recruit Night. Like the drag queens on Kelly's favorite show, the skaters' personas were larger than life. Each person took up space in a way that, to me, felt both foreign and magnetic. They seemed to embody a way of being that was bigger than the kids who had bullied me in grade school, bigger than the scars on each of my feet, bigger even than roller derby itself.

Every time I passed Soup Beans on the track, I prayed for her to notice me. It was a desperate kind of yearning: another way in which I felt like the kid in the back of that red wagon. I didn't know what I wanted from her besides some small form of attention—a nod of the head or maybe a thumbs-up. It felt like too much to hope for something verbal like "You look great out there," or better yet "I'm proud of you." Still, I craved it.

Kelly, who left the track in search of some nachos, had located the concession stand and was watching me from the sidelines. I smiled at her and waved as a man's voice boomed over the loudspeaker. "This next one is going to be a backward skate!" he announced. "You heard me! Only backward skating for this next song!"

The derby players transitioned to skating backward effortlessly. Even in my tan, rented skates, Bolt made it look easy. She zigzagged backward on one foot around the kids while dancing to the beat of the song.

Still clinging to the wall, I turned myself around. I was hoping that once I was facing backward, my body would instinctively know how to propel itself, but nothing happened. I was paralyzed, too scared to take a step or even push off the wall and let my wheels carry me.

The teenager monitoring the rink skated up to me and said, "Ma'am, you can't just stand here."

I couldn't recall ever being called *ma'am* before.

"I can't skate backward," I told him.

"Then you have to get off the rink."

I told him I was trying. Across the rink at the snack bar, Kelly motioned for me to join her. I checked to see that no one was coming before making my move to the nearest exit. As soon as I transitioned to the carpet, however, I knew I was going to fall. My feet flew out from under me and I landed on my right wrist. Miraculously, it didn't hurt; I knew right away I hadn't seriously injured myself. My ego was much more bruised.

"Oh my god," one of the moms said, jumping up to check on me. "Are you all right? That was a hard fall."

The familiar heat of humiliation spread over my cheeks. This was not the kind of attention I wanted. Had Soup Beans seen? I checked over my shoulder and was relieved to find her still engaged in conversation with another one of the moms.

"I'm fine," I said, hoisting myself back to a standing position. "I'm fine."

Kelly's face was contorted in concern when she reached me, still holding the plastic nacho container. I repeated that I was fine, perfectly fine, and grabbed her hand. Originally, I was going to say that I wanted to find Bolt, trade back our skates, and leave, but I didn't want my last action on skates to be the fall. What if I was too afraid to put them back on? It felt too important to risk it.

Kelly used her finger to scrape out the remaining nacho cheese and then threw the tray in the trash. I held on to her sticky hand as we made our way back past Soup Beans, past the skate rental, past the crowd of party guests who were gathering around a huge cookie cake. The adrenaline from the fall powered me toward the track. I held my breath as we neared the gate where I had fallen. This time, I knew how it would feel to step off the carpet and onto the rink, and I was determined to make it look effortless.

4

PELVIS BREASTLY

After the on-skates meetup, I offered no verbal con-firmation—either to Kelly or to myself—that I had decided to pursue roller derby, and I never defined what *pursuing* meant. The possibility of joining the team casually had not occurred to me; playing for fun wasn't an option. I knew inherently that I wanted to achieve the highest level of gameplay possible, make the All Stars team, travel the world . . . I just never admitted that to myself or to anyone else. Something more primal was driving me: low-level panic. There was a voice in my head that wanted desperately to be noticed and seen—to belong in a way I never had before.

It didn't occur to me to go to a skate shop to buy my gear, and even if it had, I wouldn't have been able to afford it. Soup Beans had mentioned that a typical Fresh Meat starter package, which consisted of skates, a helmet, pads, and a mouth guard, cost in the neighborhood of five hundred dollars, but I simply didn't have that kind of money to spend. Even though we had moved four months earlier, our apartment was filled with unpacked boxes of books and binders

and art. The things we did have—a couch, a bed, a table—
were donations from Kelly's sister, who was moving abroad.
The threat that our money would run out before Kelly found
a job was too real a possibility to ignore.

When I got the first installment of my graduate school
stipend, I budgeted one hundred and fifty dollars for skating
equipment—grossly low by any standard, but the best I could
do at the time. One hundred and fifty dollars was groceries
for two weeks if we could stretch it. We were also saving up
for a desk that Kelly could use for applications and I could
use for schoolwork; I felt guilty using that money for derby,
but Kelly was encouraging.

I launched a full-scale investigation for beginner skates and
spent so long weighing the pros and cons that even Kelly got
exasperated. "Just pick one," she told me. "You're thinking too
hard about this." The skates I eventually settled on were the
cheapest I could find online: Riedell R3s. They were ninety
dollars and the description claimed they were "the perfect
combination of performance and value for beginner skates."
Unlike the skates I had borrowed from Bolt at the meetup,
they weren't leather but vinyl, and they were "heavily pad-
ded to fit like a sneaker." Had I asked any experienced skater,
she would have warned me against R3s. Rarely did they last
longer than a year; if the cheap nylon plate didn't simply snap,
the boots themselves were sure to fall apart. The wheels that
came with them were cheap and slippery on any surface.

I found a helmet at Walmart. It cost about half what the
leading derby helmet online cost and the only difference was
that the holes on the top were square instead of round. I told
myself no one would notice, which is what my mother had
always said about the off-brand sneakers and clothing we always bought. Rarely, growing up, did I find that to be true.

I turned to Goodwill for the rest of my gear. As a kid, I'd often notice knee pads and other skating equipment, though we mostly bought clothes. Since my mother prided herself on her frugality, she allotted herself only a dollar and ten cents of spending money a week, which she used to buy a can of Diet Coke at the public library, where she was the administrative assistant. She read somewhere that hoarding five-dollar bills would make you a millionaire, so if our gas or grocery change ever consisted of fives, she'd take them and stash them in the largest cupboard of her desk.

My dad worked as a mechanic all my life, but he preferred the title "automotive technician." His spending habits were only slightly less bizarre than my mother's, although he was a lot more limited. Though he made more than my mom made as an administrative assistant, my mother would always seize his paycheck and, a day later, hand him a stack of bills, which she called "his allowance." With it, she expected him to pay for the large pepperoni pizza we picked up on the way home from church every week and a two-liter bottle of Diet Coke. The rest of his allowance was split into gas money and tithe. At least, that's how he explained it to my mother. I often saw him leave cash tucked under windshield wipers and into Christmas cards he'd hand to near strangers. He did it occasionally for people who came into the shop—single moms, elderly customers—or simply wouldn't charge for the work he'd done on their car. He once gave a waitress at our local diner a one-hundred-dollar tip.

IT HADN'T TAKEN much convincing to get Kelly to come to Goodwill with me. She was eager, as always, for a break from applying for jobs. She was also keen on the idea because we had a specific goal; there was nothing Kelly hated more than perusing.

The Goodwill Kelly and I found in St. Louis was a warehouse lined with frames and mirrors and filled with dozens of dumpster-sized plastic bins. Each held an assortment of things like toys, household appliances, and holiday decorations, and every item was coated with a slightly sticky residue. Most of the other shoppers wore latex gloves, which I immediately envied. They sifted through the bins with a methodical precision, and I wondered if any of them were looking for anything as specific as adult knee pads.

Every time Kelly or I saw something that looked vaguely pad-like, we'd yell to the other, but it almost always ended up being an oven mitt or a dark seat cushion. Occasionally we would find a few Barbie-pink child-sized pads, but nothing that would fit me. While we searched, we threw ideas for possible derby names back and forth.

"What about Shania Pain?" she called.

"Soundtrack of my fucking childhood," I responded. "What about Lady Macbitch?"

"Too profane," she said. "They wouldn't be able to say it in front of the children."

"What would your name be, then?" I asked. It was difficult to imagine Kelly coming up with something for herself that wasn't profane—so much of her speech relied on one-syllable expletives that, with a slight variation in tone, could carry a range of connotations. I also expected her to pick something that revolved around her obsession with yo-yos and yo-yo tricks, which she practiced religiously every day. She often set up her phone to record the tricks and archived her videos on a private Instagram account that was hidden even from me. "It's just for me," she once told me. "I don't need anyone else's eyes on it."

To my surprise, Kelly didn't choose a yo-yo name. "I always thought if I were a drag queen and a little bit heavier, I would be Natalie Portly," she said. "But that doesn't really work for derby. For derby, I would be Fibonasti. Like Fibonacci from math. Nasti for short." When I commented that it hadn't taken her very long to come up with that, she said, "You don't think I've been thinking about this since I went with you to Recruit Night? I fucking love puns."

We left Goodwill empty-handed, which put me in a bind. With my skates, helmet, and mouth guard I was already at my one-hundred-and-fifty-dollar mark, but I absolutely needed wrist guards and knee and elbow pads. I considered reaching out to Soup Beans to ask if there was some kind of gear loan program—or if she or anyone else on the team had old pads I could borrow until I saved up some money. The prospect was terrifying. Even if it worked out, it meant that at least one person would know I was broke, and if borrowing racing suits in high school had taught me anything, it was that I didn't want people's pity.

There was a second option, although I genuinely dreaded it: call home and inquire about my mother's old wrist guards and pads. I had been in elementary school when I stumbled upon them while looking for one of my bug catchers in the garage. When I asked my mom what she used them for, she simply said, "Everyone skated in the eighties." My dad later confessed that she had broken her wrist roller skating. She never went to the doctor, though, so it was impossible to know for certain. There was no one my mother loathed more than doctors (except perhaps dentists). Her own par-

ents had distrusted doctors so much that they'd avoided getting my mother medical attention for her appendix until it
was an emergency. Instead of internalizing the message that
doctors were necessary and helpful, she'd somehow learned
the opposite lesson, one that she passed on to us in many
ways. Why wouldn't she go to the doctor? I had wanted to
know. Dad responded, "Why would she? It was clear the
thing was broken; X-rays would only confirm what she already knew."

The guards and pads I coveted had been purchased after
my mother's injury and were essentially brand-new. Even
with safety equipment, my mother could no longer skate
without paralyzing fear. It made me sad to think about, but
part of me thought maybe I could bond with my mother
over skating. We had so little to talk about these days, and
surely she remembered how exhilarating and freeing it felt to
skate.

I thought about trying to avoid a family call by texting
Cam; it was possible she could mail the pads to me in secret
and my parents wouldn't suspect a thing. It probably wouldn't
work, though. I could just picture her running to my parents
and ratting me out within minutes of getting the text; it had
happened before. Ever since I had left home last year, she had
been tightly allied with them and publicly opposed to all my
decisions . . . and I wasn't sure I could blame her.

"Call tonight?" I texted my dad. I still hadn't responded
to my mother's email from four days ago asking me if I was
dead, and sometimes if I took too long to respond, she
wouldn't acknowledge me at all, especially if she caught a
whiff that I needed something. My first few weeks in Bowling Green, when I desperately needed my social security
card to get a job, she ignored my requests. It took weeks of

appeals to my dad for him to send it to me. I still don't know if she ever found out.

Dad's response came two hours later. "Free after church. Skype?" I groaned. I should've known he would want to Skype. Even if my mother wasn't speaking to me, she would sneak a peek at the screen. If it appeared I'd gained weight or was wearing something unflattering, like a crop top, her opinion would almost certainly get back to me via my dad. In college, I'd taken to calling her only in the semi-dark so all she could say was "Why don't you turn on some lights, kid? You're ruining your eyes!"

As I confirmed the time with my dad, I visualized myself climbing into a suit of armor. In college, this was a strategy I used (along with applying heavy makeup and wearing my baggiest clothes). Sometimes, if my imagination was vivid enough, I could picture her comments bouncing off me like arrows hitting metal. There was an added incentive this time, though—and an extra mission. Get the pads. Get out. Get to play roller derby.

OVER SKYPE, my father looked old, which made me wonder if I looked older too. I hoped so. Though we could hear each other perfectly, the video kept freezing, and I harnessed these moments to analyze his features. Maybe it was the Denver Broncos baseball cap, which cast his face in a gray shadow, or maybe I had just never noticed the wrinkles around his eyes and mouth before. It had only been three months since I'd seen him last. He had come to St. Louis to deliver some of my belongings: a lamp I had purchased at a garage sale as a kid, some clothes I had left the day I ran away, even a small loveseat and a recliner that sat unused in their basement. It was an incredibly kind gesture, one Kelly and I greatly appreciated, but his visit had been very awkward. The drive was a long, boring eight hours, and he had slept on a blow-up mattress in the spare room. For the most part, we didn't talk about my mother and her disapproval. We didn't talk about her at all, really.

Six weeks after I left home to move in with Kelly, I met up with my father for a hike, to talk about how to move forward. He had been wearing the same Denver baseball cap and jeans, cinched with a tight belt, that were a few sizes too big for him. "So, what are you going to do about Mom?" he had asked me. He told me that she was fuming, which made me feel terrified, but that she had spent a lot of time thinking about things and "maybe she has changed."

"She told me she can't remember being that hard on you, and I told her I wished I had a video recording of all those times I saw it happening and didn't know what to do to stop it," he said. Then, his voice softened. "Listen, I know why you left. I want to apologize for not intervening all those times. What I'm trying to say is—I should have intervened."

It had been incredibly validating to hear those words. I wrote them in my journal and read them every day as proof I wasn't overreacting or crazy or weak. Some friends thought I should be angrier at my dad than I was—his complicity, his passivity—but I mostly just clung to him for the potential of a loving parental relationship. It was just so much more complicated than that. I had always seen him as one of the kids.

As my dad tried to fix our Skype connection, I focused on his bookshelf: the rosaries on the top shelf and, leaning against a few empty beer bottles, the small container of holy water I'd collected for him from Mother Cabrini's shrine.

The parts of his personality these trinkets represented seemed immune to change, which was refreshing, given that my mother told me I was destroying her. My dad would still read and reference *Rediscovering Catholicism* and *Scrawny to Brawny* no matter where I lived. He would wake up early and sit in his chair to pray and meditate regardless of who I slept with. There was something both fragile and resolute about my father; he embodied a lifestyle founded on and fueled by ritual.

I couldn't see my mother, but I knew she was listening to our conversation just out of the frame because whenever the screen froze, my dad assumed I couldn't hear him and reported back to her. "She looks happy," he said. If my mother responded, she didn't speak loudly enough for me to hear.

When our connection improved again, my dad turned back to me. "I couldn't hear you very well. Did you just ask me how's work going?"

"Yeah," I said. "I just wanted to know what's new with you."

Dad thought carefully about this for a moment and then went on a short tirade about how he was getting all the shitty work at the dealership: whoever doled out the assignments wasn't doing it fairly. I could hear the frustration in his voice, which was usually measured and calm. Every question I asked, every possible solution, he waved off. "Just something I have to deal with," he said.

"Well, this will cheer you up," I said with feigned confidence. "I'm trying out for roller derby." At that moment the screen started freezing, catching his face in various states of worry.

When the problem resolved, he asked, "What did you say you're trying out for?"

"Roller derby," I said, less confidently than before. "Do you remember that movie we saw when I was in high school? *Whip It?*"

His eyes lit up momentarily, but then the spark of recognition was clouded by something I couldn't identify.

"Yes . . ." he said slowly. "Isn't that the movie where those big girls beat the crap out of each other on roller blades?"

"Basically," I said. "I mean, there's rules. It's not exactly like that anymore."

For a moment I thought the screen had frozen again, but when he blinked, I realized my dad just didn't know what else to say. Our conversations were usually structured around him asking questions and me answering them. When that framework broke down, neither of us knew what to do.

Finally I said, "Is there any chance you could look in the garage and see if you can find Mom's old knee pads and wrist guards? I think they're in one of those green bins."

"Are you sure you want those?" my dad asked. "They haven't been worn since 1985."

"I definitely want them," I said.

At this, I heard my mother slam the recliner back into place. It sounded like she was ambling off toward the kitchen. This was her new strategy for expressing disapproval nonverbally, and it terrified me. What if she convinced my dad not to send the pads to me? What if she somehow forbade me from joining the team? It seemed like she had the power to do anything and I was at her mercy, just like I had been as a kid.

When she returned from the kitchen, she stuck her face in front of the computer's camera and pushed my dad out of the frame.

"You're just asking for trouble, kid," she said. "Why would you do something that dangerous?"

It was the first time I had heard her voice in several weeks and it had the immediate effect of making me feel stupid. Was joining the team a terrible idea? *Was* I asking for trouble? This was coming from someone who had suffered a pretty bad roller skating injury. Maybe she was just trying to protect me. Maybe she really had my best interests at heart. But also, wasn't it a double standard to tell me roller derby was dangerous when she encouraged my sister to continue tearing up her shoulder at swimming? Last time I'd talked to Cam, Mom was taking her to the doctor for a cortisone shot every twelve weeks—the most frequent the doctor would sign off on—to dull her swimming-induced pain. During the worst of it, Cam couldn't even reach her arm above her head. They both knew that cortisone shots were essentially Band-Aids: they would numb the pain, but whatever was wrong in Cam's body would keep getting worse.

I could just picture what would happen once I ended the call. I could hear her saying *I knew this was going to happen. I knew that crowd would rope her into something dirty like this.* I had overheard hundreds of these types of conversations over the years. Something I said or did would light a fuse in my mother, and once they were alone, she would let the bomb explode on my dad. She'd confront him in a shrill, high-pitched whisper, filibustering until he made his way to the kitchen for a drink. Once he had a beer in hand, he'd begin to offer comments like "I know" or "You're right."

Part of the reason I'd overheard so many of these conversations was because our bedroom shared a wall with the living room, where they'd stay up and talk about us after we had gone to bed. Even as young as elementary school, I learned that it was easy to find out what my mom thought of me—all I had to do was turn off the light and wait. "I think she's just a slob," she said to my dad one night. "And I'm running out of ways to try to beat that out of her." Another night, she said, "I don't know how to impress upon her that what she thinks and what she wants mean relatively little in the grand scheme of things. Do you know what I mean? She thinks she's the center of the goddamn universe."

Hearing these things made me feel insignificant and afraid. It made me feel like I had no one I could talk to about the things I daydreamed about while walking home from school or the goals I had for the future. It made me realize I couldn't trust my mother or my dad, who, at night when they thought I was sleeping, seemed to treat me no better than the mean girls in fourth grade. A pack of them had started shouting, "Lesbian!" at me in the hallways, and I didn't know what that meant. At least they were saying it to my face, I reasoned.

My dad surprised me when he continued our conversation as though my mother hadn't interrupted.

"Didn't the main girl in *Whip It* have some sort of dorky name?"

It took me a few seconds to realize what he was referring to—once I remembered the thread of our conversation from before I felt a surge of excitement. *This is your chance,* I thought. *Don't blow it.*

"I have a whole list of names!" I said, pulling a notebook out of my bag. "It's a tradition to choose a new name in roller derby, and you're supposed to pick something fierce or intimidating." I scanned the list to find a couple of good ones to share. Lots of people probably would have been embarrassed to share any of these names with their dad, but I knew he would love them. When he was outside of my mother's orbit, my dad was very playful. My sister and I were frequent targets; his jokes often made us cry. He once switched us into each other's beds while we were sleeping. Another time, he sent me a fake college acceptance letter telling me I had won a full swimming scholarship, complete with a fake water-mark. More than anything, my dad loved toilet humor. There was no way, I thought, he wouldn't love the smarmy names I had come up with.

"What do you think of Oliver Fist or Vagina Woolf?" I asked.

Dad stared at me blankly. It was in moments like these that I felt everything I had in common with my family had been eradicated by my college education. It wasn't that he didn't appreciate the humor—he just couldn't place the ref-erences.

Scanning through my list of names, I tried to recover quickly.

"I was also considering something like Pelvis Breastly."

Not only did my dad understand that name, he laughed so hard the computer slid right off his lap and the camera pointed upward at the ceiling. I grinned, glad he couldn't see how delighted I was that he was laughing.

"So you'll mail the pads?" I asked.

He nodded, wiping the tears from his eyes.

In the background, I heard my mother shout, "Did you turn on our blankets?" There was no heat in the attic where they slept. Every night before bed, one of them had to go turn on the electric blankets so they wouldn't freeze to death in their sleep.

My dad straightened the computer. Eyes locked on me he

said, "I'll do it in just a second." Hearing that, I felt something inside of me sink. He was right there, on my screen, but I felt he was gone.

Sometimes I went down a rabbit hole imagining what my life would've been like if I had been raised solely by my father. He had wanted to be a stay-at-home dad, but my mother convinced him he'd be ostracized by all the stay-at-home moms. "They'll be automatically suspicious," she told him. "They'll think you're a pedophile. A sex offender." When we lived in Alaska when I was little, I clung to my dad. It was my dad I called for. It makes sense now, knowing my mom's distaste for babies; he probably held me against his skin, slept with me on the couch. I'd seen pictures of me strapped to his back or sitting on his shoulders. What would have become of us, I thought, if my mother hadn't started relying on me more and more for emotional support? Would we be closer? Understand each other better? What would've happened if he hadn't faded into such a non-presence in my life? And where would that have left my mom?

"Sounds like Mom is ready for bed," I said. Dad stretched and yawned loudly. We both knew they never went to bed at the same time, but he agreed that he should probably end the call.

"Night, Dad," I said.

"Good night, Pelvis," he said, and the camera blinked off.

5/
FRESH MEAT

W hen I crossed the threshold of the Skatium on my first day of Fresh Meat, the first person I encountered was a scrawny, shirtless man lighting a cigarette with a blowtorch. His cargo shorts hung loosely from his body, and I was so shocked by his hairy butt crack that, at first, I didn't notice the cigarette dangling from his lips or the blowtorch he was raising to his face. The sudden whoosh of the flame caused me to jump back in alarm, but when our eyes met, the man's expression suggested this was the most normal Sunday morning activity in the world.

Fifteen or twenty skaters were already sitting out on the track, and when I joined them, I asked about the man with the blowtorch. One woman craned her neck to catch a glimpse of him as he walked past the bathrooms, twirling the blowtorch like a baton.

"Oh," she said. "I think he's the dude who lives behind that red door over there." She pointed to the space between what used to be the two locker rooms on the opposite side of the rink.

"People live here?" one recruit asked.

Ginger Assassin, the skater with big red hair, whom I recognized from Recruit Night, answered. "Oh yeah. They used to be squatters, but I heard the owner rents out the old locker and storage rooms for two hundred bucks a month now." She lowered her voice and pointed to the area where I had seen the strange cleaning lady vacuuming. "If you go look behind those Coke machines, you'll see someone draped a hose over a doorframe. There's a Styrofoam cup, with holes poked in it, duct-taped to the end of the hose. You know—for showering." Her comment was met with wrinkled noses and confused stares.

Another veteran skater pointed to a small window overlooking the track. It was dark, but there were several illuminated lava lamps visible from where we were sitting.

"That's where the DJ Booth Man lives," she said. "He's been here the longest, I think. Anyway, don't let him catch you fucking with the stereo over there. And also, don't touch his cat—it's the one with the pink collar. The rest are strays."

Everyone laughed uncomfortably. There was something ominous about the Skatium and its inhabitants. At Recruit Night, when Alice mentioned her theory about the place being a drug den, I had thought she was joking, or at least exaggerating, but it was starting to seem like a legitimate possibility.

Most of the people who trickled in after me took a seat quietly in the circle, but there was one exception: a short woman with blue hair who was being trailed by two young boys. When she arrived, she began introducing herself to all the new recruits. When she got to me, the ghost of a laugh was still in her eyes. "I'm Taryn," she said. "Short for Taryn ItUp."

I was surprised when Taryn sat and the boys started vying

for a spot in her lap. The possibility that any of these women were mothers hadn't occurred to me. Taryn didn't look like any mom I had ever encountered before. Both her arms were covered in brightly colored sea-creature tattoos. Her fingernails were tinted blue from the recent dye job.

"Mom!" one of the boys yelled. "I want to go to the bathroom! It's so cool in there! There are planets on the walls and somebody painted all the toilets black!"

Taryn whispered to us, "I try not to bring them here, but sometimes Logan's dad, Doucheface, drops him off and I just don't have a choice." We all laughed, but I laughed the hardest. I already knew this woman was someone I wanted to know.

Just as one recruit started to ask Taryn when the coach would arrive, the door to the Skatium opened again and a woman with long legs and a dark pixie cut walked in. She strode onto the track with the air of someone who was in charge; I respected her before she even said a word.

"Did you all give them the rundown on the Skatium?" she asked the vets. Ginger nodded. "Good," she continued. "The first thing you should know about the Skatium is that we have to put up with a lot of bullshit here. I'm just going to hold on to the hope that one day we'll be able to afford a place to train where we don't have to worry about getting stabbed by a meth addict or breaking our legs on one of these disgusting balloons from last night's rave." She bent down and picked up a deflated cream-colored balloon, which looked suspiciously like a used condom.

Our coach introduced herself as Flux, short for Flux Decapitator, and explained that she was on the All Stars team and just one of the many trainers at Arch Rival. We went around the circle to introduce ourselves; it seemed a few recruits had already bailed. There were now twelve of us, including the transfers. I was happy to see Nurse Pain, the mom of the birthday girl from the on-skates meetup.

Flux instructed us to take our skates out of our bags so she could teach us about changing wheels and bearings, but while she spoke, I became distracted by her shirt. In big letters it said SORRY, WE DON'T SKATE STRAIGHT. I felt a surge of excitement. In college, after Kelly graduated, I had been the only non-straight person on our swim team. Our romance had been a particularly juicy source of gossip for the other swimmers, not only because of our age difference but because we were the only same-sex couple to date within the team. My gayness was always the first thing new recruits learned about me and the way I was identified on the team. It was something I knew about Kelly before even meeting her, too. Being in Ohio was even worse. We had no queer friends and didn't know any queer people. Making queer friends was one of our goals in St. Louis, but so far, the only gay person Kelly had met was a motherly lesbian usher at the Fox. We were both putting a lot of pressure on derby to change that.

As Kelly would later observe, not only was Flux queer, she was also incredibly charismatic. All her lanky limbs were covered in carnivorous plant tattoos—Venus flytraps and cobra lilies and big floating bladderworts. She had an eyebrow piercing and dimples that formed whenever she smiled, which was often. And even though we were sitting cross-legged on the floor, she still wore her helmet, letting the buckles dangle as she fiddled with her high-top skates.

After instructing us how to change our wheels and adjust our toe stops, Flux passed out a sheet of paper listing all of the league requirements, including the practice schedule, which specified that Sundays would be devoted to basic skills, Mondays were for strategy, Tuesdays were a co-ed practice with the men's team, and a four-hour block on Thursdays would be divided into a basic practice, followed by scrimmage, followed by an invite-only advanced practice. I snagged on the co-ed bit; I hadn't known there was a men's roller derby team in St. Louis. I made a mental note to avoid Tuesday practices at all costs. Being hit around by men while I was still learning to skate seemed like a terribly bad idea.

Nurse Pain scanned the paper and raised her hand. "I'm sorry," she said. "The woman I met at my daughter's birthday party didn't say anything about practicing this much. Are we expected to come to all of these?"

Flux shook her head. "Some people do," she said. "But you're only required to do five a month—ten hours on skates. We do expect that each skater volunteers a minimum of once per quarter at one of our community-outreach events. I usually skate in parades and walk shelter dogs."

Nurse Pain nodded and opened her mouth to speak, but Flux wasn't finished.

"Oh, you also have to volunteer on one of our committees. I'm an artist, so I'm on production committee. Most of the newbies just start out on bout committee." Flux pointed to Taryn ItUp, the quirky woman with the two little boys. "Taryn heads the bout committee and we would be so fucked without her. She runs all the games, makes sure we have officials, and manages volunteers. She's just incredible." Taryn smiled and blushed.

When Flux finished speaking, I stared down at the practice schedule, mentally calculating the hours I'd have to do my homework if I committed to three practices a week. Could I make it back from the Skatium on Thursday nights in rush-hour traffic to make it to the weekly departmental reading? Would I still be able to grade student work and finish all the books I was assigned?

Blades of Glory, the hairdresser from Recruit Night, broke the silence by voicing a concern I hadn't even considered. "What if—what if we can't do it? Physically?"

The skater sitting next to Flux asked if she could answer. I recognized her from the photographs on the Arch Rival website: Tutz. Her hair was dyed platinum blond and she was wearing a thick headband with pizza slices on it.

"Listen," Tutz said. "When I found roller derby, I weighed over three hundred pounds. I had to have special pads made before my first day of Fresh Meat because the extra-large ones wouldn't fit around my knees or elbows." She explained that she'd gotten lost in Springfield one day and saw a roller rink with a sign that said ROLLER DERBY HERE. "It was like a fucking crack in the universe," she said. "I went to a bout, and there were women of all sizes being idolized by a crowd of people. Each body type was appreciated and doing something totally badass."

Tutz explained that we didn't have to think of ourselves as athletes to start playing derby. She said we didn't have to have any previous experience with sports or even be in good shape. "If you're here to learn roller derby, that's enough," she said. "Whatever skill level you're at, we'll teach you. It doesn't matter why you're here—whether your goal is to be on Team USA or whether you just want some new friends."

At this, Taryn ItUp interjected. "Or if you're a mom and just want a few hours to yourself!" Several of the recruits nodded and clapped.

"Exactly," Tutz said. "Don't worry about not being able

to skate. The more you skate, the more your body will get used to skating. The more you hit, the more your body will get used to hitting."

While Tutz spoke, Flux smiled and nodded vigorously. She told us that Tutz had recently been interviewed by *Women's Health* magazine and that if we wanted to know more about her story, we should read the article. At this, Tutz waved away Flux's suggestion and said, "I pretty much just summed it up anyway."

LATER THAT NIGHT, it didn't take long to find the article. The story was titled, "The Life Changes That Helped Me Lose 120 Pounds and Cope with My Anxiety and Depression." Underneath were two photographs: images of Tutz before she joined roller derby and after. Both pictures were poorly lit and had been taken in a bathroom, but that's where the similarities ended. The woman in the first picture didn't look anything like the Tutz I had met. Her hair was long and dark. She was wearing a white, underwire bra with thick straps and leggings that she'd pushed low to expose her stomach. In the second picture, Tutz wore a sports bra and yellow, polka-dotted booty shorts. Her thighs didn't touch.

I knew the photographs were intended to inspire, but instead they made me feel slightly sick. At my mother's Weight Watchers meetings, my sister and I would always browse the pamphlets while we waited. Thin women standing in their old jeans, holding the waistline out triumphantly, thin women sipping pink smoothies while riding stationary bicycles, thin women wearing heels and cocktail dresses, hair blown back by artificial wind. Side-by-side images like the one of Tutz in *Women's Health* were common, and they were always accompanied by numbers—pounds lost, calories cut, dress sizes down.

My mother was an obsessive tracker of numbers. If she came home from her weekly weigh-in with a small pin or blue ribbon because she'd met another weight loss goal, she'd greet us exuberantly. She'd order my dad to hide any foods that could tempt her and say, "Who's ready for a walk?" For an entire year when I was in elementary school, my mother didn't miss a day of walking. She walked in thunderstorms and blizzards. She started saying things like "Losing weight is just math. Calories in, calories out."

If my mother came home from a weigh-in and her number had been the same as the week before, or if she was marginally heavier, she raged. While my sister and I microwaved hot dogs for dinner, or Hot Pockets, or frozen chicken sandwiches, my mother either wouldn't eat or would settle for a single English muffin.

Another reason Tutz's pictures made me so apprehensive, aside from their obvious connection to the Weight Watchers brochures, was their extreme nature. Everything about my mom was extreme as well: her exercise regimen, her oscillating and unpredictable emotions, the way she scrutinized my body and my sister's throughout our childhood. I hated, simply based on the *Women's Health* heading, how easily roller derby could be reduced to a weight loss strategy: *300 pounds to 180—learn how finding a support system changed this woman's life!* It was too neat, too banal. It also too closely resembled the way my mother would emphasize over and over that to be the best athlete, the fastest swimmer, I needed to weigh less.

Yet there were some differences that set Tutz's article apart from meant-to-be-inspiring celebrations of weight loss I'd previously encountered, like the acknowledgment of her involvement with fat positivity groups. "I got used to being invisible and started believing that I just shouldn't exist," Tutz said. "During this time I was diagnosed with depression, anxiety, and insomnia with self-harm tendencies." Tutz also didn't create an illusion that her weight loss—or her derby career as one of the best blockers in the United States—had solved all her mental health problems. "Since I still struggle with depression and anxiety, it's really important for me to practice self-care and forgiveness."

Roller derby, too, separated Tutz's experience from the ones I'd read about in other magazines. "After a couple of months of reining in my anxiety and finding specialized pads that fit my body correctly, I went to my first practice. I'd never roller-skated before, but I knew I had found something I could be proud of for once," she said. "I was terrible at derby when I first started. But every time it knocked me down (literally and figuratively), it inspired me to get back up and rebuild myself. It taught me that there is power in my thighs."

AS I SAT ON THE Skatium floor, it was clear the other recruits were all inspired by the condensed version Tutz told us. There was a reason, she assured us, that we had come to this place—we had found our own "crack in the universe." She insisted that the derby community was special, and later, I would frequently hear this sentiment paraphrased and expanded upon in derby circles. "Nobody joins roller derby if they have a perfectly happy life," one skater told me. "Usually they're in some kind of transition or crisis. Usually they're dealing with some shit."

When Tutz finished speaking, Flux took over again. She reached into her bag and took out a stack of packets.

"You all have to pass a physical and written test from the Women's Flat Track Derby Association before you start playing games," she said. "It's called the minimum skills test, or just 'mins,' and basically we use it to make sure you're not a danger to yourself or others."

Nanny McWhee, the professor I'd seen skating on the sidelines at Recruit Night, began to complain. "I thought I was done taking tests," she said. "You must be joking." Flux offered a half smile and looked away; I was the only one to laugh. I was glad she was sitting next to me so I could lean over and whisper, "I thought I was done too."

"Are you an academic?" she whispered back.

"Sort of," I said. "I'm in grad school for writing."

Nanny's eyes lit up and she asked a series of follow-up questions. "Which one? How do you like it? When do you start teaching?"

Flux cleared her throat and asked that we focus on the minimum skills packet she was holding up. "I'll catch up with you later," I whispered.

There were five general categories outlined in the packet: Basic Skating Skills, Recovery Tactics, Balance and Agility, Pack Skills, and Blocking. Underneath each heading was a list containing dozens of requirements. *Hops over an object at least six inches (15 centimeters) in height without touching the object or losing balance, while skating at a moderate pace. Turns 180° without breaking stride, maintaining a moderate pace. Consistently demonstrates the ability, judgment, and timing to take a whip off another skater's body or clothing without pulling the other skater off-balance. Consistently demonstrates the stability to provide hip and clothing whips without getting pulled off balance.*

I couldn't fathom ever being able to "hop over an object" of any size, let alone six inches. Nor could I imagine taking any sort of "whip off another skater's body." It concerned me that in her explanation of why we needed to pass the minimum skills test Flux admitted that we could be a danger to ourselves and others. I had certainly considered the first part, but as I looked around at the others, I realized I had never seriously considered I could hurt somebody else.

Flux checked her watch and let out a sigh that blew her bangs up. "I knew I was going to talk too much," she said. "We don't have as much time to skate as I was hoping, but gear up and we'll at least go over crossovers and stops."

One of the recruits started putting on her wrist guards backward and Taryn ItUp rushed to her aid, which made me grateful I had tried on all my gear at home. It was embarrassing enough to be wearing my mother's old pads, which were of much less pristine quality than I had remembered. Although I had managed to scrub off the dust and cobwebs, there was nothing I could do about their quality: Mom's knee and elbow pads were comically thin, especially when compared to the plush, highly protective gear everyone else was wearing. I prayed no one would notice and prevent me from skating.

When we were finally all geared up and standing, Flux instructed us to start with some basic laps. She demonstrated the most effective way to skate around the track—in a diamond pattern, so that your crossovers would propel you from the inside of the apex to the outside of the straightaways.

None of the newbies could cross over, although I was

closer than I had been at the nine-year-old's birthday party. Kelly and I had since watched several YouTube videos by a Canadian skater named Miracle Whips. In a thick French-Canadian accent, she had described the process of crossing over as leaning into a fall from which you catch yourself at the last minute. Flux echoed the advice, exaggerating the movement by swinging her right leg out and throwing it over her left. She made it look so easy, but my balance was too shaky; the best I could manage was lining up my skates toe-to-heel.

"That's a great first step!" Flux shouted when I passed.

When Flux asked us to gather in the middle of the track so that she could show us how to stop, it took several minutes for everyone to assemble. Blades of Glory crashed into the wall. Nurse Pain planted all eight wheels on the track and let friction slow her down. Alice simply dropped and skidded into center track on her knee pad. The transfers, Bruise Almighty and Birdsong, were the only ones besides the vets who could successfully stop—they threw their heels out and let their back wheels vibrate on the track in perfect form. "Transfers must think they're hot shit," Alice whispered.

Instead of asking us to gather in the middle again at the end of practice, Flux had clearly learned her lesson and said we could simply sit down, remove our skates, and gather on the sidelines to talk while taking off the rest of our gear. As soon as my skates were off, a wave of relief washed over me. At the end of my first proper derby training session, I hadn't fallen. I hadn't gotten hurt. My lower back and butt hurt, which Flux had promised at the beginning of practice. I was also drenched in sweat, which gave me a sense of accomplishment. It was hot for October, and there was no temperature regulation in the Skatium other than a large fan positioned at one end of the track. My pads were completely soaked through, the inside of my helmet disgustingly moist. Some of the vets had brought towels, and as I watched them dry their glistening bodies, I chuckled to myself. Taryn, who was sitting next to me and spraying her gear down with disinfectant, asked what I thought was funny.

"Oh," I said. "I was just thinking about all the towels I took out of this bag last night. I guess it just never occurred to me that I'd ever need them again after my last swim meet."

Flux returned, wielding a clipboard, to where we were sitting on the sidelines. She tried handing it off, but Nurse Pain was too busy peeling off her wet rainbow socks to notice.

"Can I have your attention one last time?" Flux asked. "We were thinking it might be nice to assign each new skater a mentor—someone who's been around for a little while and will take you under their wing. If you sign up, we'll randomly pair you with a willing vet who will reach out to you soon."

I felt my face redden as I was handed the pen and clipboard. It seemed taboo—almost illicit—to speak of mentorship so matter-of-factly. Growing up, I had craved such a connection, especially from women coaches and teachers who might see me in ways my mother wouldn't, or couldn't. I thought if I worked the hardest, or swam the fastest, or earned the best grades, one of them might rescue me in the dramatic fashion I'd read about in books: a spontaneous adoption, an intervention, a confrontation with my mother that would make her more nurturing or loving. Nothing like that ever happened, but many of my coaches and teachers did save me in small ways over and over, sometimes without even being aware of it. They refuted my mom's assertions that I was careless and selfish. They bought me books and clothes. They let me sleep in their spare bedrooms to escape her rage. It was a professor in college who insisted I move in with Kelly after graduating. "You're a grown-ass woman now," she told me. "You don't have to follow her orders. You don't have to always be afraid."

At twenty-two, I might have been a grown-ass woman, but I still felt like a child, desperate for someone safe, a mother I never had. It seemed like a shameful thing to crave; it meant I wasn't strong enough to survive on my own even though I had everything I needed. So signing my name on a list and being paired up with an older woman who was willing and kind—it felt too easy. Unearned. I hadn't proven anything to the team or to myself, hadn't yet shown how hard I could hit or how much of a beating I'd be able to take.

Before I could talk myself out of it, I jotted down my name and passed the clipboard on. At least for tonight, my desperation was louder than my shame.

DERBY MOM

After a few practices, I began receiving a multitude of Facebook friend requests from fellow Arch Rival skaters. Taryn was one of the few skaters I recognized immediately. Her pictures looked exactly the way she had when I met her: candid and colorful. Most of them were selfies—Taryn with her two boys, Taryn with her mom, Taryn with a woman she called her "derby wife." In all the photos she grinned broadly, open-mouthed—sometimes tongue out—green-rimmed glasses framing her green eyes.

I accepted Taryn's friend request right away, and a few days later she messaged me. "So I guess I'm your mentor! Lol!" While Taryn expressed her excitement about mentoring for the first time and her willingness to help me get acclimated, I scoured her profile. I learned that she was a business analyst for a healthcare company and that she used to work in a restaurant at Universal Studios. I gleaned that she'd been playing derby for about two years, and that she changed her hair color even more frequently than her profile picture. Before blue, it had been teal with purple highlights, and before that, yellow with pink tips.

We decided to get lunch at a little burger joint near the Skatium called Stacked. I looked up the menu ahead of time to find the lowest-calorie options and went on a run beforehand for good measure. Dining out with people always made me nervous. I didn't want them to know how obsessed I was with food—how out of control it made me feel. When I arrived, Taryn and one of her sons were seated at a round table near the bar. Her hug was tight and confident. When we broke apart, she held me at arm's length and looked at me with a tenderness that seemed disproportionate to the short amount of time I'd known her.

"I'm so glad we were paired up," she said. "I don't know how they did the matching, but I'm just really happy that I'm going to get to be your derby mom."

"Me too," I said, hoping my cheeks weren't turning red. Taryn radiated a specific kind of maternal love that made me feel immediately exposed. She couldn't have known that was something I always found myself seeking out, could she? Was I wearing my damage that obviously? Even as I basked in the glow of her approval, I simultaneously felt confused, caught out, and ashamed.

Trying to cover, I said, "Have you ever done this before?

"Nope!" Her grin was unapologetic and her teeth were as crooked as mine. "You're my first."

Embarrassed, I racked my brain for something else to say, but Taryn interjected before the silence got awkward.

"I hope the drive here wasn't too bad," she said. "I suggested this place because it's pretty important to the team culture. We come here a lot after practice. They sponsor us, and our draft night is held in the back room."

"Wait—what draft night?" I asked. "Flux told us that

once we passed minimum skills we would automatically be on the C team."

Taryn nodded. "Yeah, but roller derby has two seasons—local and travel. Travel season is the competitive season. Once that's over, we launch into local season, where Arch Rival breaks into three teams that play each other in St. Louis to raise money. That's why there's a draft."

"So—is it your goal to one day move up to the B travel team?" I asked. The question seemed redundant. I expected Taryn to gaze off into the distance and divulge that she'd been dreaming about being on the B travel team ever since she joined Arch Rival. Instead, she dismissed my question by waving her hand as though swatting a fly.

"I have absolutely no desire to ever make the B team," she said. "I'm not a super competitive person. And it's too much commitment for me."

My expression must have betrayed my shock. I tried to backpedal in case Taryn was offended, but she cut me off.

"Are you one of those people who need to be at the top?" Her forwardness made me blush. "Babe, there's so much more to derby than playing at high levels! If I quit now, it would be like cutting off my arm. These people are my community. I know it sounds corny, but it's true."

The waitress arrived with her notepad, and Taryn ordered a Mountain Dew and two burgers—one for her and one for her son, Jacob. I ordered a salad, but Taryn grabbed my arm. "You can't just have salad. Or, at the very least, you have to try some of my burger. Have you ever had goat cheese and onion jam on a burger before?"

I shook my head no. Ordinarily, I would've been annoyed and uncomfortable by someone pushing food on me, but somehow, it felt different with Taryn. "I'll have a couple bites," I promised.

When the waitress left, I asked Taryn where her other kid was today.

"Oh, Logan's with his dad, Doucheface, this weekend. I have to go pick him up tonight, actually. It's a four-hour round trip to Butt-fuck, Illinois." Taryn sighed and folded her arms across her chest. "That dude is such an asshole."

Jacob abruptly stopped spinning in his chair and stared at Taryn.

"Mom, who's an asshole?" he asked. I laughed, but Taryn rounded on him quickly.

"What did I tell you about saying the word *asshole*?"

Jacob cracked a smile and stared at me as he answered. "I can only say *asshole* when I'm a rock star."

Taryn pushed Jacob's placemat to him and offered him two crayons, then turned back to me.

"But seriously, that man *is* an asshole. During the divorce he's like, 'Don't get me started on the fact that you play roller derby.' Some people don't think it's a real thing, you know? They think it's all flashy and fake—clearly they don't know how much athleticism it takes. That's been one of the biggest hurdles for me. I've never played sports unless you count high school color guard. I've never really thought of myself as an athlete."

There was a slight pause as Taryn sipped her Mountain Dew. I wasn't sure if I should comment on her ex and if so, I wasn't sure what to say. She hadn't really left an opening, so maybe she didn't want my opinion. The worst possible thing would be offending her by accident, so I instead chose to pick up where she left off.

"I've played sports my whole life," I said tentatively. "I

started competitive swimming when I was nine and pretty much all I cared about in my childhood was breaking records and improving my times. In college I started going a little psycho when I stopped getting better. It became . . . really unhealthy."

Taryn nodded and said, "Yeah, see, I don't get that. Why would you keep doing it?"

This wasn't the first time I had been asked that question. My college advisor had asked me the same thing. I would arrive in her office, hair still wet from swim practice, so exhausted I could barely pick up my legs to climb the stairs. Her kindness would make me tear up and eventually I'd start crying. "Why are you doing this to yourself?" she would ask, gently. "I don't understand."

I would joke that I was too tired to consider leaving the sport, but the real reason was fear: I was scared of leaving something that had defined me for so long and scared of losing my only friends on campus. Swimming was all I had known since I was nine years old; I couldn't just quit when I was so close to the end. I still remembered what my mother used to say when I was in middle school, swimming with the varsity team over the summer. The practices had been brutal, and the older girls mostly ignored me; I had wanted to quit dozens of times. "You're better than that," she would say. "You made a commitment for the summer and you're going to see it through."

Part of me, if only on a subconscious level, was also scared of what my mother would think of me if I quit. It didn't fully make sense to be focused on this since she had stopped coming to college swim meets once she realized I was nowhere near the fastest; she also blamed my college swim coach, Christie, for allowing me to room with Kelly on training trips and away meets. She thought Christie should have picked up on the fact we were both gay. We often called Christie "Mom" on the team, but that meaning took on a new role for me when I came out to her. I didn't tell her until after Kelly had graduated: when I came back the next fall for sophomore year, I was a wreck. My mother had spent the summer insisting that I was straight—just stupid and confused. One night she paused the show we were watching on the image of a model getting ready for the runway and said, "If you think she's attractive, that's just disgusting." Every day, she had a new theory. "It's your grandmother's fault," she once said. "The gayness can be traced back to her." The worst had been that God was punishing my father by giving him a gay sister and now a gay daughter. "He's not saying a lot right now, but your father is not okay," my mom assured me.

In coach Christie's small office, I sat across from her and willed myself not to cry. "I'm gay," I told her quietly. I didn't say, "I'm in a relationship with Kelly," as I had for my mother. I was more certain of my gayness than ever, despite my mother's attempts to convince me otherwise. "And I just had the worst summer of my life."

I handed her a piece of paper, on which I had written everything I'd been hearing from my mother. To my surprise, Christie was the one to start crying. "Oh my god," she said. She offered to get me in touch with the athletic director and one of the psychology professors, openly queer women who might be able to counsel me through. She said she knew the director of the counseling department and could get me an appointment. "No," I said. "This is enough."

In the moment, it had been—her warmth, her tears, the

way she hugged me and told me she loved me. It had been everything I wanted from my mother all my life, and as a result, I developed a deep bond with Christie that had nothing to do with swimming. On particularly hard days, she invited me over to her house to sleep in her spare bedroom. I texted her about class and work. She was the first one I called when I thought I had appendicitis—not my mother.

"We need to go to the hospital," she said. "I'll pick you up in front of your dorm in ten minutes."

What I hadn't told Christie was that my neck was also swelling. What she saw when I got into her car was a grape-sized mound on the side of my neck. Her eyes got big, but all she said was "Let's get you to the ER."

I spent all day in the hospital with Christie, who rubbed my back and listened to me talk about my mother. "She was a tennis star in high school," I said. "She knows how to play guitar, and when I was little, she would sing the most amazing country songs." I wanted her to know that my mother was a real person—not just the quotes I'd given her on that sheet of paper the day I came out. I also wanted to feel less like I was betraying my mother by seeking comfort from Christie in this moment. Christie needed to know how much I loved my mother, how much I wanted to please her.

As the sun set, the doctors found no appendicitis, nothing at all physical that would account for my level of pain. Christie asked that I speak to a social worker. "She was supposed to go home tonight," I heard her whisper to one of the doctors. "I think that's why this is happening."

I didn't want to talk to a social worker; all I wanted was for Christie to keep telling me I would be okay. A huge part of the reason I kept swimming—though I would never tell it to my college advisor—was that I wanted to be near Christie. She was the closest thing to normalcy I had. Seeing her at practice calmed me.

IT FELT ILLICIT to speak of any of this to Taryn, who already seemed to be stepping into Christie's old role. I couldn't let her know this was a pattern with me: collecting maternal figures who could temporarily fill the void left by my mom. I wanted her to think I was normal and well adjusted, someone who pursued sports for reasons unrelated to their past emotional scars. Describing my unhealthy relationship with swimming—and athletics in general—felt too complicated to try to communicate to Taryn during our first get together, so I simply shrugged and said, "I don't know why I didn't quit." She studied me for a few seconds; her look was one of pity and understanding. The vulnerable, aching feeling that had surged through me after our hug returned even more strongly than before.

When our food came, Taryn cut her burger and slid half onto my plate. It was more than I was expecting—more than I wanted to eat—but I thanked her. Would she think I didn't like it if I didn't eat the whole thing? I wondered. Maybe I could hide portions in my napkin when she wasn't looking, a strategy I had used with much success throughout my adolescence.

That thought disappeared the moment I tasted goat cheese for the first time. Taryn found it amusing that I'd never had it before.

"I've tried everything because I've worked in restaurants my whole life," she said. "I started working in my parents' restaurant when I was just ten. In a lot of ways, it was awesome. But I'm sort of angry at my parents for exposing me to all that at such a young age. There was a lot of . . . harassment. You know, from men."

Taryn's vulnerability persuaded me to ask her something I'd been wondering about. She seemed to sense my hesitation because she nodded encouragingly.

"So, can I ask you why you started derby? I mean, you said you're not competitive or whatever. And you'd never played sports before. Why now? Why this? Had you seen a bout before?"

"Yeah. My current boyfriend, Ethan, Jacob's dad, and I went on a double date to see a game with this other couple. It kind of freaked me out how much hitting there was. That was a major obstacle for me. I didn't want to get hit. I mean—who does?"

I smiled and nodded, even though I understood the appeal of a full-contact sport perfectly well. I was eager to cast aside all social conditioning—particularly those unwritten rules that governed what I as a woman was and wasn't allowed to do with my body—and embrace a new set of rules. I thought about the loneliness I had felt swimming and that I still felt now, running before the city woke up.

But it also had to do with the fact this was a kind of violence I could choose and control—and one that would leave evidence on my body. The day my mother sat me down on my bed when I was in elementary school and told me with certainty that I would die alone, it felt like a gut punch. When she left, I felt shocked that there was no physical mark on my body I could point to as evidence that something hurt. After I came out, her words had done even more damage, none of which was visible. All I wanted was proof I could see.

Taryn and I settled into a more comfortable conversation about league requirements and the upcoming event where I'd be volunteering: a fundraising gala for a local women's safe house. As the waitress set the check down on our table, I bemoaned the fact that I didn't have a dress.

Taryn snatched the check and slapped her credit card down without even checking the total.

"Borrow one of mine," she said. "I have a bunch of fancy dresses I've collected over the years."

"You don't have to do that," I said. Just as I'd been afraid to ask Soup Beans if I could borrow gear, I didn't want this to lead to pity.

"It's not a problem," she insisted. "I've always wanted a daughter." Blushing, I looked away.

A FEW NIGHTS before the gala, Kelly and I stopped by Taryn's house to pick up the dress. It was dusk, and Taryn had warned me that she lived in what she called a complicated neighborhood. Many neighborhoods in St. Louis were complicated, she said, because of the intense racial and class inequalities that so often spilled into despair and violence. On Taryn's block, there was a faint slamming I couldn't identify. Someone beating a rug? As Kelly and I shuffled up the sidewalk, I remembered Taryn lamenting the fact that her boys could both recognize the sound of gunshots. "No kid should know what that sounds like," she had said.

We didn't have to wait long on the front porch before Taryn flung open the door and pulled us in. She hugged us both and then released us into the living room, where Jacob's dad, Ethan, was lying on the couch playing with his phone and Jacob was sitting in a sea of plastic toys. It was only the third time I had met her, but it felt natural being inside Taryn's house. Everything was my level of messy—cluttered, but not disgusting—and had all the St. Louis staples of our apartment: a fake fireplace, an open floor plan, wood floors, and stained glass. It immediately felt comfortable. Ethan barely acknowledged us, but Jacob hopped up and ran over.

"Do you want a cookie?" he asked. "Do you want a Lego? Do you want to play with my robot?"

I sat on the ground next to Jacob and started connecting Legos; it had been over a year since my summer nannying for a boy not much younger than Jacob and I still missed him. Kelly remained standing. She wasn't keen on kids like I was, and when we talked about having kids in the future, we compromised on the possibility of fostering queer teens. I wouldn't get to be pregnant, which I had always wanted, but it would mean Kelly wouldn't have to deal with diapers. "I just fear I'll be a shit mom," she always said. "What if I can't love the child fully?"

"I don't think that would be a problem," I told her. "I see all the love you have for me and Lady."

I had my own fears about motherhood—most of which were still germinating. I wondered if it was even possible for me to be a warm mother, having grown up with such a cold one, and how I would break some of the patterns of my girlhood. I loved Kelly and Lady with all my heart: was that enough to prove I could love a child too? Quick as I was to refute Kelly's concerns about her own mothering capabilities, I fully understood and shared her apprehension and fear.

Jacob was delighted that I was playing with him; he started bringing me other toys and dropping them in my lap.

"He's definitely my child," Taryn said. "He'd give away everything if we let him."

Jacob grabbed my hand and led me to the fish tank; I loved the feeling of his tiny hand in mine. Would Taryn let me babysit, I wondered?

"Here are my fishies!" Jacob announced, poking at the tank each time a fish darted by. "When I play roller derby like my mom, my name's going to be Fish Man." He took a big pinch of fish food flakes, but the little tube slipped out of his grasp and spilled all over the carpet. Jacob stared at me, horrified.

I hadn't realized Taryn was standing behind us until she said, "Hey, Fish Man, it's all right." She handed me the dress she was holding. "I know it was just an accident. Just try to pick it up the best you can. I'll vacuum up the rest tomorrow."

As Jacob sank to the ground to pick up the flakes, I barely felt the weight of the dress I was holding. I was back in my childhood bedroom, looking into the fish tank my sister and I adored.

It was small—ten gallons—and it fit perfectly on the homemade stand Dad had constructed out of two-by-fours. Cam and I had planned it all out with our Magic Markers: pink and purple rocks, a floral backdrop, a treasure chest, and fake aquatic plants. We bought everything at Wal-Mart with our babysitting money, including the fish: four neon tetras bright as the highlighters in our backpacks, a pair of black mollies speckled like dalmatians, and a little albino frog that won every staring contest we initiated. Most of the fish got Harry Potter–themed names, but since the mollies reminded us of the dogs from *One Hundred and One Dalmatians,* they became Pongo and Perdita. It wasn't long before Perdita became pregnant.

The night Perdita gave birth, it was pitch dark in our

bedroom except for the subtle glow of the streetlight outside our window. From the bottom bunk, where I was eye level with the tank, I recognized what was happening a few seconds before Cam did. We squealed with delight as we observed their tininess; some of the baby fish were smaller than the nails on our pinky fingers. It was such a joyful moment I reached up for Cam's hand to give it a squeeze, but I couldn't find it in the darkness.

"I wish we could see the baby fishies better," she said.

Earlier that day, my mother had confiscated all the lightbulbs in our room. She'd been threatening it for weeks. Recently, Cam and I had been forgetting to turn off the lights before going out to play and she'd scream at us in the backyard. Did we think electricity was free? If we couldn't learn to be responsible, she'd take all the lightbulbs out of our room. We knew it wasn't an empty threat; Mom's threats were never empty. But still, one of us had forgotten to flip the switch, so this was clearly one time too many. So we sat in the dark in silent rapture straining to see the baby fish emerge from Perdita's swollen belly.

We watched together as the baby fish took their first swim—dozens of them, it seemed. Our frog, Snape, observed from the pink and purple rocks. The water glistened in the streetlight's glow. There was no warning that the peaceful moment with my sister was going to end, but then Perdita's slow movements became quicker. She seemed to twitch, and then began barreling toward a group of her children. Open-mouthed, she devoured three of her own babies.

Cam and I stuck our whole arms into the tank and began flinging the fish onto the dark carpet, splashing fish water everywhere without even thinking about what Mom's punishment for that would be. The water was cold and slick;

there was something dangerous about putting our arms into a tank full of creatures we could barely see. When my fingers closed around them, the fish squirmed inside my cupped hands.

Together, Cam and I watched the mother fish consume five more of her kids like Pac-Man. We both knew there was no way to work fast enough to save all the babies or rescue the ones gasping and writhing on our bedroom floor.

"Help!" Cam called. It sounded like she was drowning.

Our dad came in, shining a flashlight from his tool belt. If she heard us at all, Mom didn't bother coming in. Usually she sent Dad on missions like these—anything messy, anything unpleasant. "Oh boy," was all he said. We knew better than to ask for a bulb to be screwed back in: Dad never deviated from Mom's punishment, even in moments like this. All he succeeded in doing was killing several baby fish under his big boots.

In the end, we saved two. We used the cup from the bathroom sink to keep them alive and separated them from their mother until they grew as big as her. Even when we were sure it was safe to put them back in the tank together, Cam and I were fearful. We tipped them in and held our breath.

"PROMISE YOU'LL SEND me a picture when you try it on?" Taryn asked. Blinking, as if waking from a bad dream, I looked at her. It took me a few seconds to realize I was still holding her dress in my arms.

"I promise," I said. It was the least I could do—I felt overwhelmed by Taryn's generosity, her willingness to help me. I was already asking myself how I would ever make it up to her. Could she sense how much I needed a kind, maternal figure right now? Was she this giving and generous to every stranger she met?

I could hear Kelly chatting with Ethan in the living room. Jacob was still picking up flakes of fish food with his little fingers. I told Taryn that it was getting late; we should probably head out. She walked me to the door and squeezed me so tight the hanger from the dress pushed into my abdomen, but I still didn't want it to end.

I didn't try on the dress until the night of the gala. I didn't have a backup plan if it didn't fit, so I was relieved that it slipped over my head easily and zipped all the way up in the back. If anything, it was a little bit too big, but I was grateful for that. I always wore my clothes big so no one would be able to see the contours of my body.

In the mirror, I scrutinized myself. My hair, one shade lighter than pure black, hung in stringy clumps in my face. There was a zit in the corner of my mouth. My fingernails, painted black, were chipped and bitten. My legs were pasty white. No amount of makeup could make me feel better in my own skin, I reasoned, so I skipped it entirely.

As I was buckling my shoes, I remembered what my mom sometimes said about messy-looking girls we encountered at the grocery store or the pool. "That girl looks motherless," my mom would say. No one to tell her to comb her hair, paint her nails a fresh coat of ruby red to cover up the black. What she really meant was *That girl looks lost,* which is exactly how I felt.

Reluctantly, I stood under the lamp to take my picture. I hadn't forgotten Taryn's request, though it made me cringe now. "You look like Morticia Addams," my mom would frequently tell me. "Someone with your coloring really can't wear all black without looking sinister and scary."

The selfie I sent to Taryn was slightly blurry, but I didn't care. She texted back almost immediately. "You're fucking beautiful!!" I couldn't help tearing up. She couldn't know how much it meant to me to hear that—or that it gave me the confidence to leave the house that evening. All night, especially when I felt eyes on me, I repeated her text to myself like a mantra. *You're fucking beautiful.*

7/
HITTING ZONE

B y the third Sunday of the twelve-week Fresh Meat program, Halloween decorations had sprung up all over
South City. They were gorier than any I had seen before—
there were bloody scarecrows hanging upside down from
front porches, skeletons trapped in cages strung from trees.
Even in the daylight on my way to practice, it all looked so
violent and ominous.

When I walked into the Skatium, a dark figure lurking in
the shadows caused me to jump back in alarm. I dropped
one of my skates and it made a loud smacking sound on the
wood floor.

"I'm sorry!" Flux said. "Didn't mean to scare you! I'm
just standing here to tell everyone not to put on any gear and
to meet in the middle of the track."

My heart was still racing as I made my way out onto the
track. I took a seat in the circle next to Blades of Glory. "Do
you think it's a drug bust?" someone asked. "Maybe somebody finally got stabbed and we can't practice today."

Flux followed close behind me and shook her head in
response. "Nothing like that. I just don't want you to put on

gear because it's easier to learn how to hit when you're not on wheels." Everyone's response was to start beaming and cheering. I smiled too, but on the inside, I was terrified. I didn't think we'd be learning how to hit an opponent so soon. Most of us still couldn't even stand upright without falling over.

Flux requested that we tighten our circle so that our hips were nearly touching. Nurse Pain had the misfortune of standing beside her in the circle; she contorted her face in premature anguish, sensing she would be Flux's crash test dummy.

"The trick to hitting is not to stop once you make initial contact," Flux said. "You keep going. You hit *through* their body. You take their space."

As Flux wound up for the hit, Nurse Pain stepped away from her slightly. "You can just have my space." She laughed nervously. "I'll just give it to you."

Flux reassured her that the hit would be clean and she would be fine. She asked if she was ready, and Nurse Pain hadn't even finished nodding before Flux slammed sideways into her body. It was such an effective hip check that Nurse Pain stumbled into the skater beside her.

"Just like that," Flux said. "No elbows. No tripping. No punching. None of that is legal anymore."

Blades of Glory interrupted Flux for clarification. "So, hips, butt, thigh, shoulders—that's all legal hitting zone?"

Flux nodded and asked Blades if she wanted to go next. Since I was standing next to her in the circle, I widened my stance to prepare for the hit. Blades was bigger than me, and I didn't want to stumble, or worse, fall in front of Flux and all the other new recruits. Flux praised my stance and said my intuition was good; in derby, getting low was the best way to counter a hit. "Don't close your eyes though," she told me. "You want to remain alert, especially when you know a hit is coming."

Flux gave Blades the go-ahead, but when she tried to hit me, she barely grazed the side of my body.

"Sorry! Miscalculated!" Blades wound up to try again, and though this time she was effective in making contact with me, I didn't move at all. Blades threw her arms up in the air and said, "This is harder than it looks!"

She was right. When it was my turn, I couldn't perform the maneuver either. Even though I knew I had the strength to knock the woman next to me out of the way, my technique was impeded by the fact that my feet had to stay planted and I had to calculate how to lean and pop my hip. On the third try, I was finally successful in making her move, but Flux said I would've gotten a penalty for finishing the hit with my forearm.

After a few rounds, we moved to the thick plastic wall lining the track.

"This is a great way to practice hits if you don't have another human to train with," she said. Then, without warning, she crouched and slammed her body against the wall. It shuddered and made a low rattling noise. "Sometimes it's better to practice on something inanimate." *Slam.* "Something you can't hurt." *Slam.* "And something that won't"—*slam*—"hit"—*slam*—"back."

Per Flux's instruction, I aimed to initiate contact with the meaty part of my thigh. I reveled in the rattling sound the wall made each time I connected with it. The hits hurt my hip and shoulder, but it was a satisfying pain in that it had a distinct purpose: I could already imagine how it would be very useful in roller derby. In swimming, my coaches often emphasized that winning races was painful. We practiced disconnecting with our bodies with mantras like "This doesn't even hurt." In sprinting, so much emphasis was put on breath control, and we would deny the reality of the air our bodies needed by saying to ourselves, "This race matters more than taking a breath right now." More than once, I witnessed my teammates hyperventilating into swim caps or blacking out from lack of oxygen.

Using my thighs to hit the Skatium wall reminded me how self-conscious I'd been about my thighs as a kid. Before races, I compared the size of my legs to those of my teammates; mine always looked the biggest. I expressed my concern about this quietly to my dad so my mother wouldn't hear, and he demonstrated that I could make my legs look smaller by sitting a different way on the pool benches. "See?" he asked, lowering his thin body onto the couch and then pointing to his thighs. "Scoot to the edge of the bench so that extra fat won't get pushed up."

My dad's explanation only briefly satisfied me. It was too difficult to constantly monitor the way I was sitting, and I resented the fact that smaller girls could focus on their upcoming races rather than the size of their thighs. Now, at the Skatium, I felt grateful for my big thighs for the first time. I was relieved not to be one of the bony girls, slamming herself into the wall and yelping in pain. My body could withstand this kind of battering. It was made for this. *I* was made for this.

ONCE WE STARTED hitting, my Fresh Meat class of fifteen started dwindling. After two contact practices, four people were gone, including Nurse Pain and Blades of Glory.

Two weeks later, our group was down to half its initial size. As we were taking off our skates, a thin, butch woman said to me, "I'm not used to being so shitty at things. I mean, you should read my graduate thesis. It's really good." That was the last time I saw her.

I wasn't any better at hitting than the people who bailed, but I took comfort in the clear benchmarks listed on the minimum skills list and crossing them off one by one. I was excellent at weaving, at one-footed glides, and at pushes. Each time I conquered another skill, I could see the progress I was making, and as a result, I grew even more committed to learning all the skills by the time we'd be tested in early January.

I also enjoyed the literal and figurative boundaries of roller derby. The hits aimed at me were never personal; I was just a body in the way. That was one thing Flux emphasized over and over: hits should never be performed out of vengeance or spite. There were a few people in the derby world who were known for taking people out when they posed no threat, and these people were not seen favorably. Hits should always have a purpose, the most common of which was moving a player out of the way. Space was the most valuable commodity on the track. "The space your body takes up is precious," Flux once said. This was something of a revelation to me. I had never been taught to hold my ground, either literally or figuratively. "If they're targeting you, it likely means you're skating in the path they want to send their jammer through. It's more important than anything in this sport to own your space."

Flux also spent lots of time describing the difference between a good hit and a bad hit. "Bad hits happen when you're not in control of your body," she said. "They happen when you go after someone in a half-assed way. When you're not fully committed, you're going to wind up tripping your target—or yourself—and taking out more people than you intended. Maybe even hurting someone. This, by the way, is one reason we practice jumping—people will be falling left and right. It's important that you're able to maneuver around them."

It was more difficult to wrap my head around the concept of a bad hit. I had been watching so many high-level games online: top ten leagues with skaters who had been training for a decade or more.

"Watch the bozos from any of the leagues around here if you want to see what a bad hit looks like," Soup Beans advised. "It's just all about body control. You have to be in control of what your body is doing at all times."

It was also possible, I learned, to be a dangerous hit-receiver. Flux taught us how to fall small, with all our limbs tucked in so we wouldn't clothesline somebody else on our way down and our fingers wouldn't get rolled over by passing skaters. There was so much to remember I feared I was bound to forget something and wind up hurting somebody or myself. Soup Beans dismissed this worry. "Girl," she said. "You've only been skating what—three or four weeks?—and you're already safer than the entire league I skated with out in the middle of Missouri where I grew up. That's just part of starting out at such a highly ranked league!"

Flux was thorough in her explanation of the "legal target zone": the places on our opponent's body that would most safely and effectively impede her ability to continue skating. She described the places we should aim for—upper thigh, hip, chest—and we practiced them on each other. "Don't hold back!" she advised. "It's safer not to hold back. If you see an opportunity, take it."

Tutz, the woman I had read about in *Women's Health,* contributed to our training sessions by emphasizing the importance of counter-hitting, a concept that had not occurred to me. If we saw someone barreling toward us to strike, we needed to prepare to fight back. "Don't just stand there and let it happen!" Tutz shouted. "Pretend you're getting mugged! Pretend some bitch is trying to take your money!"

My first partner for an on-skates hitting drill was Stormin' Norma, a sweet, red-haired skater. The goal was to stand behind our partners and push them up track while they were plow-stopping, resisting being moved. It felt oddly sexual, standing behind Norma, who was bent at the waist and digging her heels in. I didn't know which part of her to touch. "Pick one of my butt cheeks," she told me. "And then start using your thighs to push."

When it was time to switch, I realized I felt more comfortable being hit, although my plow stops were so weak Norma could push me anywhere on the track she wanted. After that, I started trying to pair up with Taryn for every drill. Somehow, she knew exactly how much pressure I could take before falling over. She gave advice constantly— even when our heads were locked like billy goats' and I was attempting to drive her up the track. Trust your toe stops, she always told me. Bend your knees. Position yourself so that your collarbone is hitting mine and then push with all your might.

Soon, though, it became evident that I couldn't rely on the same partners for each practice because I was doing far more practices than most people—double, if not triple, the monthly minimum. It wasn't long before the other skaters began taking notice. "Do you ever leave?" they asked. "Who are you bunking with? The meth lady or the DJ booth man?"

Part of this reality meant that I had to drive directly from Thursday-night practice to the weekly author reading on campus, which was required for writing students. The first night I did this, I forgot to bring a change of clothes or any food to tide me over for the reading. I was used to denying myself food, and most of the time I would've ignored my growling stomach, but I was already starting to feel nauseous, and I wasn't sure I could make it another two hours. Thankfully, this was a practice that Taryn had attended.

"I'm embarrassed to ask this," I said to her as we took off our skates. "But do you have any food with you?"

She unzipped the front pocket of her purse and pulled out a package of peanut butter crackers. "I'm a mom," she said. "Of course I have food with me."

I took the crackers, blushing. If only she knew some way to help soothe the throbbing pain in my lower back from falling straight onto my butt earlier. As if reading my mind, she disappeared and reappeared a minute later with a bag of ice. "Just stick it in the waistband of your shorts," she said. "No one will even see."

I hugged her tightly before leaving and told her again how lucky I was to have her as a derby mom. "I have this thing where I need to help people," she said. "It's just how I function."

At school, I climbed the steps to the English department slowly. Campus looked different at night. I had overheard a few undergrads saying that WashU was on a list of campuses that most looked like Hogwarts, which wasn't much of a surprise. The buildings looked like castles—there were circular towers and gray stone and lots of stairs. The English department was saturated with life-sized oil paintings of benefactors. The room where the readings were held had stone angels in the upper corners that flanked the podium. Walking in with a bag of ice stuffed in my pants, I felt distinctly uncomfortable. There was a voice in my head pleading with me to turn around and walk out—go home and take a hot shower, cuddle with Lady, and get started on tomorrow's homework instead.

"Your hair is all wet!" My friends Klara and Tory, both writers in my program whom I deeply admired, approached. Tory was nearly thirty, tall and athletic. Klara was fifty-five with salt-and-pepper hair and big, thick glasses.

"And are your pants wet too?" Tory asked, pointing to the mound of ice, which was already melting, giving the impression I had peed myself. They were both wearing buttondowns; never had I been so envious of normal clothes. Why hadn't I anticipated that I wouldn't want to attend a reading in the same psychedelic leggings and sleeveless green hoodie that I had practiced in? Why make it so easy for other people to know I didn't belong?

"I actually just started playing roller derby," I said. My voice was quieter than usual. I didn't want anyone else overhearing. This graduate program was highly competitive, and the understanding was that we'd devote these two years of our lives entirely to our studies.

"Roller derby!" Klara exclaimed. She jabbed her elbows out in a mock display of hitting. "That's pretty tough, isn't it?" It was common for people Klara's age to have an image in their heads of roller derby from decades past.

In the stone angel room where we were standing, I could see out into the hall where caterers were already setting up a long table of delicate finger food for after the reading. Taryn's crackers had only temporarily tided me over; I was ravenous again. Would anyone notice if I snuck some grapes and cheese?

"We just started learning how to hit," I said, pointing to the mound of ice. "I took a couple hard falls today."

People around us filed into the stone angel room and started taking their seats in preparation for the reading. I still felt torn about whether to stay. I'd never heard of this author or read any of her work, but even if I had, I'd probably be too timid to ask a question or introduce myself afterward. My lack of courage was one thing I hated about myself. Why did I always get so scared to talk to other adults? What did I fear they would say?

"We should sit," Tory said, guiding us to a row of chairs. My last thought, as I trapped myself between the two of them, was that I should've washed the stink off my pads. I made myself small, praying no one could smell it.

WHAT I CAME to learn, the more time I spent at the Skatium that October, was that hitting wasn't the only danger we had to contend with: the Skatium residents were thieves. The DJ booth man blamed all the theft on "the crackheads." He insisted that it wasn't the people who lived in the Skatium who were taking our stuff, but those who wandered in, high and looking to get out of the cold. Admittedly, it was difficult for us to distinguish between those two groups. Once, a woman with a shaved head and thin lips wandered inside during our practice and right out onto the track. We didn't all see her at once, but after a few seconds, everybody stopped skating to stare. It was like some kind of Western standoff—she looked at our feet, confused, it seemed, as to why we were wearing wheels.

"Can I help you?" Taryn finally asked. The woman didn't respond, and when Taryn made a move toward her, she cowered, like a dog afraid of a beating.

"I'm not going to hurt you," Taryn said. She guided the woman away by the elbow. Once the woman tore her eyes away from our skates, she seemed transfixed by the spray-painted planets and stars on the Skatium walls. When Taryn returned, she reported that she'd seen men trying to break into our cars and ordered us to make sure they were all locked.

Our cars weren't the Skatium thieves' only target. Sometimes they'd ransack our bags. If anything remotely valuable was left sitting on the benches, it disappeared within minutes. Once, our announcer, Magilla Guerrilla, visited practice and set his phone down on the Skatium railing. When he realized his mistake, several skaters threw up their hands. "Not again!" one of them exclaimed. "We've got another missing phone!"

Just like when we'd practiced tornado drills at school, every skater on the rink seemed to know exactly how to proceed. One group split off to start moving our bags to the inside of the track, which we typically avoided because putting our bags there decreased our practice space. Another group went off to help Magilla track down his phone. The resident who had stolen it either hadn't possessed the foresight to silence it or didn't know how, because we could hear the phone ringing right outside his door.

"That's my ringtone in there!" Magilla called, pounding

on the door. "I know you have my phone, and I would like it back!"

The skater helping Magilla dialed and redialed until the man cracked open the door. He handed back the phone and said, "I have no idea how this got in here."

Sometimes it was difficult to know what posed a greater threat: simply being inside the Skatium or being on wheels, learning to hit for the first time. The members of the coaching committee rotated with Flux, and each one seemed to have an unending list of hitting drills when it was their turn to coach practice. In one, two players would stand hip-to-hip on either side of a line. When the whistle blew, the objective was to slam into each other so hard that one of us either fell or stumbled, surrendering her space. It was like a human tug-of-war, only instead of pulling, we pushed. Our bodies were the rope.

Soup Beans's favorite drill, Lunch Money, involved one player at a standstill on the track and the other hitting and pushing her relentlessly. The hits didn't even have to be legal; the idea was that one skater was a bully trying to steal the other's lunch money. "Bullies don't play fair," Soup Beans told us. "So, bullies, you can push with your hands, shove with your elbows, whatever you need to do to get that person to the ground."

Hitting at speed was even more difficult. One drill we often did with Flux was performed skating in a single-file line in which the person at the back of the line would weave through each of us, hip-checking as she went. The drill was supposed to teach us to communicate. Once she struck us, we were supposed to yell to the person in front that she was coming, but I rarely remembered to do that from the ground. Weaving through was much more fun, though I often tripped on other people's skates and Flux said my hits felt like love taps.

As I learned to use my body to compete for space, I couldn't help but recall a drill from high school swimming that my coach had dubbed Arkansas Death Match. It was always used as a punishment—in the case I remember most vividly, we had lost a meet by a few points and made a couple of foolish errors, like one-handed touches and illegal relay entries.

Coach explained the rules of Arkansas Death Match to the freshman "maggots" who hadn't played before. We had to swim one fifty-meter sprint every minute, racing in the same lane right beside our competitor. Hitting was encouraged. "Drown them," Coach said. "Hold their head under and drown them."

Coach set me against my nemesis, Riley. She won the first sprint, and that's when Coach started yelling at me. "You Froot Loop! Are you gonna let her kick your ass like that?" he screamed. "Aren't you gonna fight?"

We pushed off the wall at the same time, and I watched Riley underwater. I could see Coach screaming when I turned my head to breathe. I couldn't hear what he was yelling but I'd heard it all before. *If you swim that slow in a meet, everybody in the stands is gonna stand up—not to cheer, but to vomit.*

I timed my stroke to hit her. Our arms smacked in midair and Coach started jumping.

"Get down with your bad self!" he screamed. "You're an animal! Riley, are you going to let this piece of dog shit beat—"

We pushed off again, and Riley started hitting back. Her fingernails scraped my shoulders, and she pushed to the center of the lane, so I pushed back. I was afraid that our arms were going to lock together. I was afraid that we would tear each other apart.

When we finished Death Match, Riley wouldn't look at me. Our own heavy breathing was all we heard. And then, sobbing. On the deck, a sophomore was in full-on hysterics. She was doing squats while Coach screamed at her.

When Coach saw that we'd finished, he forgot about the sophomore. "Good girls," he cooed, bending down to pat our heads. When the other girls reached the wall, they let Coach pat them too. Collectively, we adored him. But I could feel the bruises blooming. I surveyed them in the mirror that evening, spinning to see which side was more colorful.

Maybe this is where I got my tendency to do the same with derby bruises, which speckled my arms, legs, and abdomen. When there was no practice and Kelly wasn't home, I worked on my hits by slamming into the closet door in the apartment. After ten on one side, I'd switch to the other. By the time half of my body was feeling raw and numb, the other would just be waking up and I'd start the process over again. I liked how it hurt. I liked the souvenirs the pain gave me. It was a twist on a pattern I had established as a teenager. I found ways to punish myself for my failure to justify my fear: four hours of swimming laps, running during the hottest part of the day, skipping meals, bingeing and purging. I took any excuse I could to get out of the house, out of my mother's reach. I wished her actions would leave bruises, because then I'd have proof that she had hurt me. I'd know why I was cowering. It didn't make sense to fear a mother who devoted hours to watching swim practice, a mother who professed to love my paintings and photographs, a mother all my friends adored. "She's so cool," they would say, "because she says and does whatever she wants."

IN THE FIRST few weeks of hitting, my body fought back. Matching pea-sized blisters formed on my pinky toes, which made wearing both skates and shoes agonizing. My toenails threatened to peel off. Dozens of fingerprint bruises dotted my upper arms. The first time I came to practice with a clearly distinguishable hand mark, someone said, "That's proof you're doing derby right!"

During a particularly grueling practice, I was slammed backward by another skater and hit my head hard on the track. Birdsong was quick to administer a concussion test; as a preschool teacher, she was trained in how to deal with such injuries.

"I don't think you're concussed," she told me. "But I also wouldn't skate anymore today."

I nodded. The practice was almost done anyway. I drove myself home slowly, as though the speed of my car could somehow lessen the pain in my neck. Unable to turn my head far enough to check my blind spot, I stayed tense the whole way. I worried that at any minute, someone would come flying out of nowhere and hit me over the guardrail and into the drainage channel below.

For several minutes after parking, I simply sat in the car. I couldn't motivate myself to make the twisting motion that was required to get up, couldn't turn to see if opening my door would result in it being torn off by a moving car. Once I finally got out of the car, heaved myself up the steps, and pushed open the heavy door to our apartment, I walked straight past Kelly, mumbling hello. I didn't acknowledge

Lady, whose tail was thumping on the wood floor, and went straight into the kitchen, where there was a large ice pack waiting in the freezer.

It wasn't until I had lifted both legs onto the couch that I noticed the blisters on my ankles. There were seven in total, bigger than raisins and oozing fluid. The pain in my neck completely overtook the pain in my ankles, so much so that when I rubbed the blisters with the pad of my index finger, the stinging that ensued seemed dull by comparison.

Kelly brought me a glass of water and set down a bottle of pain relievers on the coffee table without speaking. When she saw the blisters, she went to the bathroom cabinet and came back with a large brown bottle of hydrogen peroxide.

I worried about what she would say when she returned. Suddenly, the line between empowerment and brutalizing myself seemed so thin as to be invisible. I didn't know if derby was merely doing what my mother had always done to herself—distracted and numbed—or if it was in fact teaching me to feel something for the first time.

"You know," Kelly started. I cast my eyes down. "I've watched a lot of practices and I'm shocked there are any straight girls on your team. Don't you find it weird? I wonder if some of them joined derby because they missed out on experimenting in college. I mean, it's a pretty ideal situation if you think about it. When else can you vertically spoon another woman? When else can you stand behind a woman and repeatedly thrust?"

A grin broke out across my face. "Thrusting has nothing to do—"

"I'm just wondering if some of these 'straight girls' have other . . . tendencies. That's all."

I opened my mouth to argue but felt too weak to do

anything other than laugh. If I'd had the strength, I would have told her how grateful I was that she was toughing it out with me, how much I loved her, how liberating it felt to be creating our own life from scratch. Kelly joined in my laughter, and we laughed so hard and for so long that eventually my sore abs felt like they were flattening into my spine. We laughed so hard I had to heave for air. We laughed until the hydrogen peroxide on my open blisters stopped frothing and began rolling down my ankles like tears.

8

THE ROOKIE RUMBLE

In early October, Kelly and I had been invited to a grad school party on Halloween weekend. The host was a second-year fiction student I had seen on campus and at readings but never had a conversation with. Her publishing record intimidated me, as did her effortless academic-hipster style. *Partners welcome. Costumes mandatory,* she wrote in the email invitation.

I was pleasantly surprised when I read this. Kelly took Halloween very seriously, whereas I pretty much just wore whatever costume she planned for me. On our first Halloween together, we went as the two main characters from *Juno.* She fulfilled Michael Cera's nerdy baby-daddy look with the iconic sweatband and matching mustard shorts (into which she'd stuffed a sausage-shaped roll of socks). Sculpting a convincing baby bump for me had proven slightly more challenging, and in the weeks leading up to Halloween, Kelly conducted thorough research. The most successful strategy involved squeezing into a swimsuit to hold my pillow fetus in place. The result had been authentic enough to elicit disapproving scowls from the partygoers who saw me smoking outside on the porch.

There was plenty of evidence on Facebook of the great lengths Kelly had gone to in order to ensure her costume was the hit of the party in the years before we met, too. In her junior year, she'd been Kip from *Napoleon Dynamite*. Her mustache perfectly matched her dirty-blond hair, which was parted and slicked to the side. She'd worn belted cargo shorts and calf-high dad socks and thick, drugstore glasses that completely obscured her vision and, as she confessed to me, gave her a terrible headache.

One of the first things I learned about Kelly was that she never strived to look pretty—as a woman or a man. She delighted in anything gender-bending, anything drag. This was an attractive quality, though I did sometimes wonder about how much self-expression was encouraged—or, at the very least, not discouraged—by her family. As the third in her family to come out, Kelly had no doubt she would be accepted by her parents. Her oldest brother, who came out to them as bisexual, was an active member of the BDSM scene. Kelly and her sister had found handcuffs in his things when they were just thirteen and learned about "camp": a place in the woods for people in the scene to meet and have safe, adventurous sex. Later, when Kelly was researching piercers for a safety pin industrial she wanted done in her left ear, she encountered a picture of her brother on the piercing site, extra-large fishhooks in his back being pulled by someone outside the frame.

It was just a fact that Kelly's upbringing had been more accepting, more informative, and more liberal in terms of teaching her healthy self-expression. The closest I had to a creative outlet was church, for which my sister and I dressed up and applied makeup but had to strictly abide by gender norms or our mother would send us back to our room to change. My favorite plaid button-up was not allowed, nor were certain shoes that my mother deemed "mannish." I started looking at my attire as a performance, which helped me stomach feeling not myself.

For the grad school party, Kelly and I dressed as well-known artists—she as PBS icon Bob Ross and I as Frida Kahlo. Since I'd grown up mostly in white spaces, it didn't occur to me that dressing up as Frida was culturally appropriative in any way. I didn't yet have the language or insight; I was too preoccupied with gathering the necessary supplies. It had taken a great deal of planning—and a lot of time at Goodwill. Eventually, we found a beautiful floor-length floral skirt for me to wear and several brightly colored scarves to drape over my shoulders. I dyed my hair even darker and applied eyeliner pencil to highlight my existing unibrow and upper lip hair. The rings and bracelets we'd found at the bottom of the bins adorned every finger; the earrings hanging from my lobes were heavy.

Kelly's outfit was trickier, in a sense, because so much hinged on finding the right wig and facial hair, which we did, online, for $12.99. The blue button-up and khakis were easy, and I already had a big palette and bright colors to decorate it. Once I handed her a paintbrush, she looked quite convincing.

We arrived at the party half an hour after the scheduled start time, at Kelly's insistence. "I've been burned too many times," she said. "These things don't really start when they say they do." I was grateful for our lateness; by the time we found a parking spot on the street, we could hear the dull hum of dozens of people. I didn't even have to consult my notes to verify the address.

When we pushed open the door, however, I had a moment of panic that we had crashed the wrong party. Practically no one was in costume. People stood in small huddles, looking rather bored and sipping wine from plastic cups. Most people wore simple, hipster trends: plain black turtlenecks and oversized glasses, high-waisted light-wash jeans and a tucked-in white T-shirt. I had the sudden urge to turn around and walk back out the door.

Before I even left the threshold, I spotted Tory pouring herself some merlot into a red Solo cup. When Kelly and I approached, she nearly spit out what was in her mouth.

"Okay, this," she said, gesturing broadly to Kelly and me, "is amazing."

"Why are we the only ones in costume?" I asked, voice low. "The invite said costumes were *mandatory.*"

"I don't know," she said. "I was too busy to throw something together. I assume everyone else was too."

I'm busy, I wanted to say. *I made time because I wanted to fit in.* Clearly, my wanting to fit in so badly had resulted in the exact opposite. I could feel people's eyes on me. I could feel them talking about me. I wanted to go.

As if reading my mind, Tory extended her hands. "Please stay," she said. "It'll be fun."

The party dragged until we listened to some of the first-year fiction students read their work; I sat on the hardwood floor in a pool of my floral skirt, Kelly beside me. I thought their work was amazing—it was well written and poignant and immediate. Kelly found it harder to concentrate. I watched out of the corner of my eye as she pulled a crossword out of her bag and set it on the floor in front of her.

Instead of listening, she mentally filled in the answers. I smiled to myself. Not many people could do a crossword puzzle without a pen. We left not long after the reading ended.

Before bed, I made a half-hearted attempt to scrub off the makeup that conjoined my eyebrows, but the next morning there was still a dark stain on my face. I had been so tired that I forgot I had to get up early to get to derby practice. It was a unique practice—a Halloween-themed "rookie rumble" that Flux had organized to get us comfortable with game-play. I was worried. It had only been four weeks since I had laced up my skates for the first time as an adult. My balance was questionable even when no one was trying to barrel into me. Illegal moves and their corresponding penalties were a mystery.

It was Nanny McWhee who first voiced the concern that once we passed mins, we would have almost no experience with actual gameplay. "We can hit each other till we see stars," she said, "but it won't help us learn the sport." This rookie rumble was Flux's response to that concern. It'd be very low contact, she promised, with only new skaters. She encouraged us to wear costumes.

Even if I had woken up in time to get dressed up, I had no intention of wearing a costume. After the previous night, I didn't want to run the risk that I'd be the only one. I also had no idea what kind of costume would be conducive to skating in a scrimmage—something clearly black or white with space for numbers on the back. Frida, with all her flowy fabric and bangles, was surely a no-go.

Yet, Frida was still present on my face in the form of a stubborn unibrow. At stoplights, I licked my finger and tried rubbing it off. When that didn't work, I resorted to using my fingernails.

When I pulled up to the Skatium, the skin between my eyebrows was inflamed and still noticeably darker than the rest of my face. One of the unexpected benefits of having the remnants of a unibrow, however, was that all my attention was focused on my vanity instead of my nerves. I wasn't thinking at all about the rookie rumble or what I would be expected to do on skates. I felt somewhat confident in the sense that I could tell I was among the best of the pack of rookies, and I figured if they could do it, I could too.

Two things became glaringly obvious when I pulled open the heavy Skatium door. The first was that I was the only real rookie attending this rumble. Nanny McWhee skated quietly in the corner while everyone else warmed up on the track; it was clear she had no intention of playing, since she hadn't yet passed mins. The second was that I had again made a grave error as far as costumes were concerned, this time in choosing *not* to wear one.

Taryn, who was dressed as a Teenage Mutant Ninja Turtle in a shiny green dress, approached me, smiling.

"Hey babe!" she said. "Did you forget to wear a costume?"

I sputtered in response, not knowing whether to lie. Instead, I asked her where all the rookies were. "Wasn't this supposed to be a scrimmage for just us?" I asked.

"That's a good question," Taryn replied, thoughtfully. "They must've gotten scared off. You'll be fine."

I put on my gear with great trepidation, watching Nanny skate on the sidelines all the while. When I had everything on, I skated up to her. She took a knee when she saw me coming and removed her helmet, revealing a giant pair of white underpants tied over her bald head.

"Are you Captain Underpants?" I asked, laughing.

"Oh no, honey, this isn't a costume. These are my big girl panties. Derby demands it." She pulled the underwear off her head and pointed to the signatures she had acquired. "These names are to remind me I have teammates to help me through all the fear and discomfort." The way she spoke about the underwear was so profound, just like the way she spoke about everything, and I couldn't help but laugh. They were the biggest pair of underwear I had ever seen and covered with signatures like a little kid's plaster cast.

"Sign your name for me, dear," she said, fanning out a variety of brightly colored markers for me to choose from. "I'm already so inspired by your tenacity."

I chose pink and found an empty spot between Nox and Trigger. But—what to sign? I hadn't chosen a derby name yet so I supposed I didn't have a choice but to sign my legal name.

"Why aren't you playing in the rookie rumble today?" I asked. Nanny scoffed and gestured out onto the track.

"I know my limitations," she said. "I'm not stable enough for this."

Nanny didn't say anything about my decision to play, but it was hanging in the air. Did she think I was stable enough? Did *I* think I was stable enough? It hadn't occurred to me that I could say no—no to Flux, no to the skater writing big numbers on my arms with an extra-large permanent marker, or to the skater pulling me out onto the track.

Among the horde of costumed skaters was a black-and-white cow. A humming built-in fan moved the fabric of her costume in a billowy tent around her body. The numbers on her back were written with strips of duct tape. It occurred to me that it would probably be a good idea to follow her when I was out there. Surely it wouldn't hurt as much if I fell on an inflatable cow. But was she on the white team or the black team? How were we supposed to tell? What the hell was she thinking, dressing up as a cow?

When Kelly asked me later what it had felt like to be caught in a chaotic mess of bodies, I told her it was like unknowingly entering a wave pool. This had happened to me once when I was six years old. The waves only came in fifteen-minute increments, and I had discovered the pool during a period of calm. I had no idea the water would grow violent until the lifeguards started blowing their whistles and the kids around me started pointing at the waves hurtling toward us. I could vaguely hear my dad shouting from the side of the pool, but he was too far to reach, and there wasn't enough time to get out.

Other bodies hit me before the wave did. Arms scooped me up, dropped me, thrust me under. Everything I had been noticing before—the cold water on my legs, the warm sun on my back—suddenly no longer mattered. Water rushed into my open mouth and got caught in my airway. My hands turned to claws. Panic swelled in my body, even more violent than the wave, as I coughed, gasping for air, unsure I would ever reach dry land again.

The roller rink was like that wave pool. I skated onto the track with Taryn in a moment of calm. I heard the five-second whistle. After that, I was thrown to the ground, both knee pads slid down, and my skin skidded along the wood. I bit my own tongue. Someone pulled me up, threw me back down, sent me careening off into another direction. Fingernails scraped my face. Somebody else's wheels locked with mine, and I hit the ground. Hands squeezed my upper arm, dragged me forward, and threw me into the wall that was the opposing team. I had no control over my own movement.

When the whistle blew after what felt like an eternity, I literally crawled off the track. On the sidelines was a tall person dressed like a slice of pizza. Only when the pizza approached me did I realize it was Tutz.

"Are you on my team?" I asked.

"Girl," she said, not answering. "I can see you thinking so hard out there you're burning your brain cells. Try to loosen up a little."

We watched the scrimmage for several minutes before Tutz said, "Let's go in together for the next one. I want you to do two things: stay with me, and get low. It's easier for them to knock you over when you're standing straight up. You looked like a freaking prairie dog in that last round."

I nodded seriously.

"Tell me your name again?" she said.

"I don't know yet," I said.

"Girl, you're killing me. You gotta figure that shit out," Tutz said, taking my arm. "Or somebody will go ahead and figure it out for you."

9

BAD BLOOD

After Halloween was over, all of my teammates' focus shifted to one thing: the Women's Flat Track Derby Association (WFTDA) championships in Portland, Oregon. Playoffs had taken place in September in Montréal, Columbia, Vancouver, and Madison, and only twelve teams from around the world had qualified, including Arch Rival's All Stars team.

Usually at practice, the All Stars would pair up with skaters on the B and C teams to help mentor and support them in their learning, but the closer it got to champs, the more the All Stars stuck to themselves. I didn't blame them; I remembered how it felt to be preparing for the state championship in high school with only five or six of my teammates. Everyone else finished their season early and could go home directly after school, rest, sleep in on weekends, eat whatever they wanted. A huge sense of responsibility came with representing my school at the highest level, which is what I imagined Arch All Stars felt like. We'd never made it past the first round of champs before, and were being pitted against

Denver this year, a team with whom we consistently had bad blood.

Taryn and a group of B and C team skaters were traveling to Portland to support the All Stars. It wouldn't have been feasible financially for me to go, and I wouldn't yet have felt comfortable going even if I did have the money, but I couldn't help feeling a twinge of envy. How exciting it would've been to cheer on the All Stars in the same arena in which they were playing. How perfect an opportunity to further bond with Taryn and my league mates. For how little time I had been a member of the league, I already felt hugely invested in the success of the All Stars—and their representation of St. Louis. I had only lived in the city for six months, but already shared the All Stars' scorn when they recalled other teams not knowing where we were from. "Where is Arch City?" people would say. "I've heard of the Arch before but I can't remember what city it's in."

As the All Stars prepared for champs, I prepared for a one-on-one meeting with a visiting writer who was coming to WashU to critique our work. All I really knew about the man was that he was famous; I felt uncomfortable giving him work about my gayness, lest he react in any way like my parents. Most of the essays I had written in grad school were somewhat closeted anyway, but I still chose carefully. I settled on two different pieces. The first was about my visit to see a spiritual healer on my twenty-second birthday and the revelations she offered me about my mother ("She struggles to love") and about my past lives ("You were once a young girl, tied to the stake and burned"). The second essay was a lyrical piece about urine; I braided together personal, gender-related anecdotes with facts about pee, like the ways female animals use it for self-defense.

I felt nervous about the meeting, but I was too preoccupied with champs to obsess over it. A few days before everyone left for Portland, Taryn texted me and told me to bring any clothes I didn't wear anymore to the Skatium for a clothing exchange. Everyone in the league would do the same, and we would have a massive pile of clothes to give away. It was a common occurrence, she said—a delightful pick-me-up right before the big tournament weekend.

I spent several hours the next day going through my closet. When we moved to St. Louis, everything Kelly and I owned fit in our two cars. Most of what I had was clothes, flattened into vacuum-sealed bags. I was bogged down by items like the floral dress my mother bought me for college interviews, all four of my high school state meet sweatshirts, even pants that no longer fit but that I had fond memories of wearing in Texas during a college internship. For the first time I could remember, it didn't feel hard to start a donation pile. There was a voice in my head urgently telling me I needed to shed my skin, grow up, put the past behind me. An even louder voice asked if I wanted to be caught dead in some of the clothes I had dragged to St. Louis—clothes I hated wearing but wore out of obligation or in order to stay invisible.

The first time Kelly came to visit me in my hometown, I suggested she wear a dress for that exact reason. She was passing through on her way to visit her grandmother in Detroit. It had been six months since I had come out to my mother, and she had only recently stopped berating me about it every day. I reasoned that no one would suspect we were romantically involved if we were both wearing dresses. At least, that was the impression I got from my mother. Wearing a dress didn't feel particularly difficult for me. I still mostly felt like myself in a dress, but for Kelly it was uncomfortable at best. She looked like a completely different person, hair down instead of in its usual, messy bun. She also applied heavy makeup to her eyes and lips. I wasn't sure she would comply with my suggestion to wear this costume, but I learned later that even though Kelly had had a relatively smooth coming out, she still battled an internal dialogue that stressed hyper-vigilance. Even the most accepting family, I realized, didn't inoculate people against the harm of a misogynistic and ho-mophobic society. It didn't help that her first girlfriend, who had immigrated from Brazil, spoke to her mother in Portu-guese about Kelly right in front of her—"Those boots make her look like a little dyke," the mother had said.

We planned for Kelly's visit to my hometown as though it were a bank heist—carefully arranging timelines, loca-tions, and contingency plans. The place I'd chosen for us to eat lunch that day was a bridge behind an abandoned train station. The depot had been nonfunctional for as long as I had lived there, though the city council apparently had high hopes for revitalizing it. Flyers were hung in the post office and the library asking for support from constituents. The vi-sion was strong—the tracks were already laid, and they spanned the state of Michigan and westward past Chicago. Bringing back a functional train station would kickstart the economy. People would flock to my town. That was the idea, at least.

I chose the depot as a meeting place for both the solitude and the rustic beauty. Kelly wouldn't get to see much of my hometown, so I wanted what little she did see to be memo-rable. To get to the bridge, we would have to pass through a field of bishop's lace in which sat an abandoned red caboose. Under the bridge were metal beams covered in graffiti. The paint chipped easily, and a collection of bright colors fell off the walls and landed on the ground. I had a habit of picking up the little chips of paint and crunching them between my fingers, leaving the pile more pixelated than I found it.

It was difficult climbing up the side of the railroad tracks to the spot I had planned for us to sit. The ground was uneven, and the incline was steep. It was even more difficult because of our dresses, and Kelly told me so.

"I'm only doing this because you promised it won't be forever," she said. "And I know how afraid you are."

She was right—fear of being outed dominated all my thoughts, all my choices. Truthfully, it still did, even after I moved to St. Louis and joined Arch Rival. What good was it doing me to hold on to clothes that did nothing but closet me or remind me of a time when I was closeted?

THERE WERE ALREADY heaps of clothing on the Skatium benches when I arrived that evening. I carried in three full garbage bags and spread the clothes out for people to peruse, all the while eyeing pieces that I liked. Almost everything was derby related, if even tangentially. Within a few minutes, I found a pair of olive-green leggings with leather patches sewn on the knees, a purple tank top that said DERBY OR DIE, and a faux-leather jacket that was slightly too big for me but in a comforting way. I felt somewhat shameful bringing traces of my past lives to this space, where everything on the tables had such personality and grit.

Tutz arrived with even more clothes than I did. "Where are we putting the extra-large stuff?" she asked. There was no hint of shame in her voice, which made me feel even more admiration.

I was surprised by the volume of apparel that had other teams' logos on it. Flux explained this by saying she often bought a T-shirt from the host team at tournaments; sometimes there was even a clothing exchange like this one for visiting skaters. Often there would be a casual exchange of jerseys; it was just roller derby culture.

I picked up a tank with a pink safety pin on it that said London Rollergirls. "That was mine!" Flux said. "They're a great team. I just didn't like the way it fit." I held up the tank and considered it. Flux was much thinner than me; I didn't know that I could squeeze into it.

"We're going to be playing them when we beat Denver this weekend," Tutz added.

"How does it work?" I asked. "You're definitely playing Denver first, right?"

"It's a bracket. We're going in ranked eighth and Denver is ranked seventh, so we play them in the first round. Then whoever wins goes on to play London. We probably won't beat them, but we'll give them a run for their money. And anyway, putting up a fight will increase our rank for next year."

"But you're pretty confident about Denver?" I asked.

"Well, we beat Denver by three points six months ago when they came to St. Louis for our Sibling Rivalry tournament. We did it once, and we'll do it again."

I had heard about Arch's animosity toward Denver, but I had no idea what sparked it. As though reading my thoughts, Flux spun around to look at me. "You won't find any Denver apparel in here because we *really* don't get along. There's one player in particular who we all just loathe—she said something awful to Dad Bod on the track during the Sibling Rivalry tournament and we'll never forget it. Don't get me wrong—we want to win because it would be our first win at champs, but the fact that it's Denver just lights a huge fire under our asses."

I wanted to ask what the Denver skater had said that was so awful, but I figured Flux would have just said it if she wanted to. I wasn't about to pry, so instead I said, "Are there any teams we get along with well?"

"Minnesota," Flux and Tutz answered in unison, then laughed. "Minnesota is kind of our sister team," Flux said. "They have the best venue, the most fans, the biggest spirit. We're always cheering each other on."

I mentally filed away this information as I sorted through the heaps of clothing on the Skatium benches. Everything I touched, I wanted. Some of it I wasn't sure would fit me, which was a lingering source of shame in the back of my head, but I was mostly overcome by a desire to have it all. A new wardrobe suddenly felt key to shedding my old self. I wanted nothing to do with the self that had walked into the Skatium that day; I suddenly wanted desperately to reinvent her. I took plaid button-ups, derby T-shirts, the London tank. I took cheetah-print sneakers, punk-looking leggings, a fanny pack with the old Arch logo on it. I took bad tie-dye jobs and denim vests with poorly hacked-off sleeves. I took a Minnesota Roller Derby T-shirt, a belt with spikes on it, and three geometric print T-shirts for Kelly. I filled the three garbage bags I had brought and then asked to borrow another.

THE DAY OF the Arch vs. Denver game, Taryn posted a handful of pictures from Portland that made me wish more than anything that I was there. In one, she sat in the stands with Loki Doki, Pegasass, Soup Beans, Carmina Piranha, CupQuake, Fletch-A-Sketch, and Girl Fawkes: all people I knew from practice and would've loved spending time with. In another, Draggie was waving black and pink pom-poms.

Taryn offered her password for Kelly and me to watch the game live on WFTDA TV and we eagerly took her up on her offer. Before the game started, we made our own pizza and mixed drinks, tuning in right as the announcers were introducing themselves.

"Live from beautiful Portland, Oregon, hosted by the Women's Flat Track Derby Association and the Rose City Rollers, my name is Lightning Slim and I am joined here by my good friend, Mr. Whistler. Just off-screen, doing stats for us, is Ophelia Melons."

"*Ophelia Melons?*" I repeated. "Does *everyone* choose a derby name?"

As if directly answering my question, Lightning Slim began rattling off the skating officials. "While we have a few seconds, I'll run through the skating officials for this contest: Crewhead, Umpire Strikes Back, JC Chaotic, Eric Rock, Colin-the-Shots, Ogre, Lattie, Izzy Demented, and Harm-N-Killa-Brew as our refereeing staff."

There was a brief pause while two people ran onto the track to secure the sport court and the announcers recapped the results from earlier in the day.

"Nonskating officials—the NSOs—for this contest are sHellcat, DB Hubbard, Travis Sickle, Wizard of Laws, Juju Be, Amelia Dareheart, geoknitter, Sho'Nuff, Tara Byte, Danger Muffin, Doc Skinner, Mortricia, Apron, and Los Angry-Lez."

"Can you believe this?" I asked Kelly.

"Why shouldn't they get to have derby names?" Kelly

asked. "I'm much more distracted by what the Denver coaches are wearing."

The camera was zoomed in on the Denver bench: players in their dark blue jerseys and silver helmets, coaches wearing sweatbands and cutoff overalls, one side buckled and the other hanging down their backs. It was quite a contrast to the Arch Rival coaches, who were wearing professional tan blazers and black turtlenecks.

The rosters for each team were displayed and another difference became glaringly evident: no one on the Denver team played under a derby name. Most everyone was listed under their legal last name.

"That's not fun at all," Kelly said. "I'm glad Arch isn't like that."

"I actually asked Taryn about that recently," I said, recalling a conversation I'd had with her about an Arch skater who used her real name. "She said some people think it makes it more likely you'll get sponsorships. Back in the early 2000s when derby was reimagined, fierce names were everything. But some people aren't into the whole nod-to-the-past thing. All they care about is looking professional."

When the game began, Arch's four best blockers joined their best jammer, Bricktator, on the track. I had heard a lot about Bricktator but hadn't yet met her.

As the teams got into position and the timer counted down, the announcers quipped that they were lucky to be at the Veterans Memorial Coliseum in Portland—a venue in which the Beatles had once performed.

With that, the whistle blew, and the jammers were off. It looked so much calmer than how it felt to be playing—although it probably felt less so to the blockers smashing into each other and shoving each other off the track. Taryn had told me to focus on just one blocker and watch what she was doing, and when I did, the game slowed down significantly. Most of the time I watched Tutz, who had written, in big letters, FOR FUN on her thighs. Pretty soon I could anticipate her next move—or, at the very least, rationalize the moves she made. She always seemed to know where her teammates were, how many seconds were left on the clock, where her jammer was and where the opposing jammer would be coming from.

What impressed me most, within the first thirty minutes of gameplay, was Bricktator. I knew she had a background in figure skating—Taryn had told me she was known for wild, pirouette-like moves on the track to evade the blockers, but it was another thing entirely to see it live. "What a maneuver by Bricktator!" Lightning Slim yelled after a particularly amazing jump-spin to remain in bounds. "I can't believe she spun on one foot like that after taking a hit to the hip! And with a little half smile too—something you don't always see from such a focused player."

The score remained close, but Arch stayed ahead, 83–64, at halftime; Brick was the highest-scoring jammer of the game. "Things are shaping up to be a battle of endurance, Mr. Whistler," Lightning Slim said. "A lot of grinding hard jams that are very low scoring. That's my prediction for this half."

He wasn't entirely wrong. Some jams ended with no points scored on either side because the jammers would get out of the pack within seconds of each other. Other times, they were both ground down by incredible blocking that prohibited anyone from being declared lead. Most jams were in the single digits: every point mattered.

I wasn't sure how enthusiastic Kelly would be about watching a full sixty-minute game, but I could tell she was invested right from the beginning by the way she leaned forward in her chair, a characteristic move when she was watching something good. When a ref made a signal we were unfamiliar with, she would look it up and report back to me, insisting that we pause the game so she wouldn't miss anything. "Damn!!" she yelled at the screen, pushing the plate with her pizza crusts onto the coffee table. "Arch is killing it!!"

Even though I was looking for animosity on the track between the two teams, I didn't see it. When the whistle blew, ending a jam, both teams pretty much just ignored each other, skating off to their respective sides as if they had blinders on. In other games, it was common for Arch to high-five or chat politely with the players on the opposing team; sometimes, if a particularly good song came on before the whistle blew, they would even initiate a dance party to pass the time. None of that was on display here, but as far as I could tell, neither was anything that could qualify as bad sportsmanship.

With four minutes left, Arch led by only five points: the slimmest margin yet. All it would take was a particularly good jam by Denver to cinch the win. Every muscle in my body felt tense. I knew how badly Arch wanted this win—how much they had trained for it. Would winning this game help put St. Louis's name on the derby map? Maybe people would stop asking where Arch Rival was from if we finally got the honor of playing London.

The next two jams went in our favor, widening the lead by twenty points. With a minute left, Denver put up their best jammer, Klein, who was declared lead and scored nine points, but it wasn't enough to make up the deficit: Arch had won its first championship game.

After the game, my Facebook thread was flooded with celebratory memes and declarations of team spirit. Taryn messaged me from the arena itself, ecstatic. "DID YOU SEE?" she asked. "TELL ME YOU SAW." I texted her back immediately and wished I had more derby friends to text. I was on speaking terms with many of them—they knew my face from practice—but sending a random text about this game would likely just be seen as weird or overeager. How long would it take, I wondered, to feel comfortable reaching out to share our joy over the A team's success? How long before I could call them friends?

GETTING BACK TO reality after WFTDA championships was a bitter pill to swallow—even worse, I imagined, for those who had actually gone to Portland and played. Arch had predictably lost their game against London in the semifinals, but the loss didn't seem to dampen anybody's spirits. The pictures from the after-party on Sunday night looked wonderfully lively and not at all sober. How could anyone return to their normal lives—lawyer, teacher, hairdresser—after something so grand and incredible? All I wanted was to train for as long as it took to make the All Stars team. How was I expected to focus my attention back on grad school?

The English department sent my essays to the visiting writer two weeks before his arrival. They put him up in a private apartment located off campus and scheduled one-on-one appointments there to discuss our work. We were supposed to show up, knock on the door, and stay for an hour.

The prospect was intimidating to me. Still, I came right on time and stood passively on the front porch. I was wearing a black skirt with a baggy, holey sweater and black combat boots, blue eyeliner, and thick mascara. I'd gotten the entire look, including the makeup, from the recent clothing exchange and left my apartment feeling good, but suddenly I worried it was too grunge for a meeting with a famous author. As this thought was occurring to me, the man opened the door.

"After you," he said. He gestured up the stairs, and I shook my head. If I went first, he would be able to see right up my skirt.

"Go ahead," I said.

"No, I insist." I felt myself blushing as I tried to discreetly pull down my skirt. I could feel him following me, closely.

The apartment was small and filled with bookcases; the author led me to a couch and gestured for me to sit. I couldn't help feeling alarmed by our aloneness. If I screamed, would anyone be able to hear me? Why was I suddenly thinking about screaming? The author sat right across from me on a tall chair at a table with a desktop computer. Our knees were nearly touching.

"First things first," he said. "How old are you?" I felt myself blush again, felt sweat accumulating under my arms and between my legs. How old could I pass for, I wondered? Would he be able to sense I was lying?

An uncomfortable silence passed before I gave him my real age: twenty-two.

"That explains it!" he said. "You're just a baby."

I felt heat in the area around my eyes: one of the first signs that I was going to cry. Something about this meeting felt very wrong. *You can't cry in front of this man,* I thought. *It's simply not an option.* But maybe I could leave? Simply get up and walk away? Would he try to stop me?

The man extended a hand and put it on my knee. His touch was hot, and I squirmed underneath it. "What did you study in undergrad?" he asked.

"Math," I said quietly. "Math and art."

"Oh this is perfect," he said, removing his hand from my leg. "Now I can put this in terms you'll understand. I read your pieces, but they're just not 'adding up' to anything. Sometimes it takes us time as young writers to develop a compelling voice—a voice with charisma and power."

I could hear what the man was saying, but my gaze was fixed on the hand that had been, just moments earlier, resting on my knee.

"Here's another math thing I think you'll understand. If I were to perform a statistical analysis on this piece about the healer, I would find that there is far too much sobbing. A reader can only tolerate sobbing every twenty pages or so."

He handed me a printed copy of my essays, on which the only marks were circled sections with quips like *Please no more sobbing!*

The man remained silent as I scanned through the essays, but I didn't know what to say. After a few minutes, he asked for the one about urine back. "See, this is difficult for me to say, but I think you'll understand. Piss is just such a repellent thing to write about. This essay is really just not successful on any level. I'm not sure any amount of editing can change that. Do you know what I mean? No use for me to sit here and go through it with you."

He handed me the essay and leaned back in his chair. I stared at him—his lanky body taking up so much space in the room while I squeezed and constricted mine into the smallest possible space. Finally, I asked him if we were done.

He checked his watch. "Well, it's only been ten minutes, but I really don't have anything else to say. Just keep working on building that voice."

The writer patted my knee twice more before I stood. He walked me back downstairs and showed me out. The door hadn't even shut before I was crying. I held the essays to my chest and let my tears fall on his comments—*Please no more sobbing!* My legs felt weak, and when I saw a tree stump by the side of the road, I sat down on it. Then I realized I was shaking.

Nothing even happened, I told myself.

I skipped practice that evening, which was entirely un-characteristic. As Kelly gathered her things to go rock climb-ing, I curled up on the couch and pulled a fleece blanket up to my chin.

"Are you sure you want to skip?" she asked. "Roller derby usually helps you feel better about stuff. Maybe you could pretend somebody is that author and just beat the shit out of them."

When I told her I was sure, she offered to bring me rock climbing, but being suspended dozens of feet in the air seemed even less appealing than being on skates. Besides, I was glad that Kelly had found a rock gym that she liked and that she was meeting people there who would belay her. I wasn't sure I could ever trust a stranger not to drop me.

Once she left, I started eating and didn't stop. I ate every-thing I could get my hands on: mixing-bowl quantities of cereal, tortilla chips and salsa, granola bars and cookies. I dropped globs of peanut butter on my new sweater. I didn't even sit down to eat; I ate everything standing upright in the kitchen, directly underneath the bright light, like the albino gecko I once had as a kid. I ate until my stomach bulged, and I felt so much shame as I was shoveling the food into my mouth that I could barely tolerate living inside my own skin.

The whole time it was happening, I knew it was going to end with retching into the toilet. I rushed into the bathroom and just as soon as I put my hand in my mouth, I felt the food already coming up. My body seemed to know from experience what I expected of it.

When I was done, I stared at myself in the bathroom mirror. I hadn't bothered to turn on a light, so my reflection was illuminated only by the lights in the kitchen. My hair, which earlier that afternoon had been in a crown braid, was a frizzled mess. My blue eyeliner was smeared from crying. My clothes were lumpy, splattered by food and vomit. Half a day earlier, I'd been convinced these things could change me, make me feel more powerful. Now, I wasn't sure I would ever feel powerful again.

10/
THE HAPPIEST SEASON

The minimum skills test was slated for the first week of January, so I skated almost every day of December. From what I could tell, about ten people would be trying to pass the test. Only about half were rookies who had started Fresh Meat with me back in October; the rest were veterans looking to make a comeback. Hakuna Renata was the most intimidating of the lot. She wore leopard-print knee pads and rarely smiled. Rhino Might, an ex–All Star, and her ex-wife, Ven Detta VanGo, would also be retesting. Taryn told me they had stopped skating when Detta became pregnant with their little girl. The women were returning to derby now that their child was a few years old, but after their separation they preferred not to speak.

It shouldn't have really mattered who was testing with me; there was no cap for how many people could pass at one time. There was, however, a finite number of spots for people who could be drafted immediately after passing mins—and that number was undetermined. It all depended on how many players each local team wanted to pick up, and that wouldn't be known until right before the draft. This was the reason I was telling myself I felt competitive, even with those like Renata and Rhino who had been playing at high levels for years. It was possible, I thought, that their stellar performance could make me look worse by comparison, and then I would be relegated to another twelve-week Fresh Meat training session. Repeating the process would mean I wouldn't get to participate in the local season at all this season.

I could tell it made Taryn uncomfortable when I talked about mins and the draft, an experience, she was convinced, that would be fraught with disappointment for me.

"Very few people pass mins in three months," she told me, "and even fewer are drafted right away. You should be prepared for the possibility of not passing and not getting picked."

"I know," I said. "Trust me, I'm not getting my hopes up."

This was patently untrue: the more time I spent on skates, the higher my hopes shot. I was operating under the belief that the hard work I put into learning my skills and improving my endurance would immediately pay off. I knew that hard work didn't guarantee success. Nothing, especially in sports, was ever fair. But that didn't stop me from barreling toward my fantasy of making it onto a local team the only way I knew how: putting in more work than anyone else.

Part of the pressure I felt to get drafted came from the fact that I would be seeing my family for two days over the holidays, which, however brief, usually set me back in a number of ways. Most often it prefaced some sort of mental breakdown in which I would question all the decisions I had made in my life and all my current aspirations. Having something concrete to set my sights on through Christmas could mean the difference between sinking or swimming.

What I worried most about, however, was getting sick, as

I usually did after visiting. This year, I would be driving to Michigan with Lady on Christmas Eve, staying through Christmas, and flying out of Detroit the day after to attend Kelly's grandpa's funeral in North Carolina. I felt very nervous about leaving Lady with my mom while I was at the funeral (she wasn't shy about telling me she didn't like her) and made my sister promise she would let Lady sleep in her bed and send me frequent text updates. It would be downright miserable to be sick in North Carolina, and even worse if I drove back to St. Louis under the weather. I couldn't risk being sick for mins testing, which meant I had to find a way to stay sane and balanced during the visit.

As the temperature dropped, fewer people lingered at the bus station beside the Skatium. I often wondered where unhoused folks went. Were there shelters nearby? Somewhere warm they could stay? In Detroit, where we sometimes went ice skating in the winter, people slept on benches no matter how cold it got.

Once, I arrived at practice and noticed a grocery cart left in an embankment between the station and the rink. In it was a pink covered baby carrier. There was frost on the baby blanket and tiny icicles hanging from the metal cart.

I felt frozen in the warmth of my car. Should I get out to make sure there wasn't a baby in the carrier? Was I prepared for whatever I would find?

Carmina Piranha beat me to it. She pulled over, switched on her hazards, and made the trek over to the grocery cart. Tentatively, she peeked under the baby blanket. Aware that I, too, was watching, she raised the blanket so that I could tell the carrier was empty. I very rarely prayed, but I said a quick prayer that wherever she was, the baby was warm.

Two weeks before Christmas, I heaved my heavy duffel

bag up the little hill to the Skatium and found that we were locked out. A small congregation of skaters was huddled close for warmth. Taryn was in the middle; I stood next to her and we laughed whenever someone pushed her way out of the pack to pound on the door.

"He's either not here or he's too high to hear you," Taryn said. Even though I had only been training at the Skatium for three months, I knew she was right. The DJ booth man frequently forgot to unlock the doors, but it usually didn't take this long for him to stumble down to let us in.

Fletch, a bushy-haired All Star who was scheduled to lead practice, began kicking the door. "We've been out here for fif—teen—god—damn—min—utes." The door shuddered with each kick but eventually she threw up her hands and turned her back to the door. "Wanna make bets on what he's gonna say when he finally lets us in?" she asked.

Everyone laughed; we all knew he would first offer a vague excuse, something like "Lost track of time," and follow it up with "I gave a couple of you girls my number a while back. Why don't you just call me?"

By the time the DJ booth man arrived, our practice should've already started. Taryn saw him first; he was rounding the corner of the old storefront of the pub.

"You girls are early tonight," the DJ booth man said, pushing past us to unlock the doors.

"No, we're not, actually," Taryn said.

"What time is it anyway?" His eyes were red and watery. Everyone but Taryn slid past him into the Skatium. I heard her confronting him gently, but firmly.

Fletch sat down next to me on the cold cement to put on her gear. "It boggles my mind that we just beat the number seven team in the world and we have to practice at a place like this." She pointed up in the rafters above the track. "You can see the fucking smoke. People were smoking in here."

Birdsong, the skater who had transferred from Chile, pointed toward a nearby bench where several chicken bones were scattered. "God, I hate this place," she said. "We're all either going to die of lung cancer or build up our immunity so much we'll survive the apocalypse."

"Want to know what I hate most?" Fletch continued. "It's the way he calls us *girls*." She lowered her voice an octave to imitate the DJ booth man. 'You girls don't hit each other too hard today! Don't leave any teeth out on the rink for me to clean up later, okay, girls?' Does he call the dudes who skate here hockey *boys*? If anyone's losing teeth, it's those idiots. They don't wear helmets, let alone mouth guards."

This wasn't the first time I had heard skaters complain about the "girls" issue. Piranha had erupted into a similar tirade a week earlier, and I chimed right in, hoping my support would buy me social capital. I was eager to agree with almost anything derby folks said—anything to speed up the process of being accepted and integrated into the league.

Even though I would never tell my teammates, it didn't bother me to be called a girl. In many ways, I still felt like one. I was used to being the youngest in the room, as in grad school, and often I felt like a child in those spaces. As a freshman, I hung out with the seniors on the swim team, which is how I met Kelly. Most of my friends were older, including a ninety-one-year-old neighbor I exchanged letters with in college. My mother, in all forms of correspondence, continued to address me as "kid." When I turned eighteen, four years earlier, I told her, "I'm an adult now." She scoffed and told me no one thought eighteen-year-olds were adults; it was just the age at which you were old enough to buy lottery tickets and cigarettes. This news came as a relief: there were still so many things I didn't know how to do, so much I hadn't figured out. It also seemed to emphasize that adulthood was something I had to earn over time—not something I could simply claim.

"Does he think we're a bunch of prepubescent kids?" Piranha asked, stuffing her foot into a roller skate. "We're not kids; we're full-grown women! It's fucking insulting!"

I tried to let myself take on her anger as my own, but mostly I just felt preoccupied with saying and doing the right things.

A WEEK BEFORE Christmas, Kelly and I huddled together on the Skatium benches to watch the holiday scrimmage. Unlike the Halloween scrimmage, the holiday scrimmage was open to all genders and included players from surrounding leagues, so until I passed mins, I couldn't participate. I wasn't upset about that, though; watching was entertaining enough. Almost everyone was wearing a costume. One woman had wrapped herself in tinsel. Soup Beans strung blinking lights through the holes of her helmet. Ginger Assassin had stuffed her mane of curly red hair into the hood of a white sweatshirt, pinned little felt circles to her front, and heavily dusted her face with frosty white blush. Kelly shrieked with delight when she saw Ginger's creative snowman outfit.

When I heard Draggie yell, "Does anyone have any tape?" I rummaged through my duffel bag and handed her a roll.

"You're the best!" Draggie said. She pulled out a pair of reindeer ears, stretched the headband over her helmet, and began taping them down.

Even though she was skipping a day of rock climbing to

be at the scrimmage, Kelly was wholeheartedly invested. She asked me the names of people she didn't recognize, and most people she did recognize came up to her to say hello. Everyone, it seemed, loved Kelly, especially Soup Beans, who called us "dreamboats" and drew a big heart shape in the air around us. I was struck by how open I felt around them—how easy it was to be out. There were so many queer people on the team it felt like the norm: there was nothing unusual about us, nothing exoticized.

From the sidelines, it was easier to see the nuances of the game. Flux had been telling us to spend time watching old footage—one component of mins was a written test on the rules of the game—but I had been too preoccupied with learning the physical skills. With Kelly asking me questions, I began to realize how much I had picked up naturally, but also that I still had gaping holes in my knowledge bank.

A group of four green blockers and our red blockers lined up on the track. The jammers wore a big star on their helmet covers (which old-school skaters still called "panties") and positioned themselves behind the pack. When the whistle blew, they barreled into the walls formed by the blockers. They jumped, juked, and spun to try to get around them, and after about fifteen seconds, the green jammer was successful in breaking through.

"So now she's the lead jammer," I told Kelly. "She's going to sprint around the track and try to get around the blockers again. For every person on the red team she passes, she gets a point."

"I know that much," Kelly said. But then, a few seconds later, she asked somewhat sheepishly, "What's the benefit of being the lead jammer if both jammers can score points?"

"Only the lead jammer can decide when to end the jam,"

I explained. "It's a huge advantage to be the lead jammer because you can call it off before the other jammer gets any points."

As the green jammer hit the red wall again, one of the refs whistled sharply and called her number.

"What happened?" Kelly asked.

"She got a penalty but I'm not sure what she did to deserve it," I admitted. The hit had looked perfectly legal to me. Maybe she had initiated the hit with her head? I truly didn't know, which made me especially thankful I wasn't playing.

After two minutes, the jam ended, and Kelly and I both noticed the music playing; it was Andy Williams's "It's the Most Wonderful Time of the Year." Kelly reached for my hand and I rested my head against her shoulder. We never showed tenderness in public, never held hands lest someone catcall us or throw something out of a passing car. Once, when Kelly was visiting me in New York, we kissed in the back of a movie theater, but that was only because we were on the highest plane, looking down on all the moviegoers like gods.

The skaters lined up again, and as the jammers hit the walls once more, blockers were flung like pool balls off the track. People shouted from the sidelines, "Get up! Get up!" Short, piercing whistles indicated the referees were sending more players to the box, but sometimes the skaters disputed the claim. "That was not a track cut!" SheKill O'Neal yelled. "She was totally in bounds!" While she was arguing with the ref, a skater skidded out of bounds so fast and hard she knocked the distracted ref on her ass. And all the while, Williams's calm tenor proclaimed over and over that it was the hap-happiest season of all.

"I'm never going to think of this song the same way again," Kelly said.

ON OUR LAST practice before Christmas, I arrived at the Skatium and found several of my teammates wearing what appeared to be figure skating costumes. Before I had time to ask anyone about the rhinestones, a small woman with straight brown hair approached me. I recognized her immediately from champs in Portland.

"We haven't met before," she said, lowering her outstretched hand to where I was sitting on the Skatium floor. "I'm Bricktator, or Brick, or Tator, or Mom. A lot of skaters call me Mom because I like to keep all my ducks in a row."

I remembered the footage from champs in which Brick would complete several scoring passes, racking up the points, and return to her bench only to give what appeared to be a pep talk to the next jammer in line. She spent exactly no time celebrating her own success and seemed to focus all her energy on mobilizing, complimenting, and pumping up her teammates.

It was impossible to ignore the WFTDA commercials in which Brick was featured, however. In between gameplay, a reel would play of the most well-known skaters in the sport, and there she would be, launching herself over the apex to score a grand slam. I recognized some of the other skaters too, just by the frequency with which people talked about them. There was Scald Eagle, who painted her face to look like a bird of prey, and her sister Brawn Swanson, who wore a furry mustache. Both women played for Portland, the number one team in the world. Then there was Freight Train of Austin, who posted hip-hop dance routines on her Instagram that I couldn't help but watch in their entirety. Lady Trample of Melbourne, Scald Eagle's girlfriend, was a ramp skater and had started an international organization called Chicks in Bowls. Tracy Akers of Denver (real names only) was my favorite blocker to watch on these commercials, aside from Tutz. Nothing, though, was more exciting than seeing that Arch Rival jersey.

"You're wearing a Kalamazoo College sweatshirt," Brick said, pointing to my chest. "And you have an orange duffel. Did you go to K?"

I nodded. "I swam there," I said, pointing to the Speedo insignia on my bag. "I probably should've returned this bag after my last season."

My comment was met with a bark of laughter. "How weird!" she said. "A school of twelve hundred, six hours away, and two of us end up playing on the same roller derby team. What are the odds? I played soccer at Kalamazoo. Forward. I was pretty aggressive on the field. It was one of the things that prepared me for derby."

"What else besides soccer?" I asked. It surprised me that anyone felt prepared for derby.

Brick laughed and pointed to Bolt and Flash in their tutus. "I was a figure skater. That's why everyone's dressed up. I'm leading practice tonight, and I'm going to teach you all a routine. Post champs we like to do something that's a little less serious but still hones our skating skills. I guess it's the equivalent of football players learning ballet."

If those wearing figure skating dresses looked ridiculous upon walking into the Skatium, they looked even more ridiculous once they put on their bulky pads. Sequins reflected off their shiny helmets; the sparkling tights vanished at the shins under their tall socks.

"Bolt!" someone called. "Do a spin for us!"

Bolt stopped in place and twirled, arms above her head in mock ballet form. Pushing her blond curls back, she flashed a big smile, exposing her black mouth guard.

"All figure skaters on the track!" Brick called. By the time we circled around, her face was devoid of any humor. "The most important thing is to smile at the judges," she said, pointing to the empty bench on the far side of the Skatium.

We all waved to the imaginary judges before starting our warm-up. Taryn, who was wearing a shimmery purple top, looked particularly exuberant. Brick led us through a series of glides that began relatively simply on one foot, and grew increasingly difficult as we skated backward, again on one foot, weaving through obstacles. I felt embarrassed, not sure how long I could hang with the experienced skaters. Again, I was the only rookie at practice. Would Brick tell me when I should stop and instead practice skills off to the side?

"Don't forget to use your toe pick!" Brick called, cheerily.

Fletch fell forward and nearly hit her nose on the ground.

"Goddammit, Mom," she called from the floor. "It's a toe stop, not a toe pick, and we're not fucking ballerinas."

"I don't care who you fuck," Brick said, skating backward past Fletch. "Just use your toe pick."

The All Stars communicated with such ease; there was so much history, so much humor. It made me envious watching them; I longed to be part of that club. The B and C team skaters too had such a connection; they trusted each other, and they were still not quite sure about me.

After warm-up, we progressed to jumps.

"Think about it like kicking a soccer ball," Brick explained. She demonstrated kicking an imaginary ball, then pushed off the ground with her other skate and spun upward. We all applauded, mouths agape, when she landed on one foot.

As we began jumping, Brick accused us of being too noisy. "All I hear is thuds and clacking," she said. "Figure skaters are light on their feet. You're all landing like a pile of bricks. Poise. Grace."

I looked over at Fletch, who was biting her lip in concentration, and debated trying to make a joke. When she landed heavily on both feet, I decided to give it a try.

"Did you hear what she said, Fletch?" I asked. "Poise. Grace."

To my delight, Fletch smiled broadly and flipped me off with both hands. "I could kick your ass right now," she said.

Another chance, another risk. "But could you do it gracefully?" I asked.

She let out a cackle and I felt warmth spreading over my body. "You're a real piece of work, you know that, rookie?" she said. I just beamed in response, delighted that my teasing had paid off. So many of the skaters were friendly, but not yet my friends. After practice, they sometimes moved away from me to gear down with the All Stars "in-crowd." If I was paired with any of the All Stars skaters during practice, I could feel them going easy on me, for which I was grateful—but it felt particularly humiliating. Most skaters didn't joke with me the way they joked with the others. We did our drills in near silence and high-fived robotically when we were told to. I'd been wondering for weeks how to break the ice with people who didn't know how committed I was to the sport and the league.

Not long after, Bricktator gently suggested I stop before

the routine got too difficult, which was good, because I probably would have kept going and risked injuring myself. I expected that when I was excused, I would just retire to the sidelines and quietly practice my minimum skills, but Brick had other plans.

"How would you feel about operating the music for the routine?" she asked, handing me her phone. "We're skating to 'Circle of Life.' It's all queued up."

Again, I felt myself flush. I was half-mortified, and half-relieved that I wouldn't be sequestered to the sidelines. Did she think I was a danger to other players? Incompetent? Likely to mess up the carefully choreographed routine? I had heard people talking about other new skaters in such a way. Was this what people thought of me?

Still, I was relieved that I was off the hook for the routine, which had certainly gotten too complicated. Offering a way for me to stay involved with the practice meant so much, especially when I thought my belonging hinged on being physically capable of performing the routine. I told her I'd love to help out with the music.

When the team heard the song to which they would be performing, they jumped and clapped. Some started laughing too hard to even focus on the routine. They got about halfway through, but it looked like a sloppy junior high talent show number and Bricktator made them start over.

"The second row of people have to rise up on the fourth beat!" she called. "Then we all stay standing until I give you the next cue. That means you, Fletch."

Manning the music was more difficult than I expected because of how frequently Brick wanted to start over. Sometimes the music had barely started when someone messed up and Brick shouted, "From the top."

When ten minutes were remaining in the practice, Bricktator deemed that the routine was ready to perform all the way through. Taryn handed me her phone, which she had already set to video mode. "I have a feeling we're going to want to remember this," she said.

It wasn't just the routine I wanted to remember. I wished the video recording could capture the feeling I had of a threshold opening, an arm being extended to me from these skaters to join their world. I was so close. It was the feeling of being awake, and wanting to stay awake. It contrasted so strongly with the end of my swimming career, when I often practiced with my eyes closed, playing a game with myself to see how many strokes I could take without looking—how far I could go pretending to be elsewhere. The last thing I wanted to do now was shut my eyes. When I was skating— when I was with the people of Arch Rival—I so often longed for something more powerful than a video recording and something more reliable than memory. I never wished to be anywhere else.

The skaters did the routine in one take, laughing and high-fiving each other and me. As we were all taking off our gear, I saw Bruise approach Taryn and whisper into her ear. Taryn announced that on the way into practice, Bruise's car had slipped into a ditch. "We need everyone to help push!" she called. No one hesitated. We all traipsed past the DJ booth man, who was leaning against the Skatium entrance with his arms crossed.

The car had slid off the slippery road and was resting in the embankment by the bus station. "I'm just so embarrassed," Bruise kept repeating. "I'm not sure what happened."

"Hon," Taryn assured her. "We got this."

Around me, twenty skaters found a spot on the car to rest

their hands and widen their stance. The metal was cold, but I liked it; I was still riding the high of being included, feeling accepted. This was one task I could participate in without the nagging uncertainty and self-consciousness that usually accompanied skating. This was something I knew I could do.

As Taryn counted to three, I had no doubt that we would be able to push the car back out onto the road. It was as if we had already done it. I would have bet my entire meager savings and all the money I had yet to earn in my lifetime. That was how confident I was in the collective strength of these skaters, their persistence, their capability. That was the feeling I wished to bottle: my contribution of power to a task that, to an outsider, might have seemed impossible.

11/
OLD HABITS

The morning of the minimum skills test, I roller skated in my apartment while Kelly was getting ready for rock climbing. I was nervous, and I wanted to practice some skills again before I'd be tested on them later. Kelly found my last-minute preparation completely unnecessary and told me so. "You're doing that thing where you get way too intense," she said.

I knew she was right, but that didn't stop me from continuing to practice my shuffling in the living room while she changed into her rock climbing clothes and gathered her things. I was struck by how much this test setup reminded me of swimming—even when swimming had become toxic. There was a familiar rawness in my stomach: adrenaline that was starting to gnaw at my insides and made me think unsavory thoughts about my competition. In this context it didn't make sense—there was no maximum for how many could pass—and yet I found myself mentally comparing myself to Nanny and Rhino and Renata. It made me feel so unclean. So far, the derby environment had been nothing but supportive and synergetic, and I was bringing in a cutthroat energy that had no place or relevance.

When I had seen my family over Christmas, it had been hard not to get sucked back into their way of thinking: winning above all else. My sister, a senior in high school, who had been systematically breaking school records for the past four years, had so much pain in her shoulder she could barely lift her arm above her head. My mom's solution for this hadn't changed: it was cortisone shots, which would dull the pain but not fix the problem, which was likely overuse. Meanwhile, my mom was losing weight at an alarming rate by starving herself and exercising obsessively, which she roped us all into on Christmas Day. We hiked five miles in the snow before breakfast, which for her was a single soft-boiled egg. My dad was no better, emphasizing my mother's thinness and his pride in her. Both of them looked like they were withering away.

Being in North Carolina at Kelly's grandpa's old beach house was a full 180-degree pivot. The food was abundant and rich—shrimp and big slabs of steak, five kinds of cheese, and honeydew wrapped in prosciutto. No one here was withering away. When it came time for the burial, we traipsed out to the deck that overlooked the ocean. "It's fitting that we do it here, in the shallow end," Kelly said. "Grandpa Boyd couldn't swim." Kelly's dad sliced the bag holding what was left of his father; I expected him to say a few words and scatter the ashes over the ocean, but he simply turned the bag upside down and dumped the ashes in a pile on the sand.

"I figure doing it now at low tide means we can watch the ocean take him away," Kelly's dad explained.

So we waited. Half an hour passed, and the pile of ashes

was unchanged. The ocean barely touched the base of the mound. Kelly slowly sank to sit on the deck and I did the same. Her uncle exited the deck and we saw him smoking down on the beach. After forty-five minutes of watching the unchanged pile, Kelly's mother jumped as if remembering something. "Smokey!" she said. She returned with a small jar of ashes—Boyd's dog—that had been sitting inside the beach house for years. She unscrewed the lid and emptied the dog's ashes on top of Boyd's.

"Why don't we all just go inside and watch this from indoors?" Kelly's dad suggested.

The next day, the mound of ashes was mostly unchanged. "Grandpa's still there, Dad," Kelly told him solemnly. She snapped a picture of the pile and saved it on her phone while her father stared stoically out the window.

When I picked up Lady at my parents' house and prepared to drive back to St. Louis, my mom told me, "She's a different dog without you here." I asked what she meant, and she continued, "She's a better dog in every way. Doesn't whine. Doesn't bark. Not so clingy."

"Sounds like she's scared of you," I said.

"She should be," my mother said.

Getting back into my car to drive back to St. Louis was the easiest thing I had ever done. I wished Cam good luck with the rest of her swim season, but I hadn't told her about the minimum skills test so she couldn't wish me good luck in return. I hadn't talked about roller derby much at all, as it seemed to upset my mother. We didn't talk about school either, since she didn't like hearing about the "boring" academic world. I mostly just listened to them talk about food— which foods were highest in calories, which were surprisingly low, which were best to eat in the morning, which made you the fullest for the fewest calories. Both nights I was there I purged into my childhood toilet.

Maybe I should have expected not to be able to dip in and out of my old reality without it changing my outlook, even temporarily, about the minimum skills test. I should've anticipated how it would affect me and my thinking, but I didn't, not even when I noticed I was driving more aggressively than usual into South City. I pulled up to the Skatium and slammed on the brakes, heaving up the parking brake so I wouldn't roll backward into the street. No one was there but me.

Generally, I avoided being alone at the Skatium, but today it felt important to have some solitary time to talk to myself before the test began. In swimming, my mantra had always been "I will win," and that's all that was going through my head—even though the point of mins wasn't to win, it was to prove to the coaching committee that I wasn't a danger to other players. That I could give hits. That I could take hits. That I had learned the requisite skills to move on to strategy, plays, and scrimmages. And yet, my thinking hadn't changed at all. *Beat them. Do anything it takes.*

Soon other Fresh Meat and alumni skaters arrived; the committee members were the last to show, led by Tutz. I wished she was wearing her pizza costume again, which made her look significantly less intimidating. She did have on extravagant makeup: pink eyebrows and black lipstick and swirls of eyeliner on her cheeks that contoured her bone structure. It wasn't unusual for Tutz—I'd gotten used to her posts on social media in which she'd imitate the makeup styles of various drag queens—but it did make me feel like I was in some kind of derby-themed Hunger Games.

The coaching committee hopscotched through our outstretched legs and various pads littering the floor and headed straight for the bench overlooking the track. Each member of the committee had a clipboard on which was a list of skills awaiting a check mark. It reminded me of the "suggested sins" checklist my catechism school teachers used to give us while we were waiting in line for confession. On it had been common infractions we could use to jog our memories as we prepared for the holy sacrament. *Have you lied to your parents? Do you ever cheat in school? Have you taken something that doesn't belong to you?*

I had practically memorized the minimum skills list, but seeing it in Tutz's hands unnerved me. As she waited for us to finish putting on our gear, she wrote our names at the top of the page. As I slid my hands into my wrist guards, I visualized a column of check marks under my name. That was the outcome I wanted. Penance for failing to complete all the required skills would be another three months as Fresh Meat, and I was done doing penance.

At the end of the row of gearing-up skaters was Nanny. I saw her sliding her rainbow knee pads onto her legs with her eyes closed, and I approached slowly so as not to startle her. Even as I got closer, I wasn't sure what I wanted to say.

"You ready?" I asked. The energy in the Skatium was palpable. I thought it would be impossible not to be infected by it, but Nanny looked at me solemnly.

"No," she said. "This is my fourth time taking this test and I'm no better than I was twelve weeks ago. I'm starting to think I'm just too old for this. I'm old enough to be your mother."

I nodded and watched her cradling her helmet like a baby doll. I hadn't anticipated she would need comforting before the test, and I felt woefully unprepared and slightly impatient.

"I'd be proud of my mother if she were trying out for a roller derby team," I said. It was the honest truth. It would be hard watching her hit the ground—I would worry about her—but that wouldn't stop me from telling everyone I knew.

Nanny fiddled with the bottom of her T-shirt, which featured a rainbow toilet and the phrase YOU CAN PEE NEXT TO ME. I had personally heard some of the trans skaters compliment her on it, which made Nanny smile brightly. Her Facebook was full of left-leaning memes, particularly about education and the way in which the government was trying to roll back funding for it. She often wrote statuses about the classes she was teaching and the challenges of being a Black woman academic. When she heard I would be teaching my first college-level class at the start of the new academic term, she sent me all her syllabi and lesson plans. "This ought to get you started," she said.

It was somewhat painful looking down on her wringing the bottom of her shirt and fiddling with her mouth guard in fear. This wasn't the Nanny I knew. When she looked back up at me, there were tears in her eyes. "I'm not sure I can do this," she said.

I sat down next to her. The intensity I had been feeling at home and on the ride to the Skatium was starting to leak out. I hoped that I could reignite the spark when it was time to perform.

"Can you pretend they're your students?" I asked. "The members of the coaching committee, I mean. Maybe they wouldn't intimidate you so much if you went onto the track the way you enter your own classroom."

Nanny sniffled and admitted that my idea was a good one. "One thing I love about derby is being a student of it. I love asking questions. I love not having to know the answers."

"That's not what today is," I said, reaching for her hand. "Today you're demonstrating all you've learned. You're performing."

"It's a damn test is what it is," Nanny said. "I thought I was done taking tests."

"Are we ever?" I joked. She cracked a smile, slid her mouth guard into place, and buckled her helmet. For a second, she had her helmet on backward, but she realized her mistake and corrected it.

"Let's do this," I said.

WE WERE FIFTEEN minutes into the minimum skills test by the time Taryn arrived. She pulled me to the side during a water break and hugged me.

"Jacob puked this morning," she said.

"Jesus, you should've stayed home."

"Nah, his dad is with him. He'll be okay. Besides, I knew you needed me this morning more than he did."

I opened my mouth to say . . . something. "Thank you" didn't seem like it would cut it. I felt both flattered and guilty that Taryn had prioritized me over her sick kid. I also wasn't sure if what she said was true—did I need her as much as Jacob? Sometimes the knowledge that I had someone in my corner, even if they weren't physically present, was enough.

As I started to thank her, Taryn slapped my butt and pushed me back out onto the track. Flux began calling out drills, and the judges began scribbling notes onto their clipboards. I could tell Flux was trying to structure the testing as much like a normal practice as possible, but there was a new intensity in the way she talked.

"Three quick laps!" she barked. "Now three quick laps backward!"

Even though she wasn't being tested, Taryn performed all the drills with us. She skated behind me and whispered tips out of the corner of her mouth like a ventriloquist. "Bend your knees. Push your skates out, not back. Keep your arms in while you spin." When it came to jumping, I didn't need her guidance. I'd practiced jumps so many times I could launch myself into the air with almost no fear.

The endurance test, the twenty-seven laps in five minutes, was not among the skills I worried about. It had been the first skill I passed successfully, and I had done it several times in practice leading up to mins testing. Still, when I lined up on the track with Nanny, Rhino, and the rest of the people testing, I felt my heart beating loudly. Nanny gave me a look like *Are we really doing this right now?* and I gave her two thumbs up—something I'd never done to a competitor before. Maybe I was getting better, I thought.

The first minute felt utterly wonderful. Taryn called out that I was ahead of pace, the wind blew back my hair, and I felt completely capable. By the third minute, I had started slowing down. Each lap, which I was completing in about ten seconds, seemed exactly the same and everything was starting to look blurry. "You're still above pace but don't slow down any more!" Taryn shouted as I passed.

Her words gave me a burst of new energy. I'd been competing against the proverbial stopwatch my whole life, from sports to my body, down to even the most monotonous chores. It was simply the way my parents had programmed me to operate. When we were young, my dad used to give Cam and me each a plastic bag for dog poop and set a timer, and the sister with the heaviest bag at the end of fifteen minutes would win a quarter. It lit a fire under us and gave us a purpose. Showering had been the same way. As a young kid, I used to shower with my mother. She claimed it was to save water, but I think she enjoyed the thrill of trying to beat our record of three and a half minutes. Before we stripped naked, she would retrieve the timer from the kitchen and set it on the bathroom sink. "This time we'll be under three," she'd say. As soon as I turned on the water, she cranked the little dial: our equivalent of a checkered flag.

The first few seconds were always the most agonizing because I had to wait for my mother to wet her hair; there was nothing I could do to make use of that time. I once tried scrubbing before it was my turn under the stream, but the soap skidded along my dry skin and caused little pink bumps that looked like poison ivy. After that, I would just squint my eyes, stare up at the ceiling, and try to detect shapes in the cracked plaster until it was time to trade places with Mom.

When it was my turn, I sidestepped my mother as she lathered her hair. It was like an intimate tango in which our bodies never touched. We knew the routine without speaking: whose turn it was under the stream, who was responsible for uncapping the conditioner, who had to retrieve the bar of soap if it slipped out of our hands. This made me feel very close to my mother—I knew what she expected of me, which was to beat the timer, and I could predict all her movements. I liked knowing what she looked like with no clothes on: the appendectomy scar slicing her lower stomach like a Cheshire Cat grin, her small breasts, her wiry pubic hair. I never saw any of the things she insisted were there: flab under her arms, excess skin hanging around her belly like an innertube.

It was fun, this routine of ours, and I looked forward to our game as long as we were winning. The possibility of losing the race simply wasn't an option. In the shower, the ticking was drowned out by the water smacking our backs, but that didn't matter. I could hear the clock in my head, somewhere behind my teeth. I learned exactly how much time was in a second and how, when I was in a race, the seconds passed in a frenzied blur. I learned that I couldn't let too many slip by if I wanted to feel good about myself.

It wasn't an altogether different feeling from skating the twenty-seven in five. Each second mattered. With each stride, I could hear the ticking; I knew exactly what was expected. I had to average about ten seconds a lap to pass. Being on the track with so few skaters made me feel exposed—not naked, but not fully clothed either.

Somewhere during the fourth minute, I lapped Nanny. She was clinging to the inside lane, sometimes not even crossing over and not skating the diamond shape that we were taught. Her breath was extremely labored and she could barely pick up her legs to take a stride.

"We're almost done!" I called back to her. "You're a boss-ass bitch!" I heard her bark of laughter, but she was too out of breath to say anything else. When the test was over, she collapsed on her back and rolled from side to side, massaging out the knots in her body. She told her counter not to tell her whether or not she'd passed, but I knew she had because I had done twenty-nine—two laps more than I needed to—and only passed her once.

The hardest part about mins testing, I knew, would be the contact drills. Before we moved on to hitting, Taryn pulled me to the side of the track. Her hair, which she had recently dyed red and orange, was coloring her sweat. It looked like she'd been slashed at the back of the neck; streams of perspiration snaked under the seams of her tank top and down her body.

"This is where you get to show them how strong you are," she said.

Despite her words, at first I spiraled out of control whenever I was hit. It took a few minutes for me to remember I could hit back.

"Where's the aggression?" Tutz shouted from the bench. "Stop being so goddamn polite."

Her comment—a variation of something my mother had been saying all my life—caused a switch to flip inside me. When Flux next blew the whistle and it was my turn to hit, I pinballed aggressively from person to person, leaving my targets rubbing their arms and hips in pain. When I felt my hips collide with theirs, I used my ass to flick them out of bounds. I dug my shoulders into theirs and took their space.

"Ten seconds left!" Tutz shouted. I knew I needed a grand finale. A perfectly timed spectacle. I waited until we passed the apex and were skating directly in front of the coaching committee. Then I sped up to Taryn and hurled myself toward her. She wasn't looking. She didn't know I was coming. The side of my body hooked the side of hers, and I used the back of my upper arm to force her off the track. I heard a strained groan as she fell. Her lower back hit the track first, followed by her head, which made a terrible smacking sound inside her helmet.

"Atta girl," Tutz yelled, clearly impressed by my hit.

Taryn didn't pop up right away, and the sight of her sprawled flat out on the grimy Skatium floor filled me with terror. I was genuinely afraid I had permanently injured her, that in a matter of seconds we would be calling 911 to report a severe concussion. Why had I once again let my desire to win take control of me?

After a few minutes, Taryn lifted her head. She unbuckled her helmet and massaged her temples. When she saw me leaning down, she reached for my hand. "Sick hit," she said. "That was exactly what you needed to do."

Except—I wasn't sure. Had my hit been justified? Had it even been legal? She certainly hadn't been looking, and while I knew I could hit while my opponents were distracted, I didn't think it was quite as accepted for casual drills at practice. The whole thing felt dirty; I felt disgusted with myself.

Taryn must have been able to tell how I was feeling because she grabbed both my hands. "Stop freaking out, babe," she said. "I'm fine. Seriously. That was exactly what you needed to do."

Never had pain and exhilaration seemed so knotted together as in that moment. There was the ache in my hip from my contact with Taryn, the throbbing in my toes from my cheap, ill-fitting skates, the sting of watching someone I loved hit the ground—and worse, knowing I was the reason. To then help Taryn back to her feet and have her hug me: it didn't make any sense.

On the drive home, I felt very confident I had passed the test. Since I had memorized the sheet, I knew exactly what was expected. I knew it backward and forward. Still, I felt a surge of elation when Tutz texted me and a group of others that we had made it. To my delight, Nanny was also on the list of skaters who had passed. All these feelings—exhilaration, confusion, delight, elation—bloomed in my body, unbridled, as I found a parking spot in front of my apartment. I turned off the car, breathing heavily, and screamed.

PART II

12

ABOUT A MILLION JOANS

One immediate consequence of passing mins that I hadn't anticipated was that everyone wanted to know my derby name. By making it past the first major obstacle in the derby world I had proven myself, in a way; the culture seemed to dictate that I deserved to be called something fiercer or funnier than my given name.

As I drove home from practice the following week, I let the naming conundrum consume me. Choosing a name felt like even more pressure than performing well on the track. As my wipers whisked the snow off my windshield and my tires skidded around in the slush, my thoughts whirred with possibilities. Ice sculptures adorned the strip where I always ran with Lady, and Nativity scenes hadn't yet been taken down from Christmas; every church I saw had some variation of the manger scene displayed on its frosty grass. Whenever I passed by one, I was flooded with memories of the last chance I had been given to rename myself: the holy sacrament of confirmation.

At thirteen, I had been enamored with the prospect of a fresh start—particularly of casting aside the selfishness my mother so frequently accused me of. I was convinced that taking a new name would give me a chance to be someone else, to develop qualities that could help lift me out of the constricting circumstances of my life, not least because my given name had always felt like wearing a formal gown to a barbecue. Neither of my parents particularly liked it; it had been a compromise because they couldn't agree on any other name. I didn't even know the correct pronunciation, and neither did my parents. Sometimes they spoke it with a long *a* and other times, the *a* was short. They always called me Gabe—never Gabby—something my mother assured me I wasn't. The possibilities of a new name I was free to choose, therefore, were endless and exhilarating; imagine how devastated I was when I found out we could only pick a saint's name. "Choose a saint you admire," our teacher said, "or a saint who inspires you. Do some research. You'll be bonded to this person for the rest of your life."

I wasn't keen on being bonded to anybody, much less a saint. Institutional religion had never been more to me than an inconvenience. I memorized the prayers, the chants, the responses, but I didn't understand them. Mass and catechism were just periods of time in which I allowed myself to run rampant in the fields of my imagination. And saints annoyed me because they weren't born holy—somehow, they had managed to achieve sainthood despite being born with original sin. Even at thirteen, I knew I was too deeply flawed to ever qualify. No saint, I assumed, had ever lied their way through confession. None had lusted after their teacher—or a person of the same sex, for that matter. And as far as I knew, none of them fought with their mothers, or left their dirty underwear on their bedroom floors, or sneezed into a bowl of Campbell's tomato soup before serving it to their sister. In short, I thought of a saint as something I would never be: a good human being, never mind a perfect one.

As I began my reluctant quest for a suitable saint name, my parents were subjected to dozens of tirades about how annoyed I was at the Church for limiting my options and irritated at my teachers about the subsequent essay we had to write once we settled on one. It didn't take long for my mother to get fed up.

"Did you know your grandmother's name isn't actually Joan?" she asked. "It's Joanne. But of course you didn't know that because you think you're the center of the universe."

She informed me that my grandmother's teachers, the nuns, refused to call her by her given name and switched it to something more Biblical. She hadn't even been given a choice.

"Why didn't she go back to being Joanne after she finished school?" I asked.

"I don't know. Maybe after thirteen years she felt more like Joan."

Learning about my grandmother's misfortune amplified the pressure I felt about choosing a new name. The risk of being robbed of the opportunity to name myself was motivation enough for me to stop complaining and pick one, even if my choices were limited.

Some saint names I liked until I did a little research. I had almost settled on Saint Blaise—a name I liked for its spunk—but then a quick search on Catholic Online revealed that Blaise was both a man and a doctor: two attributes that turned me off before I even found out he was the patron saint of wool combers. The same thing happened with Saint

Gwen. I liked the alliteration with my given name, but then I found out Gwen had three breasts, and that was not a rumor I wanted circulating around the eighth grade.

I eventually landed on Anne, not because I was particularly enthralled by Mary's mother, but because my favorite character in literature was Anne of Green Gables. It was a quiet form of rebellion, naming myself not after a saint but after a fictional character just as vain and troublesome as me. I picked Anne, whose first true friend was her own reflection in the windowpane. Anne, who accidentally dyed her hair green and got her friend drunk on homemade currant wine.

I approached the task of choosing a roller derby name by examining my other obsessions, both past and present. Besides Anne of Green Gables, I adored several other literary icons: Ramona Quimby, Junie B. Jones, Hermione Granger. I loved Jo March from *Little Women*—her masculinized nickname, her habit of writing stories late into the night. On the film side, I was enamored of Brandy in Rodgers and Hammerstein's *Cinderella*. I watched *Balto* so many times the VHS tape simply stopped working; it always reminded me of my first memory: sitting in a dogsled with my dad in Anchorage at the start of the 1997 Iditarod.

Kelly either hadn't heard of or didn't identify with most of my childhood heroes. As a kid, she didn't read as much as I did, but she did develop an affinity for adult movies like *Clue, The Thomas Crown Affair, My Fellow Americans,* and *What About Bob?* The first movie we watched together was *Little Miss Sunshine.* "There might be something there for a derby name," Kelly had said. "Little Miss Fill-in-the-blank?" The second was *The Rocky Horror Picture Show.* Kelly wanted me to know how weird and sinister her taste in movies was—we checked them off one by one. *The Silence of the*

Lambs, Children of Men, The Phantom of the Opera, The Village. She told me how her parents forbade her from reading *The Silence of the Lambs* when she was fifteen but how she simply wrapped it in the dust jacket from *Seabiscuit* and read it in secret.

Another important decision was whether I would choose a clean name or something a little more scandalous. Kelly worried about the announcers having to say my name in the arena in front of children, but I was willing to risk it if enough people told me the name fit my personality. One thing I knew for sure was that I wanted to draw inspiration from a badass woman from history. My graduate school friends, Klara and Tory, helped me make a list and then we twisted each name into something fiercer, funnier, or gayer. We came up with Amelia Queerheart, Queera Barton, and Mauler Superior. For a while, Emily Prickinson was a top contender, then Kelly's favorite, Shania Pain. I didn't trust my own instincts enough to make such a large decision, so I asked everyone I knew for input and created a mental bar graph of their responses. When I finally settled on Annie Chokely, it wasn't because I felt a particular kinship with her; Annie had simply topped the leaderboard. But the more I read and researched, the more convinced I became that Annie Oakley was the perfect muse for me.

There was something comforting about forming a persona around a legendary sharpshooter from Ohio. Annie's talent was discovered at an early age, a fact that fit my roller derby fantasy, as I longed to be "discovered" too. She was swept up and accepted by Buffalo Bill's Wild West show—an entity about which she knew very little—and carved out a life for herself among the performers. Annie was attracted to showmanship, and although I had never "performed," outside of the kid's choir at church, I was attracted to that too. Like Annie, I longed to transform my athletic ability into a spectacle. I dreamed of being met with whistles and applause.

I wrote ANNIE on a strip of duct tape and stuck it to the back of my helmet. My handwriting made it impossible for anyone to tell how unsure I still was about the name. It was bold and wide and underlined; each letter took up so much space the tape had to wrap around the sides of my helmet. *Here I am,* it seemed to say, *the sharp shot, the main act.*

Unfortunately, neither the tape nor the name stuck. Right away, a skater called Annieville Horror made it perfectly clear she did not appreciate sharing a first name with me. "There are already two Annies here!" she told me. "It's going to get really confusing with another one." The prospect of three Annies was bad enough, but there was another, more pertinent, reason to reconsider my choice of name: I just couldn't get myself to respond to it. On the rare occasion someone called me Annie, it was usually to warn me of imminent danger. By the time I realized there was another player hurtling toward me at top speed, she had already knocked me on my ass.

Shortly after I gave up on Annie Chokely, a tall veteran skater approached me at practice to introduce herself. She asked me my name first, and when I shrugged, she flashed a smile that exposed a perfectly white mouth guard.

"What's *your* name?" I asked.

"Derby name or real name?" she responded. This was new: no one had ever volunteered their real name to me. This phenomenon made for awkward conversations when people I knew outside of roller derby—people in my graduate program or people who I met at the gym or at grocery stores—inquired about mutual acquaintances. I didn't know

Sarah, but I knew Bricktator. I couldn't point out Wendy or Leah, but I was friends with Nox and Piranha. Sometimes skaters further complicated things by changing their social media accounts to display only their derby name. The Facebook profile for a skater named Lola Blow, for example, gave no indication that she ever responded to anything else; she played as Lola, worked as Lola, and dated as Lola. The name Lola was tattooed onto one of her feet and Blow on the other. I only learned her given name, Jasmine, when I was flipping through old team paperwork. How long did it take, I wondered, for Jasmine to become obsolete and for Lola to take her place? If I shouted "Jasmine!" from the other side of the street, would Lola still turn her head?

The tall woman told me her given name, but I instantly forgot it. I would not forget her derby name, though: "Everyone here calls me Peg. It's short for Pegasass." I laughed, and Peg flashed another smile. "Some people like to pick really tough or intimidating names. I'm just not that kind of girl."

Peg urged me to pick a name fast—otherwise, someone would call me something randomly and it might stick, even if I didn't like it. "Names are really hard to change," she said, gravely. "Last season, T Dawg tried to change hers to Bad Mutha T, but there was no going back." She also informed me that once I picked a name, I had to register it both with the Women's Flat Track Derby Association and on a name registry called Derby Roll Call.

I already knew about the WFTDA but investigated Derby Roll Call's website when I got home from practice that night. Its singular purpose, it turned out, was to register and track roller derby names. The interface resembled a social media page. A banner scrolling along the top of my screen announced that the number of names in the registry had reached 32,153. Under the heading "Recently Registered Names," I found Thunderpants with the B-Town Brawlers in the UK. Under her, Raven Lunatic with Greensboro Roller Derby. Buns of Steel had recently registered with the Bembeltown Rollergirls in Germany and Eye Roll with Montréal. All of these declarations were made within a few hours; the list was so long that I scrolled and scrolled and only managed to see those who had registered in the last month. There was Slaughterhouse Thighs, and Dr. Shocktopus. Miss Calculated in New Zealand and Trauma Hawk in France. James Smackavoy, Green Bean SMASHarole, Hufflebuff, and Deadly LongLegs.

I assumed that the primary purpose of a worldwide registry would be to avoid duplicate names, and in some sense, I was right. Hydra, the Texas Rollergirls skater whose personal spreadsheet became the first international master roster in 2004, prohibited duplicate derby names and even similar entries. The first worldwide derby name registry, Two Evils, maintained the trend, requiring skaters to check the "uniqueness" of a name before submitting it to the master roster. Duplicate names were rejected unless the administrators were provided explicit written permission from the skater who'd claimed it first.

But in 2011, Derby Roll Call pushed out Two Evils as the dominant roller derby name registry, and a new era of naming began: one that acknowledged and allowed for duplicates. On the Derby Roll Call website, a large heading reads, "Wait, you allow duplicate names?" and underneath is the site's policy: *Yup. Given how many people are finding out about derby every single day, it's inevitable two people will come up with the same name at the same time. Who are we to decide who got there first? The site's approach is to accept this duplication and try to inform everyone about the situation.*

One Arch skater, a Harry Potter fanatic, selected the name Hermione Danger. It sounded familiar to me, so I searched it on Derby Roll Call and found there were fourteen people registered under that name. One was in Boulder, another in Madison, Western Sydney, Sweden, and several more sprinkled throughout the UK. I noticed that none of them had the same number, which was how fourteen skaters with the same name could coexist. If two Hermione Dangers ever ended up in the same bout or the same team, their numbers would differentiate them enough to avoid logistical problems in the penalty box and on the track.

Fourteen Hermione Dangers, however, raised another question for me: did these skaters pick the subject of their persona based on admiration alone, or did they all share certain personality traits of their namesake? Maybe they were all bookish and clever, or maybe they resembled Hermione Granger physically. It was fun extending this logic to other names and trying to imagine the skater who owned them. Was Taser Swift a singer? How much could Hulk Smash Her bench? My suspicion about Lunatits was confirmed when I noticed her number was 42H. But exactly how small was Tiny Tear-Her? Did Marilyn Meanroe take pride in her sex appeal? Did these people name themselves from the qualities they already possessed, or the ones they hoped to grow into?

More important, what traits did I want to highlight in myself? What did others think of me? My fifth-grade teacher once ironically named me Patience for Pioneer Day—she was the first to tell me that patience is a characteristic I lack. My mother was always telling me how I was feeling: "You're not scared, you're embarrassed. You're not shy, you're just being coy." When she insisted I was selfish and self-absorbed, I took everything she said to heart. For other information about myself, I looked to those around me. Just like with my derby names, I formed a mental bar graph of the adjectives people used about me. Seven votes for creative. Nine for competitive. Four for smart. By that logic, I was more creative than I was smart, more competitive than creative.

Still, I felt unsure what my defining qualities were. I was short, but not too short. I liked visual art, but literally dozens of skaters on the team were artists too. What about me was worth highlighting in a name? If I picked something literary, would the reference fly over my teammates' heads as it had with my dad? God forbid I pick something elitist or politically incorrect; that's why I needed other people to tell me I was on the right track.

Many Arch skaters did not struggle the same way I did with choosing a name for their key qualities. CupQuake, for instance, made a living as a baker. Another whose occupation was exposed by their derby name was Sinister Minister, who went by Sin. Both Big Red and Ginger Assassin had distinct, fiery hair, and Bruise Almighty, even more than the rest of us, was perpetually speckled black and blue. Other names revealed positions. Blockers included Goldie Blocks, a woman with blond ringlets, and Chewblocka. The jammers often aimed to highlight their speed and agility: on my team, there was Flash, The Jukes on You, and Bolt Action.

Derby Roll Call also clued me in to a crucial element of derby culture of which I'd been ignorant: skaters aren't the only ones who rename themselves. The registry included names of referees, photographers, and announcers, and volunteers in a variety of other roles. I wasn't surprised, then, when I was introduced to Mr. McWheely, the team photographer, who had two pinup girls in roller skates tattooed on his biceps. The skating refs, colloquially called zebras, displayed their derby names on their jerseys: Ninja Sass'em. PhDiva. Spin Diesel. Even the non-skating officials, whose job it was to time penalties and release skaters back onto the track after serving their time in the box, had names. Steve, one of our most dedicated non-skating officials, always wore a track jacket with his derby name, Count Stephanos, on the hood.

WE WERE AT our favorite burger joint, Stacked, when I presented Taryn with a list of name options. I had drawn a thick line through Annie Chokely and written a note next to Pelvis Breastly: *Dad likes this one.* There were other symbols too—a triangle for names I thought were witty, a check mark next to names I liked for their intensity.

Taryn scanned my list; her eyes stayed locked on the page even when she took a bite of her burger. Suddenly, she slapped my notebook shut and handed it back to me. "You're really overthinking this, babe."

I felt my face flush. It wasn't the first time someone had accused me of thinking too hard. I remembered how fraught looking for skates had been—trying to find the right equipment on such a small budget had become an obsession: it was all I thought about, and Kelly had noticed. Trying to make friends on the team had been an equally painstaking process: I thought about every move I made, everything I said. Tutz had told me to loosen up a little, which was particularly brutal advice for someone whose mind got in the way of letting loose. I wanted to be in control of everything that happened to me and everything around me; I wanted to know what the results would be if I made certain choices, wanted to know how those choices would impact the people surrounding me and my place among them.

"What feels right?" Taryn asked me, still holding my notebook closed. "Just go with your gut."

"How did you choose a name?" I asked.

"Well, everybody makes a list, and I did too. You're just agonizing over it more than the rest of us. What do you like? What speaks to you?"

"I like Georgia O'Queef or Emily Prickinson. Joan of Spark is pretty cool too."

"You have to pick one that'll sound good short," Taryn told me. "People will just naturally shorten it when they're yelling at you from the sidelines. If you're not careful, you could end up Queef or Prick." We both laughed. "Joan of Spark is my favorite because then you could just be Spark. That's badass."

I envied Taryn's easy decision-making skills: her intuition. The more time I spent around her the more I coveted her confidence. Naming myself just felt like another test for which I was unprepared.

When I got home from lunch, I consulted Derby Roll Call and found there were about a million Joans in derby. Joan of Arsenic was registered with the Rockin City Roller Girls. The Nottingham Hellfire Harlots was home to Joan of Dark. Joan of Snark was with Black Hills Roller Derby. Then there were the Joans whose name did not derive from the French martyr; Joan Jetsetter, Militia Joan Hart, and Joan Threat. But there was no Joan of Spark: a fact of which I immediately informed Taryn.

"How do I know if it's right?" I wrote. "How did you know?"

"I just knew," she texted back.

That night, while waiting for the pasta water to boil, I wondered about the significance of taking the name my grandmother had been given. Could it be a way of reclaiming both my Catholic upbringing and the way the Church had silenced me—both as a woman and as a gay woman—all my life? I thought there might be something freeing about taking something destructive and twisting it: strength reaped through parody.

One thing I could say with certainty was that I loved the way the name sounded on my tongue: sharp and angular and electric. It unnerved me to speak it out loud. Joan of Spark was explosive—a bundle of dynamite that could self-destruct at any time. So ten years after resisting taking a saint's name, I chose one willingly. I picked Joan who heard voices, Joan who chose to stay chaste and who sacrificed her life for God. She exercised the kind of self-discipline my mother exalted, but did so in the service of her own vision. She managed to serve her own truth—not her mother's. She was history's tough girl. I whispered the name before I officially claimed it on the derby name database, and again as I ordered my team jersey, and again as I texted Taryn to inform her of my decision.

"My derby kid, Spark," she wrote back. "Love your face."

I didn't realize how scared I was of Spark until Taryn used the name for the first time. Spark symbolized a new version of myself, one from which I was unsure I could ever return. Spark was aware that she was putting her body in harm's way. She was open to the possibility of getting torn, or broken, or beaten. Yet, despite the risk, she knew that the roller derby track was actually the safest place she'd ever been, and she acknowledged that the place she used to call home was the most dangerous. Spark wanted to move forward, and intellectually, I wanted that too, even as, emotionally, I often held myself back. I wanted to untether myself from my hometown, from the bulky clothes I wore to hide my body, from my mother's casual cruelty and homophobia. Joan of Spark wanted an identity that wasn't informed by any of these factors. She wanted to start over, just like my thirteen-year-old self.

13

DRAFT NIGHT

After passing mins, I learned that Arch Rival's semian-nual Draft Night was scheduled for the first week in February, so I would only have about a month to physically and mentally prepare. Unlike travel season, during which Arch Rival was divided into teams based on skill, skaters of all abilities shared the track during local season. The three local teams affiliated with Arch Rival—Smashinistas, M80s, and Stunt Devils—would make their selections based on per-formance during a scrimmage on Draft Night, where the draftees would take turns skating with each team.

Given the level of skill and talent in the draft pool, it was pretty evident that I wouldn't be chosen for a local team this time around. All of the people coming out of retirement were vying for placement, in addition to the few of us who had just passed our minimum skills test, which meant there were three more draftees than open spots. Taryn corrobo-rated my suspicion in the kindest way possible. "Passing min-imum skills in three months is pretty much unheard of," she said. "You should be really, really proud of yourself for ac-complishing that. Do you realize what a big deal that is?"

I told Taryn that I was pleased with my mins performance, but I didn't want to be counted out entirely. I wasn't
sure what I would do if I didn't get drafted—hanging out in
the liminal space between being cleared for contact and
being selected for a team seemed particularly demoralizing.
Had I not passed mins at least I would have something to
work toward. Not being picked for a team just meant that
my league mates didn't yet fully believe in my abilities or see
me fitting in well at this point. It would confirm that I didn't
fully belong, and I wasn't sure I could stomach the inevitable
humiliation and disappointment I knew I'd feel—whether or
not I deserved to get drafted.

Then I found out that Nanny had taken her name out of
the pool of potential draftees. She was aggressively pulling
her skate laces tight and knotting them into triple knots
when I approached her at practice to ask why.

"You okay?" I asked.

"You always seem to catch me at the worst times," she
said, tears welling up in her eyes. "I'm fine. It was just a hard
morning with my kids. That's all."

I thought about saving my question for another time, but
Nanny was already looking at me expectantly.

"I heard you're not putting your name in the draft," I said,
hoping that was all I would need to say. Nanny returned her
gaze to her skates and remained silent. "I was just wondering
why not?"

When Nanny met my eyes, her tears had dried and there
was a slight smile playing across her lips. "Why would I?
There's no way I'd get picked right now. I barely passed mins.
Why put myself through the agony of being judged again
when I know I'm just setting myself up for failure?"

A pit began forming in my stomach. I understood where

Nanny was coming from. Abstaining from the draft altogether might at least give me the illusion of power over my own destiny, a sense of control over my fear of rejection, I considered. But even as attractive as that sounded to me for a moment, I knew I wouldn't make the same choice. Not because I was braver than Nanny, but because I was more afraid. There was simply too much at stake: my sense of belonging, my identity, independence, self-sufficiency, and power, my means of exercise, a source of queer role models, even my clothing style. I wasn't choosing to face my fear of rejection. It was just that I'd been too long hardwired to see the hardest, riskiest, highest-stakes choice as the only worthy one. Opting out would mean failure to me just as much as not being drafted would.

WHEN GRAD SCHOOL started back up again after the holidays, Tory and I began walking to class together. We lived only two blocks apart, so it was nice to meet at the end of the street and traverse the wintery landscape to our fortress of a school. She was about seven years older than me, straight, and wanted a baby immediately; I hadn't anticipated that we would hit it off so well. It turned out we had a lot in common: our fathers were both mechanics, we grew up working class in Midwestern towns, and we were both academically and athletically at the top of our graduating class. Tory ran cross-country for a Division I school in Greenville, South Carolina, and thus understood the dedication and neurosis of athletic pursuits like derby. She said she and Klara had been talking about coming to watch me play, so I invited her to the Draft Night scrimmage.

Most of the time, though, we talked about school. We

talked about homework assignments like flash fiction stories that had timelines of only fifteen minutes, weekly workshop letters we had to write to our peers, and the dozens of books we had to read. One day we got on the topic of last semester's visiting writer, and I felt my heart start to beat faster.

"Maybe this is weird," Tory said, "but he loved me. He said I had very writerly instincts."

"What did you give him to read?" I asked.

"I thought carefully about it," she said. "I read a blurb about him and I knew I didn't want to give him anything about family or trauma, so I chose something that was about being in the bathtub with my boyfriend. Something I used to apply to grad school—not anything I wanted any real feedback on."

"That's good advice," I said. I had already started thinking about writing pieces that I would be more comfortable sharing with our next visiting writer—pieces that were more distanced and journalistic, nowhere near as intimate and revealing as the ones I'd chosen before. I thought about what I would wear that wouldn't elicit any unwanted touching and how I would sit in the middle of the couch rather than at the end closest to the writer's desk. It made me sick even thinking about the next time I'd have to do one of those meetings, but at least I would be prepared.

"How was your meeting?" Tory asked as we passed by the public library. I felt viscerally reminded of the moment I'd had to answer how I found derby. What was the most neutral, forgettable thing I could say without making it obvious I was hiding something? But just as I was about to respond with some version of "fine," I felt an unexpected moment of pause. I looked at Tory out of the corner of my eye. I liked her. I had found her to be an honest and reliable friend.

Could I try to be the same to her? *I'm Joan of Spark now,* I reminded myself.

In the lengthening silence, Tory stopped walking and turned to me. "What's up?" she said, concern on her face.

I didn't tell her everything—somehow the entire story seemed too attention-seeking as I struggled to put it into words—but I did tell her what he'd said. That my topics were repellent, that I had no voice, that I was too young to write anything meaningful.

"That's horrible, G," she said to me, reaching for my arm. "You don't believe any of that crap, do you?" I felt comforted by her; it made me wonder if this was how it felt to have an older sister. If so, I thought suddenly with a flash of shame, was I failing? Cam and I rarely spoke; she hadn't confided in me since I left her at home with our mother.

"Thanks for listening," I told Tory when we got to the English building.

"Always will," she said.

I SPENT THE next few weeks doubling down on practices and working harder than ever. Then, a week before Draft Night, I fell. Badly. Falling had become just another part of practice for me by now, but this time, I fell in such a way that my right hand collided with the wheel of my own skate. I felt an intense, sharp pain—I knew right away that I had done some damage—but immediately bounced back up so as not to draw attention to myself. Attention was one of the worst things I could think of receiving when I was physically injured.

Kelly had accompanied me to practice that night because she had planned on joining me afterward for the weekly reading at WashU, but after my injury, I wasn't sure we would make it. For the ten minutes that remained of practice, my wrist guard shrank around my hand. By the time it was over, it looked like a sausage stuffed into a casing. I had to ask Kelly's help removing my wrist guard when none of the other players were looking. The ensuing pain was so strong it was nauseating.

By this point, I knew where the ice was kept and casually helped myself to a bag of it before leaving. Thankfully, no one noticed that I was cradling my hand, and when we were safely inside Kelly's car, I examined it. The swelling and the pain seemed to be stemming from the base of my right thumb; bruising had begun to darken the skin.

"Should we skip the reading?" Kelly asked. I shook my head no. I wanted to prove I was a good literary citizen. I couldn't afford to miss a reading.

"Thank god you're here to drive," I said. I couldn't imagine wrapping my hand around the steering wheel—and had no clue how I was going to hold a pencil or type at my computer to do my work.

It was impossible to pay attention at the reading, particularly because Kelly kept leaning over and quietly checking up on me. At first I gritted my teeth and assured her that I was fine, but after the reading, when Klara noticed the ice melting down my hand into my lap, I allowed myself to consider a real possibility: "I think I may have fractured my hand," I told her. She instructed me to go home and wrap the injury tightly, switch out my ice packs.

"Tomorrow's Friday so there's no class," Klara said. "You should go to the campus doctor."

Chills spread down my spine at the mention of seeing a doctor. That was the last thing I wanted to do. It was the last thing anyone in my family did. The time my mother had a serious heart attack, she diagnosed herself with an allergic reaction and didn't head to the hospital until after attending a funeral of a woman who, ironically, had died of heart failure. My mother then underwent surgery and afterward, from the hospital bed, she texted me, "Now they're telling me to eat healthy and exercise, treating me like some kind of fat person!" After a few days in the hospital, she left against medical advice.

From a few hundred miles away from my hometown in the palm of Michigan, the story had sounded crazy to me, but I knew that when I was sucked into my mom's orbit, she made everyone else seem like the crazy ones. I didn't blame my sister for going along with her plans to leave the hospital—Cam wasn't even a legal adult yet; how was she supposed to resist my mother and insist that she stay and get proper care? How different, nagged a voice in the back of my head, was that situation from the one I was experiencing at that exact moment—not asking my teammates for help, resisting the idea of getting medical care tomorrow if at all?

By the time I was ready for bed, the discoloration and the swelling had intensified. "Maybe it'll be better when I wake up," I said to Kelly. I was glad that Kelly was working at a temp agency the next day so she wouldn't be around to repeat Klara's advice about seeing a doctor, but that didn't stop her from leaving a note taped to the bathroom mirror. *Go to the doctor,* it said. *Don't be like your mother.*

The second sentence of Kelly's note irked me, but it had the intended effect—forcing me to pay attention. It was one thing for me to think it to myself, another thing to have it literally reflected back to me. I couldn't even unscrew a jar of peanut butter without excruciating pain, or flip the right turn signal while driving. Walking Lady was okay because I could hold the leash with my left hand, but all the jostling made my right hand ache. Yet I still felt an instinctual resistance to going to the doctor. I was like her, in this way—maybe even a little proud to be. A doctor would just charge me some ridiculous sum of money to tell me it was broken, and I already figured as much. I'd learned these lessons well. I'd learned to ignore pain as well as I'd learned to ignore hunger.

WHEN I WAS ten and Cam was five, we liked to scream-sing Shania Twain in the living room. She wore a strand of fake pearls, and I donned our mother's big brown hat. We shimmied our shoulders and popped our hips; we pretended our ChapStick was ruby red. Neither of us was a woman, but we sang over and over that we felt like one.

At the chorus, Cam snatched the hat off my head. Twirling, she threw it into the air. The hat spun and spun, and when Cam caught it, she began to scream. Mom came to the doorframe. Cam unclenched her fist and screamed some more. A thin wire from the brim had pierced the meaty part of her hand, spanning the entire length of her palm.

I was surprised there was no blood. Cartoons and illustrations in books seemed to suggest that the worst types of injuries involved copious amounts of blood. If there had been blood, I might have backed away instead of coming closer to examine it. I may not have run my hand over Cam's thick hair and down her back, patting it gently. I could feel her lungs gasping for air as she sobbed, could feel the convulsions of her body as she shook with pain.

"It'll be okay," I whispered, not positive I believed it myself.

Mom sat down on the couch, head in her hands as I sat next to Cam. There was a dish towel slung over her shoulder. She was wearing fuzzy socks with her pink athletic pants. She told Cam to be quiet so she could think. "Should I just rip it out?" she asked, talking to herself but also, I understood, to me. "Should we wait for your dad to get home?" Dad was at the grocery store; Mom didn't often wait for him to make decisions, which meant that this was serious. "Run next door and get Mr. Davis. He'll know what to do."

I ran out the back door, two braids blown back in the wind, arms pumping. I hurdled over the patch of grass where the family dog usually did her business and pushed open the metal gate in the driveway.

I made it halfway to Mr. Davis's house, only two houses down from ours, when the fear started to creep in. Mr. Davis was the giant, bald varsity football coach who watched me from his porch as I walked the dog up and down the street. His bubbly wife let Cam and me swim in their pool, but Mr. Davis himself was elusive. Sometimes he would sit in the shallow end, muscles bulging, and watch us without speaking. I pictured him ripping the hat from Cam's hand, deaf to her screams. The thought made me cringe.

I sprinted back home and busted through the back door, accidentally letting the screen slam behind me, which Mom usually hated. But she didn't yell at me; she was still sitting on the couch with a wrinkle in her brow, dazed, lips moving slightly as she talked to herself. She didn't ask what Mr. Davis had said, didn't even seem to realize I'd left. Cam was still whimpering, but she called out for me when I arrived, so I sat beside her on the couch. She rested her head on my shoulder and her tears soaked through my T-shirt.

"It's heavy," she cried. "It hurts."

"You're fine," our mother said. "Everything is okay."

I got an old, dingy pillow from the couch and rested it underneath the hat. I must have looked like a ring bearer. Mom didn't move or speak again, so we waited. I imagined Cam going through her life with the hat stuck in her palm. She wouldn't be able to pin her own name tag to her shirt on the first day of first grade. She would need help painting sunflowers in art class. She would never make it through swim team tryouts—and who would she be if she couldn't swim?

Briefly it crossed my mind to call 911. Our teachers were always emphasizing that we should call for emergencies. Did this qualify? Mom's insistence that everything was okay suggested it wasn't. Finally, she decided that we would wait for my dad to get home from the grocery store before taking any further action.

"I'm scared," Cam said, big eyes brimming with tears.

"Mom's not scared," I said, pointing to our mother, who had just stood to resume washing the dishes in the kitchen sink. "Everything is just fine."

The Shania Twain CD had run its full course and clicked off by the time Dad got home from the grocery store. He saw my sister's puffy face, then his gaze flickered down to her hand, and then he started to back away, which is what he usually did in crises. "No no no," Mom scolded. "I'll put away the groceries. You go deal with that." Dad approached us with his flashlight. He talked about the risk of pulling, of getting the wire lodged further, of a second wire we might not be able to see.

It seemed like a lifetime of waiting while Dad examined Cam's hand. She whimpered whenever he moved it, and I rubbed her back. "It's okay. It's okay," I whispered. When Dad suggested the emergency room, Mom sighed in defeat. "I wish you would just yank it out," she said. "It would save us so much money." I couldn't help being annoyed with him, too. If he just took care of it, we wouldn't need to go to the hospital and Cam would be better sooner.

On the drive to the ER, Cam was hysterical. Everyone else was silent. I couldn't see Dad's face in the driver's seat, but Mom was staring pensively out the passenger window. When we arrived, the doctors said that Cam needed to be sedated. "How did this happen?" the nurse asked. I was the only one who saw the accident, but Mom spoke over me.

"My kid impaled herself trying to catch an old hat," she said.

"How long has it been lodged in her hand?" the nurse asked. A long time, though none of us knew how long exactly. "Why didn't you come right away?" she asked. Mother ignored her question entirely.

The wire was lodged so deeply that two doctors needed to work together to get it out. I watched from between my fingers. One man held Cam's limp hand; the other gripped the hat like a steering wheel and turned. We cheered when the blood-stained wire was finally free.

When the doctors started to leave, Mom raised her voice. "Is this the weirdest thing you've ever seen?" she asked.

Mom's face told me I should feel curious and somewhat prideful about the accident. That feeling only intensified when the doctor responded, "I've seen some pretty wild stuff in here, but this may take the cake." Mom grinned and so I grinned too—just a little at first, then more broadly, with all my teeth.

"That doctor is going to be talking about us for a long time," Mom assured me, and from the look on her face I knew that was the goal: be the best, or the most unique, even at getting injured. Make them talk.

IN TELLING ME not to be like my mother, I understood that Kelly was asking me not to be stupid. She was asking me to trust doctors and acknowledge the personality traits I shared with my mom that would make getting help contrary to my nature. But it was still grating to hear that line coming from someone who had two doctors as parents—someone who had been taught to trust the medical establishment from birth.

I waited a whole week to have my hand examined just to make sure it wouldn't get better on its own. Kelly was both concerned and annoyed. Every day I put off going to the doctor, she voiced new, horrifying medical possibilities. "You could have a bone spur," she told me. "You could lose functionality in that thumb."

The morning of the local season draft, I finally went to the clinic on campus. Kelly's persistence had started to work on me, and since the pain hadn't dulled, I felt more confident that I wasn't overreacting. It was important to me that I had proof of lasting severe pain to back up my complaint. Ever since my foot surgeries, I dreaded ever again being in a situation where it might be suggested that my pain was psychosomatic. The idea of having to defend or prove my experience was unbearable. I wasn't sure I trusted myself enough to defend anything.

Sick undergrads surrounded me in the waiting room; I tried not to breathe as I cradled my arm. The nurses took a keen interest in the way I had injured myself. One of them diverted entirely from health-related questions and instead peppered me with questions about roller derby. Another postulated that "to play a sport like that," my pain tolerance must be higher than average, which was an inference that immediately worked to my advantage. They automatically added two numbers to my pain scale so that when I reported my overall pain at a four, it became a six.

"I used to love watching roller derby," my radiology tech confessed. "You girls really take a beating!" He lowered his voice so nobody else could hear. "I'm not really supposed to tell patients what I see, but your break is crystal clear. The bone isn't where it's supposed to be."

How proud my mother would be to hear that, I thought. She would likely speculate about this radiology tech going home and telling the story to his family over dinner. *You won't believe who I treated today,* he would say.

When the doctor came into the room, the first question he asked me was when the injury happened. "I can tell by the calcium buildup it's been a while," he said. "I would've suggested surgery a week ago, but now you're pretty much dealing with a question of cosmetics."

Instead of telling the doctor honestly how long it had been—eight days—I reacted to the second part of his statement. "Are you asking me if I want a thumb job?" He laughed in a way that seemed pained.

"I would highly encourage you, the next time you experience this amount of pain, to seek medical care immediately," he told me. "This isn't something you can really fool around with."

I nodded and shifted my eyes to my lap. He instructed me where to go to get a cast custom-made out of a hard plastic material. "You'll be able to remove it for showering," he said. What he didn't say—and what I didn't explicitly ask—was if I could also remove the cast for the Draft Night scrimmage. I didn't tell the doctor I had plans to skate that evening, but I did ask when I could get back on skates.

"You don't skate with your thumbs, do you?" he said, chuckling. I smiled and jumped down from the table, but he wasn't finished. "I mean, the answer is no, you absolutely shouldn't skate. But I've been asked questions like that enough by people like you to know that you're going to do whatever you want anyway."

He wasn't wrong. What caught my attention was the phrase "people like you." What kind of people did he mean? People like my teammates, who often continued their activities as usual, post-injury, despite the risk? People like my mother, who took pride in the severity and uniqueness of our injuries growing up? Was this where family background and my derby family converged?

TORY AND KLARA met Kelly and me at the Skatium that evening to watch the scrimmage. "Is my car going to be okay out here?" Klara wanted to know. I told her if she parked close enough to the building it would probably be fine, even though we'd had a recent surge in smashed windows. I didn't want her to leave; having an audience gave me energy. I watched Tory beam as I skated the oval backward: I'd been sent off the track five months ago precisely because of my ineptitude at this skill. Through their eyes—and the eyes of the other family and friends who had come to cheer on the draftees—I could appreciate how much I'd grown.

As delighted as Tory and Klara were watching me warm up, I couldn't quite decipher what Kelly was feeling. Somewhat surprisingly, she hadn't voiced any concern about my taking part in the Draft Night scrimmage with a broken hand. "Now that you have the information, it's your choice what you do," she said. "What bothers me isn't that you take risks with your body that I wouldn't take—it's that you bury your head in the sand when something's wrong."

"Are you scared for me?" I asked, gently.

"Of course I'm fucking scared," she shot back.

"I'll be careful," I said.

"You're playing a full contact sport on roller skates," she said. Then, as if swatting away a fly, she waved her hand and said, "You know what, it's fine. I'll just distract myself by explaining the game to Tory and Klara."

Her lack of concern was a relief, since she had spent a full week making it perfectly clear she thought I was being unreasonable by not getting it checked out. As for burying my head in the sand? Well, it seemed like my hand would eventually heal just fine despite my delay.

When I saw Taryn getting her skates on, I skated to the side of the track. We had been texting about my hand, and unlike Kelly, she didn't see much cause for alarm in terms of me participating in Draft Night as long as it was well protected.

"Let me see," she said, reaching for my injured hand and turning it to make sure it was fully covered.

"It feels fine," I said. I couldn't bear the thought that she might try to stop me from participating once I had gotten this far. This night was too important to me to sit on the sidelines; it was the last confirmation that I was truly a part of this kooky, queer group of misfits.

"I'm so glad, babe," she said, reaching her arms up from where she was sitting on the floor to hug me. "You're going to do so awesome."

I expected Draft Night to be as chaotic as the Halloween scrimmage had been: the hazy, underwater feeling, bodies slamming into me from every direction, frantic yelling from the sidelines to get up quickly when I was pushed down. All of that did happen, but I also found I had a new awareness of where my body was in relation to everyone else. I helped make a wall with my teammates to block the opposing jammer from getting through and scoring points, and once I even successfully hit an opposing player out of bounds.

"Yeah, Joan of Spark!!" I expected the call to be coming from Kelly—or from Klara and Tory—but, surprisingly, it came from Nanny. She was sitting near my friends on the bench, bald head reflecting the light of the disco ball.

"Miss you out here!" I shouted.

The hardest part of the evening wasn't protecting my hand, but rotating among the three teams. The physical pain was dull in comparison to the discomfort I felt at the beginning and end of every thirty-minute period. As soon as I started to feel comfortable on one team, it would be time to move on. Players who had just been my allies became my rivals. Between each period, I skated over to Kelly for help changing shirts—green for Smashinistas, red for M80s, and blue for Stunt Devils—and I was so sweaty that it was difficult wriggling free, my helmet and protective pads only complicating things further. She had to peel my shirt off me and then help me pull the new color on. I was comfortable changing shirts in front of my derby friends, but I was very aware that this was the first time my grad school friends had seen me in nothing but a bra. I pushed aside my self-consciousness, reminding myself that I must at least look athletic with all the training and careful food monitoring.

It was hard to tell, in an unscored scrimmage, which team was dominant, though it seemed to be between the Stunt Devils and the Smashinistas. Taryn's team, the M80s, certainly had talent, Tutz especially, they just seemed to have less chemistry. The blockers often didn't re-form fast enough to catch the opposing jammer; they would still be spread out around the track, and when they realized she was circling back around for more points, they couldn't get together in time. The M80s did, however, seem like the most fun. They wore red plaid cutoffs and denim jeans; their pre-season photo shoot had been "lumber babe" themed. Taryn had proudly shown me shots of the players posed in a dense forest, swinging axes and hatchets. In one of her photos, Tutz stood like Captain Morgan with one leg propped on a tree stump, holding a handsaw behind her head and flexing her big biceps.

The Smashinistas were my least favorite team, although I still would have gladly accepted placement there. They were all clad in camouflage shirts that said GOOD HAIR DON'T CARE, and though I liked them individually—Draggie, Bolt, Smarty McFly—as a team they were cocky, loud, and what I thought was unnecessarily aggressive.

Deep down, I could admit to myself that I wanted to be on the M80s. Red looked good on me. Taryn and Tutz were two of my favorite league mates. The M80s looked like they had so much fun. The Stunts were a little more serious, which intimidated me. If I was drafted onto the Smashies, I would be happy just to be included.

After the scrimmage, the three local teams gathered on the track as all the draftees de-geared. It was strange sitting just out of earshot, knowing that they were ranking their choices. They'd meet the rest of us at Stacked, the burger joint where I'd first met Taryn, once they'd made their decision; the league had reserved us a space where the draft selections—and the celebrations, at least for those who had actually been drafted—would take place. By the time I had taken off all my gear, Tutz and the rest of the M80s were already disbanding, which wasn't surprising. Taryn had told me they only wanted to add one player to their roster and that player would likely be returnee Rhino Might, who was not only the physically biggest and most powerful out of all of us, but also had the most experience, having played for the All Stars several seasons back. The Smashies were engaged in what appeared to be a heated debate; they were likely to take three to replace a few retirements and get back to a standard sixteen-player charter. The Stunt Devils reportedly only wanted two. On the other side of the track, Bricktator was leading the Stunts through a series of post-scrimmage stretches. They seemed to be calmly discussing draftees while moving from pigeon pose to downward dog.

Watching the three teams discuss draftees, I thought about how my performance must have looked to them. I felt decent out there. I was glad, also, that I didn't have the "star" role on the team as jammer. Blockers relied on working better together. Their successes and failures were shared, which eased my mind to a considerable degree.

When I had finished de-gearing, I found Klara and Tory and thanked them for coming. "You're a badass!" Tory told me, throwing her long hair over her shoulder. "I can't wait to see you play in your first game."

"We'll be there," Klara said. "Just tell us when and where."

I hugged them both tightly. In high school and college, all my friends were on the swim team and I had very little confidence in building and maintaining relationships outside of sports. I figured the same would be true of derby, so to have friends that I had made and sustained on my own felt nothing short of a miracle.

I met Kelly outside; the car was already warm by the time I got in. I thought it was possible she'd still be frosty toward me, but the fact I had made it through the scrimmage unscathed seemed to put her mind at ease. It seemed like she had thought carefully about what to say when I entered— something that wouldn't be untrue, like *You looked great out there!*, or too hopeful, like *I can't wait to see which team you get put on!* I'd already explained that the likelihood of being drafted was minuscule, but that I wanted to go to Stacked anyway. I had claimed that if I didn't get picked, I would be happy for the other skaters. I planned on faking a smile and celebrating with them, but we both knew it would be difficult for me to feel anything beyond disappointment. I only hoped it wouldn't show on the outside.

"It's crazy to me you didn't know how to skate a few months ago," she said as I clumsily buckled my seat belt. "Remember when Tutz had to hold both your hands while she taught you how to skate backward?"

I laughed and tried not to tear up. Her warmth and support sometimes felt too overwhelming, and I was so thankful she hadn't brought up my hand again, which was throbbing uncomfortably. "I'm so grateful you came to watch," I said, leaning in to hug her.

By the time Kelly and I got to Stacked, Nanny and several of the M80s had already arrived and were in the middle of preparing a special room in the back of the restaurant. In addition to the twinkle lights strung up around the windows, Tutz had set up a disco ball in the corner, which rotated on its axis and cast splashes of color on every wall. Magilla Guerilla, one of the local season announcers, was prepping his microphone and rehearsing his opening lines.

Gradually, the room filled with skaters. Cruella Belle-Ville arrived with patriotic-themed gifts for the new additions to the Stunt Devils. The Smashinistas arrived in one large, camo-clad herd. Taryn plopped down beside me and ordered a large basket of fried pickles and a Mountain Dew. "Is your hand still broken or did all that derby somehow snap it back into place?" she asked.

I allowed her to examine my injury, wincing when she touched it, and even more when she said, "Are you going to go easy on it from here on out? Maybe take a few weeks to let it heal?"

I told Taryn I would think about it, but I knew that if I got drafted onto a team there was no way I would be taking time off. Out of the corner of my eye, I saw Kelly shaking her head at Taryn. The two of them shared a moment of mutual frustration with me that I pretended not to notice. Then, the team captains entered and Magilla cleared his throat.

"Arch Rival Roller Derby, it's time for our local season draft!" The crowd cheered and I felt myself stiffening. I was glad I hadn't eaten anything yet or it would inevitably be threatening to come up. My vision was starting to blur slightly. "This is one of the most exciting days of the year," he continued. "So we won't wait any longer!"

Gil turned to Tutz, the M80s captain, who pulled the microphone in Gil's hand to her mouth. "M80s will only be selecting one new addition," she bellowed. *You already know this one isn't going to be you,* I reminded myself, blinking to try to clear my vision. "And that lucky person is . . . Rhinoooo Might!" Rhino, who was sitting at the table behind me, pushed her chair out as she stood, causing it to squeak and then tip over backward. She made her way to the front of the room, pumping her arms in the air and motioning for the crowd to cheer.

A tidal wave of disappointment engulfed me, followed by an awful sense of shame that this was my gut reaction. Desperate to appear any way but how I really felt, I forced a smile that I hoped didn't look like a grimace. *Everyone* had known they'd pick Rhino, including me. It shouldn't have felt like a surprise. I didn't even think I deserved it more. What was wrong with me?

As Rhino made her way up to the makeshift stage, I clapped numbly, avoiding eye contact with Kelly and Taryn. Even though I had always known it was a long shot at best, I hadn't been able to stop myself from fantasizing about being on the same team as Taryn and Tutz. I had even—and I suddenly felt a wild sense of relief that I'd never slipped up and told this to anyone—already worked out what I would wear at the team photo shoot: cutoff denim overalls and one of Kelly's red plaid shirts underneath. I'd have my hair tied back like Rosie the Riveter and I'd flex my biceps for the camera.

As the applause died down, Tutz explained that each team had a tradition of welcoming new members, and the

M80s liked to draw a unibrow on people's faces with red permanent marker.

"Good thing that's not me," I whispered to Kelly, grasping for a semblance of carefree humor. "I have class tomorrow and that shit doesn't come off."

"We know, Frida," she whispered back. But she squeezed my hand underneath the table.

Once Rhino was marked, Magilla pulled her over for an interview.

"Welcome back to Arch Rival, Rhino!" he said. "So, tell us, how long has it been since you've skated?"

"I guess 'bout three years," Rhino said. "Played for the All Stars for years but had to stop for the birth of my daughter. It's good to be back!" Beer sloshed out of her mug as she raised it while nodding to the crowd, which triggered another round of whooping.

I was grateful for this pause before the next team announced their selections. I needed to get my head together. I had known tonight would be tense for me, but I was doing worse than I expected, and I definitely didn't anticipate how sickened I would feel by my seeming inability to be happy for my teammates' success. One of the things I had grown to love about derby was how joyful and purposeful the players looked when they were in their element. I'd felt radiant when they'd nailed the "Circle of Life" figure skating routine. I had cheered without reserve when the All Stars had beaten Denver. *See, you're not* all *bad,* a small voice in my head piped up. As Rhino answered a couple more questions, I looked around the room and saw real, unfettered pleasure etched on face after face. I *was* happy for Rhino, I realized. Maybe it wasn't an uncomplicated happiness, but it wasn't untrue, either—I loved that this was a sport that embraced returning players, moms, people in all stages of life. And I was happy for Tutz and Taryn, too, that their first choice was so clearly thrilled to join the M80s. Rhino's win didn't have to feel like my loss, even though, right now, it did feel a little bit like that. So much felt like it was at stake for me. But I didn't have to *stay* in that place, right? I wasn't my mother. Was I? I wanted to be someone who could feel genuinely thrilled by another person's success, even if we were up for the same prize. *I'm not there right now,* I thought, *but maybe I can try to practice with the next draft picks.*

Once Rhino was ushered offstage, the captain of the Smashinistas, Rock Slobster, took Tutz's place. Her hair, which was parted down the middle, hung like long navy-blue drapes.

"This was a hard call," she said into the microphone. "But Smashies will be taking two people." *Two?!* I thought with panic. I'd thought they were going to take three—that meant there were even fewer available slots left than I'd hoped. I took a deep breath and slowly let it out. *This is not a reflection of your self-worth,* I told myself. It didn't feel true. "Welcome to the squad. . . ." She paused for emphasis, and her teammates started using their fingers to drumroll on the table. My pulse quickened. "The Wicked Witch of the Midwest and Ven Detta!"

Ven Detta looked visibly relieved to be on a separate team from her ex-wife, Rhino. I heard her say to Bolt as she walked to the front of the stage, "This will do!"

The Smashies swarmed Detta and Wicked, and immediately began chanting "One of us! One of us!" They branded each woman with a bushy stick-on mustache.

I was starting to feel like I might hyperventilate with anxiety, except for the fact that I was forcing myself to take steady breaths. I couldn't help calculating: six remaining draftees, two more spots. I couldn't tell what was more important to me right now—getting chosen, or giving the impression that I felt calm, casual, and reasonable about the whole thing.

Finally, Cruella Belle-Ville, captain of the Stunt Devils, took the stage. Her dark hair was wet from sweating through the scrimmage, which heightened the contrast of her natural white streak. Without preamble, she said, "Stunts have decided to draft . . . Hakuna Renata and Joan of Spark!"

I didn't move. The first thing I thought was that this must be some kind of a joke. I felt Gil's gaze turn to the table where I was sitting, and Taryn started slapping my arm. "That's you!" she said. "Your name is Spark! Get up!" Kelly pulled me to my feet and hugged me tightly. In shock, I turned toward Taryn. There were tears in her eyes as she hugged me, too. She gave me a nudge in the direction of the podium, and as I took my first fumbling steps forward, it was as if the volume on the cheering suddenly got turned up, and it started to sink in. They'd called my name. I'd been drafted. Behind me, I heard Taryn say quietly to Kelly, "I *really* didn't think that was going to happen."

Magilla began speaking quickly into the microphone as Renata and I made our way to the front of the room. As the clapping and hollering quieted, I could just make out what he was saying.

"And there you have it. Hakuna Renata, who is coming out of retirement after a year-long hiatus, has been drafted to the Stunt Devils along with newcomer Joan of Spark!"

Bricktator presented royal blue gift bags with red and white tissue paper. Renata reached in and pulled out an American flag bandana.

"We're going full on Evel Knievel theme this year," Cruella told Gil. "Don't look for us in purple, derby fans—we'll be in royal blue now!"

As Cruella spoke, I followed Renata's lead by digging through the gift bag until I located the bandana. By the time I found it, Renata already had hers tied around her neck and was grinning broadly.

I suddenly experienced a wave of panic. Tying a knot wasn't something I could do with a broken hand. The M80s had their red Sharpie unibrows. The Smashies had their stick-on mustaches. This Americana bandana was supposed to be the way I accepted my placement.

As I set my gift bag down to get a better grip on the bandana, I heard Magilla say, "Having a little trouble there, Spark?"

Standing in front of a boisterous crowd of skaters and trying to force my swollen, broken hand to function normally, I shook my head no. I needed to do this myself. I needed to prove that choosing me wasn't a mistake, that I wouldn't be an instant liability. Every movement was excruciating, but I forced myself to smile. Finally, I succeeded in tying the knot. Applause broke out. I couldn't tell if the tears welling up in my eyes were from pain, or from giddiness at finally having a home.

14/
DEDICATED AS FUCK

After the draft, I added two extra days of workouts to my already jam-packed training schedule. When I'd finally gotten off the stage and was greeted by my Stunt Devil teammates, Bricktator told me that the jammers sometimes ran the bleachers and practiced agility at WashU on Saturday mornings; even though I wasn't a jammer, I was welcome to come.

"WashU—like where I go to school?" I asked. I couldn't picture this group of weird, eclectic skaters anywhere near the stuffy academic world to which I belonged. I felt protective of my teammates—and worried about what my peers would say if they saw me gallivanting around with people who clearly weren't students or teachers.

"Yeah, they usually leave the gate to the track unlocked and we just slip right in," Brick said.

The next Saturday morning, a dusting of snow coated the track. Brick had already arrived with an armful of exercise equipment: medicine balls and resistance bands and little hurdles. Ida came next—a jammer on the All Stars team I didn't know very well—and then Loki, a third All Stars team jammer who was wearing silver metallic leggings that looked better suited for space exploration than a mid-February outdoor workout. I couldn't help checking the area beyond the gate to see if anyone I knew was walking past. For a brief second, I thought I saw my grad school advisor, but it turned out to be a cafeteria worker. I wasn't sure if what I felt was relief or disappointment: part of me *wanted* people from WashU to know I belonged to an entirely different world—that I was special, in a sense.

The workout was murderous; we hopped on one foot up the football stands, we chased each other around the track, we did broad jumps and squat jumps and lunge jumps. I had to abstain from the medicine ball throws because of my injured hand, which was still in a brace. By the time the workout was over, my body was literally shaking. "Breakfast?" they suggested.

We all piled into our cars and drove to a nearby bakery. Inside, I felt my muscles start to relax, though I still felt intimidated at the thought of casually hanging out with three of the best jammers in the league. As our eggs and potatoes were served, I asked Brick why she had invited me.

"We invite a lot of people," she explained. "But most people don't have your drive. I recognized it immediately and knew if we invited you, you'd come out."

I blushed, and simultaneously thought about my exercise regime and Kelly's reaction to it. "Do you think this is starting to be a problem?" she had asked. She was referring to my insistence that I couldn't miss a practice—the rigidity of my training schedule. It was the most intense exercise routine I had maintained since college swimming, where I survived mostly on bananas, except for when I went berserk and gorged myself in the school cafeteria, only to throw it all up later in the dormitory toilet. My eating patterns weren't drastically different now: I still struggled with moderation and with allowing myself to feel full and satisfied. I still hid bulimic episodes, like the one I had the night after I met the visiting writer.

My new identity as a Stunt Devil helped me justify keeping my body in a perpetual state of exhaustion, which emphasized to me that I didn't have a problem, as Kelly suggested. I started noticing changes to my lower body: my calves bulged, my thighs hardened, and my butt lost its jiggle. My stamina came back, seemingly in reserve from all my years of swimming, and I found I was able to complete three hours of intensive training and still maintain my technique. This all made me feel unbelievably proud—like I had a purpose, like I was moving forward instead of back.

My hand steadily healed; I found the right combination of athletic tape and bandages to hold it in place, and as a result stopped worrying so much about getting reinjured at practice. I was much more concerned with game strategy, which Cruella began pulling me aside to teach me. Soup Beans placed an immediate order for my jersey. Since all three teams practiced together until the week of the game, Taryn could offer me pointers. "If you expose your side or chest like that in a real bout, you're absolutely going to get blown up," she said. "My teammates love taking that inside line, and if you're standing there like that, they'll just fucking slam into you like a freight train."

Of all the obstacles I'd passed so far—Fresh Meat, mins, Draft Night—my first game was the one I'd been looking forward to the most since I sent those initial emails to Soup Beans about joining Arch Rival. It was the opportunity I'd wanted to see my name in lights, to showcase how far I'd come. The closer it got, however, the more it became about simply surviving rather than thriving. In the glorified version of my first game that played in my head, there were no All Stars to compete against and no long-standing rivalry between teams—just me, skating backward with my arms out like Tonya Harding and being showered by bouquets of roses. The closer I got to the first game, the faster that fantasy dissolved.

"It's going to suck," Soup Beans assured me, pulling at the hem of her cheetah hot pants, which were riding up like underwear. "All first games suck. Just focus on making it out alive."

One welcome distraction was that Kelly was coming to more practices. She had found a temp agency and was working at a law firm digitizing old legal documents for eight hours a day. "My only friends are you and NPR," she told me. That wasn't entirely true: she had acquaintances at the rock climbing gym—but I could tell she was starting to sink into the loneliness of the job.

One day when Kelly had joined me at practice, a guest skater was visiting from LA on business. She plopped down beside me to begin putting on her gear and Kelly, who was standing above us, began asking her questions. It was entirely uncharacteristic of Kelly to strike up conversations with strangers; I was happily surprised that she was conversing with someone who wasn't me.

"Name's Drive Bi," the woman said. "I'm here representing LaunchCode, a nonprofit that specializes in connecting people with math and science backgrounds, especially women, to careers in technology."

Kelly's mouth hung open temporarily, and then she dug through her fanny pack for her phone to take notes. "Well—I'm a woman with a math background looking for a career." It seemed almost too good to be true: LaunchCode offered free coding classes (one of which focused entirely on educating female-identifying people), and had hundreds of employer partners who wanted to hire LaunchCoders.

"I've only taken one coding class," Kelly confessed. "Do you think I would still qualify?"

Drive Bi nodded vigorously. "We love math people. They make the best coders. You might not even need to take any of the LaunchCode classes—we might just be able to get you in the program and placed with a company immediately."

On the way home, LaunchCode was all Kelly talked about. While Drive Bi and I had been practicing our grapevines and ride-outs, Kelly had been feverishly googling the organization. "I truly can't believe something like this existed three miles from our apartment and I didn't know about it," she said.

After Kelly filled out an application for LaunchCode, she immediately began studying. When she was at the law firm scanning old legal documents, her phone was propped up displaying coding problems for her to think through while her hands were busy. She was then set up with an interview in which she could talk about her coding experience and show them some of the projects she had been working on back in college. The results came back almost immediately: LaunchCode wasn't requiring Kelly to complete any of their basic coding classes—they were recommending her for employment with one of their partner companies.

The news made Kelly emotional, which was far from typical. "I was just starting to think I'd never find anything," she said. "And then this miracle skater named Drive Bi—of all names—comes and changes my life. It's just too much."

Not long after she was approved for the program, Launch-Code helped Kelly get hired to do programming at a pharmaceutical company. Out of the twenty-four people offered an internship, only six were women. The starting salary was triple my stipend, and we suddenly didn't have to worry about scraping together enough money for rent and food. Neither of us had expected it would take so long—nearly nine months—for Kelly to find a permanent job, but we also hadn't anticipated how perfect the role would be for her, and how big a change it would make to our financial situation. For the first time since moving to St. Louis, we could breathe a little.

As our lives were improving, however, Taryn's was deteriorating fast.

The texts came fast and furious; we stayed up well into the night. "It's over," she wrote. "Between me and Jacob's dad." He'd been stealing money for drugs out of her wallet, out of the kids' piggy banks. She told me she found a picture of another woman in his dresser, a used condom that was not theirs on the bedroom floor. Those weren't the only reasons for the breakup, though.

"I think he was jealous I have derby," Taryn had texted. "I had some girls over to watch derby footage one night, and Ethan made some comment about how they were all such freaks. I couldn't believe it. I thought: these are my people. And it just kept getting worse and worse after that. He asked if I'd 'gone lesbian.'"

I felt a rush of compassion for Taryn coupled with gratitude for Kelly and her unfaltering support of me and derby, even when I'd broken my hand.

. . .

WHILE I WAS legitimately sympathetic to Taryn's situation, particularly the daunting task of telling her kids about the breakup, I was also somewhat relieved that I could finally be the one to comfort her. I asked about her father, and about her difficult coming-of-age, working first in her parents' restaurant and then in various restaurants at Universal Studios, and about the shame surrounding her relationships with men. In speaking openly about her recent voyage into eye movement desensitization and reprocessing therapy, she allowed me to step into the role of listening and confirming and consoling. It was a reversal of our typical roles, and it seemed to create a new, more peer-like balance between us.

Taryn couldn't afford her place without Ethan and would need to move somewhere smaller with the boys. "How can I help?" I asked. "I can help you look for places, pack, move your stuff, whatever you need."

"I just want to focus on derby for a bit," she said. "It's the only thing bringing me joy."

AS MY FIRST game got closer and closer, the biggest mental hurdle I faced was confronting why I had been picked over skaters who seemed entirely more worthy. Unlike several of the others, I had never played in a game, and although I had passed the skills test, I still struggled with forward-to-backward transitions, which were vital for moving quickly from offense to defense.

About two weeks after I'd been drafted, we were practicing a skill that involved transitioning from forward to backward and catching the jammer with our chest. Every time I tried to move to backward skating, I fell straight on my butt.

It was demoralizing, and I had to excuse myself briefly to get a handle on my emotions. Cruella met me by the sidelines. "Why did you even pick me?" I asked. I was close to tears. My body hurt from falling so many times in such rapid succession. "We picked you for your work ethic," she said. "You never miss a practice. You're the first on the track and the last off. You're dedicated as fuck." Most of the other draft-eligible skaters were indeed more skillful and more experienced than me—she admitted as much—but she said my trajectory was unparalleled.

"You're going to get this skill and soon you'll be laughing," she assured me.

I appreciated the sentiment but accepted Cruella's reasoning with a great deal of skepticism, preparing myself for the moment when she would yell, "Gotcha!" and announce that picking me had been some kind of dare. I'd never heard of an unseasoned player being picked over an experienced one because of promise alone.

For a week I repeated what Cruella had told me, trying to convince myself to believe it. I showed up at practice every day to work on my transitions, but it wasn't until my third week as a Stunt Devil at Thursday night practice that I found out my intuition had been correct. There was an entirely different reason I had been voted onto the team.

That reason was my ass.

"We're just a team of really small people," Pegasass told me, leaning on the rails during a water break. "We needed some big girls to fill out the team—literally. And you're the densest person I've ever met. Your cells are just really close together. You know how I mean that, right?"

I did know how she meant it, but I felt my stomach sinking. My dense body was one of the primary reasons the Stunts had voted to add me to their roster? I could tell this was a phrase I'd be repeating in my head for weeks, if not years, even knowing Peg was genuinely not attributing any negative value to what she'd said.

I flashed back to my third week of Fresh Meat, when Soup Beans casually called me a beefcake. I asked her what she meant and in response, she'd just tugged at her shirt and repeated the phrase. "You're a beefcake. The best people are beefcakes. I'm a beefcake and I'm fucking fabulous."

When I was a swimmer, it had been so deeply ingrained in me that there was a normative, ideal body type for winning races. When I was a child, I almost fit it. I have always been dense, but there was a time I was also lean and streamlined. I looked like I belonged in the water. By the time I started playing roller derby, that was no longer the case. I retained the broad shoulders from my swimming days, but my breasts had fully emerged, as if angry I'd stuffed them into ill-fitting suits for twelve years. My torso was thick, my thighs beefy.

When I arrived at the pool for the first practice of my sophomore swim season, Coach had interrogated my mother about my weight. They made no effort to hide the conversation from me or my teammates; as we did sit-ups on the pool deck, they discussed my body.

"What *happened*?" he asked.

My mother shrugged. She knew he was referring to my recent weight gain. "She's up to 130 now," she said. "Maybe 135." She was right. She always knew what I weighed: that skill she had developed by weighing women at Weight Watchers.

Though I had developed a habit of wearing baggy clothes,

a swimsuit was not conducive to hiding my body. My mother's eyes would linger on my hips and thighs. She would often say, "If you just lost ten pounds you'd be faster. Just think about it. It's physics. Less weight to haul from one end of the pool to the other."

I spent over a decade trying to win races, and that logic became my law. It was the lens through which I saw myself: my body as a vehicle to win, my body as something of which there literally needed to be less.

This thinking was at least partially informed by the Catholic Church. In catechism, I learned I was at war with my body; I needed to control its impulses, measure its intake, and monitor the space it took up. *Gluttony,* when spoken by my teachers, had the same intonation as "non-procreative sexual intercourse." *Gluttony,* I thought as I gorged. *Gluttony,* as I vomited, wiping my mouth and flushing the toilet. Something to do with self-denial and non-indulgence. To the Catholics in charge of my spiritual education, the very fact of occupying my body was irreverent.

"How'd you gain all that?" my coach asked me. The other girls stopped their sit-ups, and I felt my face flush. "What were you last season—119, 120?" He looked to my mother for confirmation and she nodded. Then he looked back to me, expecting an answer.

"I don't know," I said. "I've been doing everything the same."

I couldn't explain it to my coach or my mother, but inhabiting my body recently had started to feel strange, and when I looked at photographs of myself from the previous season, I could see the difference. All my straight lines had been replaced by subtle curves, my boniness pushed out by softness. This realization may have been my first understanding of loss, a loss which I grieved and tried desperately to reverse. The winners, I realized, were the girls whose bodies still looked like those of children—the tall girls, the flat girls, the girls whose training was compatible with their genetics. That's why, when Soup Beans and Pegasass commented on my thickness, I had no point of reference for what they were saying. Were thick skaters advantaged in derby? Were curves merely soft surfaces for competitors to bounce off of? Did it help to *not* have a swimmer's body?

I approached Taryn with my questions, disoriented. "How are you doing?" I asked, not wanting to launch into a tirade without checking in on her first.

"As good as I can be right now," she said. Then, laughing, "You look like you have a lot to say."

"I do!" I exclaimed. "Is this some crack in the universe where skill and experience don't matter if you're harder to move? Should I try to gain more weight? Would that make me even more valuable?" I was speaking quickly, agitated. I needed to know exactly what I was supposed to be striving for.

Taryn put her hands on my shoulders. "It sounds like you're asking what the ideal body type is for roller derby," she said, gently.

"No," I snapped, even though that was exactly what I was asking. "I'm just trying to be the best teammate I can be. And since that seems to be mostly about body size, I might as well focus on that." I felt angry. Or embarrassed. Or confused. Maybe all of those.

"You're overthinking again," Taryn said. "This isn't like swimming. In derby, you can't win on your own. We need walls of bodies, and it just happens that the Stunts have a hole in their wall that you fill perfectly."

"So then I'm right," I said, feeling suddenly on the verge of tears. "I'm—"

"No, that's not what I'm saying," she continued patiently. "What I'm saying is that you can play this sport—even the same position—and be any freaking size there is. Take Tutz. She started playing derby when she was three hundred pounds. And Pegasass? She's tiny. And guess what? They play the same position and they're both fucking amazing."

"How is that even possible?" I asked. What I really wanted to know was which body type was best. How was I supposed to know what I should try to look like? How was I supposed to know when to feel comfortable in my body if there wasn't one permanent measuring stick? I thought about college, when my friends and I would try to predict swimming winners based solely on their bodies. I thought about my mother, who lost interest in coming to meets once I'd gained weight and stopped winning.

Taryn pushed up my chin until I met her gaze. "Listen," she said. "The only requirement in derby is that you can stand. And that you can get up when you're not standing."

15/
THE ENEMY

The night before my first game, I washed all my pads and doused them in disinfectant. I picked up my jersey, which had been shipped directly to Soup Beans, and ironed out the bandana the Stunts had given me at Draft Night. I practiced tying it around my neck. I dropped off tickets at Klara's and Tory's—we had talked in hushed voices about the game during a discussion on Henry David Thoreau. "You going?" Tory had asked Klara. Her response: "You bet."

In the morning, I took a long shower. I folded at the waist and felt the rush of blood to my head, grabbed on to my ankles to target the tightness in my legs. When I was a competitive swimmer, I used to bend over before races to visualize myself winning. There was something about being upside down. Something about the way I could hear my heart thudding. Now, I bent not to imagine victory, but as a sort of meditation. When I stood back up again, I felt bigger than I had before: a feeling that I associated with power.

I toweled off and got dressed. My teammates had long ago convinced me to do away with underwear—too many unnecessary lines and layers. They also tipped me off to wearing two sports bras to make sure nothing jiggled. I picked a pair of sparkly red shorts from Kelly's dresser. She used to wear them, I remembered, when we were weight-lifting partners in college. Everyone had made fun of her then: for these bizarre weight-room getups, her tendency to jump right into conversations with no introductions or greetings, her plates full of brown and tan foods in the cafeteria smothered in ranch dressing. I loved all of these things about Kelly when I met her: she seemed immune to caring how she was perceived. When Kelly campaigned for swim captain, I was her biggest advocate, systematically convincing all the other lowly freshmen that despite her oddities, Kelly had our best interests at heart. As I pulled the shorts over my freshly shaved legs, I hoped to channel Kelly's courage and determination.

Next, I slathered my lids with sparkles. I lined my eyes with acrylic paint. Black shadow and winged tips. I was going for Amy Winehouse, but I looked more like Cleopatra. When Kelly saw me, her mouth fell open. "Damn," she said, stretching out the word like a piece of gum. "You look intimidating as *fuck*."

"Well, good," I said. "Makes up for the lack of knowledge."

Because all the newbies were assigned to be on bout committee—Taryn's committee—whose responsibility it was to set up and tear down for games, Kelly had arranged to catch a ride with Klara so that I could get to the venue early. Alone in my car, my fear finally caught up to me. It was horribly indiscriminate; I had no concrete worries—nothing that could've been addressed by any practical problem solving—just a shapeshifting mass of nerves festering somewhere between my chest and stomach.

On the seat beside me was a present from Kelly's dad: *The Best of Joan Jett & the Blackhearts.* He said that every roller derby player should blast Joan on the way to their games. He had been greatly enthusiastic when Kelly told him about my new sport—her mother, a little more unsure. I popped the CD in and opened my windows, even though I was on the freeway. I cranked Joan Jett all the way up and let my hair whip around my head. In my derby uniform, sparkly red shorts and aviator sunglasses, I felt like I was meeting this version of myself for the first time.

The rink at Queeny Park in Ballwin where Arch played games was unlike the St. Louis Skatium in every way. It was situated in the middle of a park with dozens of running and biking trails, playgrounds, and small creeks. My first thought, upon seeing it, was that I wished we could practice here all the time, but I knew it wasn't feasible in terms of expense or how far outside the city boundaries it was located. As I drove the winding roads, I encountered more than one person I recognized hammering ROLLER DERBY THIS WAY signs into the cold ground. I followed the arrows back to the entrance.

The inside was even more impressive. It had bleacher seating for eighteen hundred people and additional track-side options. The track was clean. There was a concession stand that sold soft pretzels and hot dogs. No one permanently resided in the locker rooms. When I walked in, the GateKeepers, St. Louis's men's roller derby team, had already begun laying the track and Taryn was standing on a chair hanging a sign that said BATHROOMS DOWNSTAIRS.

"You have orange hair now!" I said. "It looks so pretty!"

She hopped down from her chair and hugged me. "Thanks! I worried it would clash with my red M80 jersey, but I'll be wearing a helmet so who cares?"

Taryn asked to inspect my hand again, which still hadn't completely healed and needed to be bandaged and braced for the game. Then she reached into her purse and pulled out a present for me. There was a card, which she said I could read later, and a homemade three-pocket pouch stuffed with necessities: deodorant, athletic tape, several variations of painkillers. She'd sewn it especially for me and stitched SPARK on the front.

It must have taken so much time for Taryn to sew, not to mention the time and expense of gathering these materials from the store. She had so much to deal with right now—yet she had found time to make this for me. I felt a rush of affection, softness, and vulnerability.

I thanked her tearfully and pulled her in for a hug, trying to convey without words how much this meant to me. No one in my family knew that I was playing in my first game tonight—in fact, I hadn't told them anything about roller derby since asking for the pads before Fresh Meat even started. It wasn't that I was keeping it a secret—there were photos on Facebook from the Halloween scrimmage and from Draft Night—I just wasn't sure how to broach the topic. We didn't speak often, and when we did, it was mostly about things going on in their lives; there didn't seem to be space for me to jump in beyond that. And I wasn't exactly going out of my way to communicate with them more frequently. Our communication usually sent me into a thought spiral that ended in a bulimic episode; only when my stomach was empty would I feel fully in control of myself again.

"What about you?" I asked Taryn. "Are you okay?"

She pulled away and averted her gaze downward. "It's been a hard couple of days," she admitted. "I told the boys that we were moving, and they can't seem to wrap their heads around it. I kicked out Ethan already. Don't know what he's going to do without me to get his fix. Whatever. Not my problem anymore."

"Can I help somehow? Babysit?" I asked.

"Actually, yeah," she said, sounding surprised less at my offer than at the fact that she hadn't automatically declined. "If you could pick Jacob up from school occasionally that would help a lot." She started to elaborate—something about what time his school ended—but one of my teammates skated by us and bumped into me hard.

"Don't fraternize with the enemy," she told me. Taryn laughed, but I wasn't sure that my teammate had been joking.

Taryn and I agreed to coordinate the details later, and I headed to the locker room, where my teammates were in various stages of preparation. Violet sat in a corner listening to music with her eyes closed. Aggie Wartooth was smell-testing her jersey, which she had forgotten to wash after the last game. Cruella and Loki Doki were doing their makeup.

"Mr. McWheely always photographs me making faces like I'm sucking dick," Loki said, staring into her little mirror. "And they always pick those pictures to put on flyers. Hey—did y'all hear we're going to have our own billboard? Should help with attendance this season."

"I didn't hear that!" Cruella replied. "That's amazing. I hope I'm not making a duck face on our billboard. Why is it that in every picture I'm either puckering my lips or it looks like I'm pooping out a jammer?"

Cruella's comment got a few chuckles, but Loki didn't really seem to hear it. "Good news!" she announced to the entire locker room. "I haven't seen my number fourteen all week! Spark, I know you're new, but that means we're going to win. If I see my number outside of derby, it's bad luck!"

I smiled in her direction, not sure what to make of the superstitions, and opened Taryn's card.

Dear Spark,

Let me first say, I am so f'ing proud of you!!! You worked your ass off and have come so far so quickly. Tonight is your first bout—have fun!! It's gonna be scary as shit but whatever happens, just have fun. Laugh, smile, smack the ass of your teammates! I love that our paths crossed and how we are stuck to each other for life!! I cannot wait to sit in the stands one day, watching you annihilate the competition and say, "Yep, that's my derby kid!" Love your face to pieces. I know you'll be awesome tonight.

Always,
Taryn

The card made me want to cry, out of both sentimentality and fear. The line "It's gonna be scary as shit but whatever happens, just have fun" reminded me of what Taryn had told me the previous day: "They're going to go after you. They're going to try to separate you from your team and keep you behind the pack. They always go for the weakest player and try to pick her off first." Was it possible to have fun, I wondered, while being "picked off" by some of the most prestigious roller derby players in the world?

Bricktator led the off-skates warm-up, an activity for which I was wholly unprepared. We had only ever warmed up on skates before practice and scrimmages; I had come to

Queeny Park wearing snow boots. Brick apologized for failing to mention it and suggested I just wear my socks.

WE STARTED WITH lunges on the sidelines. We skipped
for distance, then for height. We threw our arms up and
screamed, bumping into each other until we'd hit everyone
else. Then we did downward dog and some ragdoll swaying
to get loose. Brick told us to touch our toes, then swing our
arms up like we were on a rollercoaster. She wanted us to
yell—to swivel our voices to match our body's movements as
a reminder that roller derby can't be played in silence.

Distracting me all throughout off-skates workout, however, was the fact that the floor at Queeny Park felt different
from the floor at the Skatium. I held out hope that the difference was only perceptible because I was doing my exercises in socks, but when I asked my teammate Nox, she
confirmed my suspicion: the floor at Queeny was a lot stick-
ier. "Now's the time to change into harder wheels if you
have them," she said.

I didn't. I didn't even know what she meant by harder
wheels. The various durometers had been so confusing to
me that Taryn had just given me a full set to replace the
cheap ones that came with my starter skates. We were about
the same weight, which she said was important when deter-
mining the durometer. Her brief lesson on wheels mostly
went over my head, but I had gathered the basics: jammers
generally liked sticky wheels because they made it easier to
grip the floor for fancy footwork and agile movements.
Blockers needed wheels with some slide, so that they could
be pushed by jammers without their skates skidding and re-

sisting, which could lead to broken ankles. I remembered
Taryn saying something about how different floors sometimes required different hardnesses, but other than that, I was
at a loss. And even if I could remember the correct combina-
tions, it wasn't like I had other wheels to change into.

Back in the locker room, we secured our knee pads and
elbow pads. We double-knotted our skates. We put on our
helmets—onto which we had painted stars and stripes like
Evel Knievel's—but let the buckle dangle until it was time to
stand up. Our captain, Aggie Wartooth, passed around permanent markers, and Flux told me to hold still while she
wrote my numbers on my arms.

One of the Stunts coaches, Grave Danger, was very pregnant. "Fuck, does it smell like puke in here?" she asked. To
me, it smelled more like feet and body odor, but everyone
nodded yes anyway. "That's what I thought."

"Yo, Danger," Shear-Ra called from the back of the
locker room. "Did you bring booze for after?"

Danger pulled a big bottle of champagne out of her tote
bag and said, "If y'all don't fucking suck tonight you have
this to look forward to."

Flux, whose hands were busy applying temporary star tattoos to Aggie's cheeks, smiled.

"Can you do me next?" I asked, heart surging, and she
nodded.

As Flux pressed the cold washcloth to my cheekbone,
Danger started her pep talk. "Tonight we're going to smash
those bitches."

Shear-Ra interrupted. "Danger—if we win can we see
your boobs?"

Without missing a beat, Danger said, "If you win, I'll let

you *touch* them." Everyone cheered, including me. It was surreal to be part of such a queer group of people—it made me feel ecstatic, overjoyed.

Not long after we stood up, and filed out onto the edge of the rink, the music started and the lights dimmed. An ex-skater wearing a beaver costume held up one end of a giant paper banner and the M80s coach, Bruno Scars, held up the other end.

"Looks like Tutz's gone even more theatrical, if that's possible," Shear-Ra mumbled.

From our place on the periphery of the track, we watched the M80s crash through the paper banner and circle the track as a team. Dressed in red plaid jerseys and denim shorts, they wielded cardboard axes and saws. Tutz had convinced everyone to change their name to fit the local lumberjack theme. The announcers dramatized each name by pulling out the vowels.

"Here we have number thirteen, Twig E Smaaaalls! And here comes number thirty-two, Snooooooop Dogwood!"

Pine as Buck followed, then Birch Please, then Taryn, who for local season had changed her name to Sequoia De-stroya. She was easy to spot in her green Teenage Mutant Ninja Turtles helmet; she was grinning more broadly than I'd ever seen. When she passed by my team, she gave me two thumbs up.

As the M80s finished their ritual, Stormin' Norma grabbed both of my shoulders. "Your only goal for tonight should be not to fall during intros," she said. "Last season, someone tripped right as the announcers called her name and broke two fingers."

"Cool," I said. "Thanks for that."

"Stop watching those hooligans," Soup Beans instructed,

and we all lined up. She handed us each a toy to throw into the audience—mine was a big rubber ball that lit up when it bounced. Then it became clear that we'd forgotten our strobe light, so Danger waved her hand in front of a flashlight instead.

Stormin' Norma was first on the track as always. The announcers, Muck and Gil, fought to be heard over our theme song, "Danger Zone," and the crowd started chanting something I couldn't quite make out. Nox went next, then Pegasass. In front of me, Cruella Belle-Ville squeezed a stuffed dalmatian puppy. When it was her turn, she puffed out her chest and howled. Once she was sure everyone was watching, she ripped off the dog's head and threw the decapitated body to the sidelines. Stuffing rained onto the track: big clumps of cloud-like innards.

Then, for the first time, I heard "Joan of Spark!" called out over the speakers. I propelled myself forward, suddenly feeling like I was onstage. It was impossible to distinguish individual faces in the crowd; the lights were too bright. I'd felt sports-related adrenaline countless times before, but this was different. In the past, it had manifested itself in my body like the feeling of being chased. It had always felt like fear. But as I rounded the track, waving with both hands, it felt like pure energy. Positivity. Warmth.

There was no national anthem. There was only a one-minute warning issued by the head official. The first pack Grave Danger and Lumber Jerk sent out for us was the power pack: our four best blockers and Bricktator as jammer. Tutz was jamming for the M80s, which surprised me because she didn't usually jam. I sat on the edge of my seat as both sets of blockers set up on the track in a tripod formation. When the five-second warning was called, our blockers slowly started skating backward so their butts were touching the M80s pack. Bricktator crouched low like a predator behind the jammer line—I felt lucky she was on my team.

When the whistle blew, Bricktator juked one direction and then went the other. The M80s pack fell for the trick, and she slipped by easily on the outside line. When she had passed all the opposing skaters, the jam ref threw one arm into the air and used the other one to point to Bricktator, indicating she was the lead jammer.

Five seconds later, Tutz crashed through the Stunts blockers. Unlike Brick's, her style of jamming didn't rely so much on agility as on brute force. She wasn't as quick, but she was strong—she just repeatedly hit people until they were out of her way.

Knowing that she was only a few seconds ahead of Tutz, Brick sped up. Her strategy now was to try to pass as many opposing skaters as possible before Tutz reached the pack and then quickly call off the jam by tapping her hips so that Tutz couldn't score any points.

As she rounded the track, Brick was going so fast she had to lift one foot to stay in bounds. As the M80s blockers prepared to meet the force of Brick's body at the apex, they began screaming. "On the *inside*! I said the *in*!" It looked as though Brick was going to swerve to the outside line, but instead she launched herself into the air. The crowd started cheering while she was still airborne. Then she landed, in bounds and ahead of all four of the M80s blockers, and the fans erupted. She called off the jam before Tutz reached the pack, beaming at us as she tapped her hips.

"That's how we start a *game*!" Danger said, drumming on her pregnant belly and kicking her leg into the air. "Four to zero, baby!"

There were only thirty seconds between jams to send out

a new pack and a new jammer. That was Lumber Jerk's job—he could barely watch the action because he was so focused on quick decision-making. Which blockers could best shut down Ida's agile style of jamming? Which jammer could match Ida's speed? Which blockers would best complement each other, physically and mentally? Sending out Bruise and Nox at the same time would be ill-advised because they were both such small people and could sometimes be overpowered by bigger skaters. Soup Beans, Cruella, and Stormin' Norma were all powerful and aggressive, but speed was their weakness, so they couldn't go out at the same time either. Loki liked to jam when Pegasass was out blocking because her style of jamming fit Peg's offensive strategy. And I needed to be matched with as many veteran skaters as possible.

"Loki, you're jamming," Jerk said. "Next pack: Peg, Cruella, Nox, Shear-Ra."

Ida and Loki lined up behind the jam line, and the packs readied themselves for the five-second warning. Confident in the pack he'd selected, Jerk turned and began scanning the bench to make his next series of calculations.

Another whistle. Another lead jammer status for us, though this one took longer: Loki and Ida were both trapped behind the blockers for at least thirty seconds before Loki found a hole in the wall of bodies and forced herself through. We jumped up in excitement—I was elated as much by the energy of the game as by the realization that I understood most of what was going on—but our cheers turned into groans when we realized Loki had stepped out of bounds and cut the track. She had to serve a thirty-second penalty.

Danger sank to her knees dramatically. Penalties were so common in roller derby that each player was allowed seven before getting kicked out of the game, but it was always worse when it happened to jammers because they were the only players capable of scoring points. With Loki out, Ida became lead jammer, but there was only so much she could do. By the time Loki was released from the penalty box, the M80s had scored nineteen points, and we zero.

"We gotta get our shit together on this next one," Danger grumbled.

Watching the game in the next few jams, I almost forgot I was here to play. As soon as he sent out one pack, Jerk started preparing the next one. Through his thick beard, his little mouth was hanging open slightly. After ten minutes— about eight jams into the game—the Stunts were winning by twelve points, and Jerk locked eyes with me for the first time.

"You ready to go in?" he asked.

The rule for local season was that all players had to compete in at least five jams per game, which usually translated to about five minutes of playtime. In a sixty-minute game, it wasn't much, but I was nervous as hell all the same. Lumber Jerk had told me he'd try to get me in at least seven, but I told him not to worry if that wasn't possible. "I want to do what's best for the team," I said. I wasn't being coy—I honestly wanted to win more than I wanted to play. I was worried that by going in more than the required amount, I might somehow skew the results of the game away from our favor.

Jerk made sure the circumstances were ideal for my first jam. He had me go out with a pack of All Stars blockers. Two of the M80s blockers were in the box for back-block penalties, so we had a two-person advantage.

I skated out onto the track, legs shaking, and heard Kelly and Tory and Klara cheering from the stands. Flux set up on my left. Shear-Ra on my right. CupQuake was the brace.

"Remember what I said?" Shear-Ra asked. "Hips on me. Sit on her. Just *sit* on her."

When I checked behind us to see who was jamming for the M80s, Tutz was dancing around in her taco shorts.

"Fuck," I said.

"Dude," Shear-Ra said. "She hits hard but at least she doesn't usually do crazy footwork or apex jumps. Just hold your ground. Brace for impact."

The five-second warning was given. CupQuake ordered us to roll backward so we were nearly touching the other pack. I realized right before the whistle blew that Taryn was right behind me, blocking for the M80s.

Tutz didn't waste any time. As soon as the jam started, she barreled straight toward me. It was the hardest I'd ever been hit. I immediately fell and curled into a ball like I'd been trained, but I still felt Tutz pushing. Then—a sharp whistle. She was sent to the penalty box for charging.

In the remaining thirty seconds of the jam, I managed to stand back up and skate back to my teammates as Shear-Ra shouted, "On me! On me!" I hadn't done anything to help our jammer, Loki, score the fifteen points she did, but after the jam ended, Lumber Jerk high-fived me. "Great job getting that charging penalty called on Tutz!"

"Yeah!" Shear-Ra said. "It's always great when we can send the other team's jammer to the box!"

Neither of them acknowledged that the only thing I'd done to help draw that penalty was be extremely unstable, and I was grateful for that. And it was true: Tutz *had* decided to keep pushing while I was down, which jammers weren't supposed to do.

I played twice more in the remaining half; both jams were less than a minute long and passed in a flurry of frenzied shouting and body-slamming. While I didn't feel as helpless as I had in the scrimmage scenarios, I was utterly useless. As soon as I realized where I was supposed to be, the action was already over; the jammer had already slipped by, or the pack had rearranged in an entirely new configuration.

As terrifying as it was to be pitted against M80 All Stars, the most frightening moment of the bout didn't happen while I was playing. As I was returning to the bench after a jam, Stormin' Norma went to stand up, but her skates slid out from under her and she hit the ground hard. The medics rushed out. The game was paused. All skaters took a knee.

From my vantage point, it looked like she'd twisted an ankle. She wasn't able to bear any weight, so the medics helped her balance on her other skate and wheeled her off the track. Fans cheered for Norma as she was rolled away; we stood up from our kneeling position only when she was gone.

At halftime a few minutes later, Kelly, Tory, and Klara came down from the stands and Kelly gave me a big hug. "It really freaks me out that you can get injured just literally falling off the bench like that," she said. "Be careful, okay?"

Tory reported that her nephew, who had come to watch the game too, had been inspired by all the tattoos and started doodling on his own body when she wasn't looking.

"Show her," Tory said.

The little boy rolled up his sleeves and showed me the scribbles on his upper arms and shoulders. He looked sheepish but proud of himself, and I thought he had a right to be—the designs were very cute. "That looks great," I told him. "I might have to ask you to do my tattoos for the next game."

During our halftime pep talk, Danger spoke while Lumber Jerk stood beside her, sipping from a Planned Parenthood cup. We were winning, 98 to 65, but the closest anyone came to mentioning the score was when Bricktator said, "We go into this half as though the score is zero-zero, got it? We can't let them rally."

The beginning of the second half very closely resembled that of the first. Jerk sent the power pack out first. Bricktator immediately secured lead jammer status and scored fifteen points in less than a minute. On the second jam, though, Twig E Smalls went up for the M80s and received back-to-back penalties, and Loki was able to make a twenty-point run. Four jams in, our thirty-point lead nearly doubled, and the game was no longer close.

Because we had switched benches with the other team and were now closer to the track, I could hear more of what was being said during gameplay. It sounded like Shear-Ra and Flux were actually *encouraging* the opposing jammer while she struggled behind them. "Only a few seconds left," Shear-Ra said. "Keep pushing. Keep pushing."

It blew my mind. When I was growing up, cheering for the competition was unthinkable, especially mid-race. I had no empathy for anyone I raced against; I saw them as the enemy.

Maybe the interactions I witnessed from the bench were a testament to how secure these players were in themselves—not relying on comparison for their sense of self-worth. Or maybe it had to do with the fact that most players didn't care who won during local season. It shocked me, in a way. It made me realize that I'd entered a completely new paradigm where there was more to playing than just winning—and though this clashed with everything I knew, and I knew I had a long way to go, it felt attractive to me. I wanted to be that kind of player, too.

Lumber Jerk kept his promise to let me play more than the required minimum, especially once it was fairly certain we would win. Kelly told me later that she thought I improved each time I went out, but I knew that couldn't be entirely true because on my sixth jam, I got a penalty for clotheslining the jammer. I knew as soon as I did it that I was going to be sent to the box. I might have known even before my arm flung out and caught her in the face. Several refs were staring right at me. In the seconds after it happened, their whistles sounded like a series of angry birdcalls. The move had been reflexive, like the way I always swung my arm out if I was making an abrupt stop while driving. My sister called it her "second seat belt," and even though I tried to break the habit, I never could.

Because I didn't leave the track immediately after my penalty was called (standing, instead, in a dazed stupor) the refs gave me a second penalty for insubordination. The jam ended as soon as I sat down, and I felt my face reddening in embarrassment. A timeout was called. During the break, PhDiva, the head referee, skated over to ask if I understood both the calls and to make sure I knew how to enter the track legally.

"I know it's your first game," she said. "And I know it's hard. Just make sure you enter behind both packs and don't touch the jammers outside of the engagement zone."

The one minute I spent in the penalty box felt like eons. I tried not to make eye contact with Danger or Jerk, worried they were mad at me for my extra-long sentence, and instead focus on the rules of reentry. About thirty seconds through,

Ida, the jammer for the M80s, got a track cut penalty and had to sit down next to me. "Are you having fun?" she asked.

It hadn't occurred to me to wonder if I was—Taryn's letter had gone completely out of my head. I told her yes before I even had a chance to think about it, but then I realized it was true: my first roller derby bout was fun like handheld firecrackers are fun. Fun like jumping off a swing when it's at the highest point is fun: a heady mix of adrenaline, exhilaration, and potential danger.

We won the game handily. I'd known going in that the Stunts were a stronger team than the M80s, but I finally found out what that really looked like: we had a higher number of skilled players, stronger braced walls, faster jammers, and we played better as a team. As was tradition, the winning team took the first pass around the track once the final score began flashing. Fans flooded down from the stands to high-five us; I made sure to crouch low to reach the children. When it was the M80s' turn, we made a tunnel with our arms for them to pass under. I slapped Taryn's ass as she went by and she immediately stopped rolling to hug me. Her teammates piled up behind her in the tunnel of arms, and still, she took her time.

"I am so, so proud of you," she whispered.

The best part of the evening was signing autographs for the kids in the crowd. I wasn't sure what the audience demographic would look like; I was surprised how many families with young children were in attendance. My parents certainly wouldn't have let me watch something so queer and violent, but these children seemed to regard us as superheroes. The merch table sold autograph books: small stapled pamphlets with all of our photographs and derby names. Almost every kid had one—they ran up to us excitedly and held out their books, asking us to flip to the page with our picture and sign the bottom. It took a few signature attempts for me to figure out how I wanted to sign as Joan of Spark, the J and S in a fancy cursive script that interlocked slightly. It had taken me years to figure out how to sign my given name, so I was surprised how natural it was to embody Joan of Spark. I didn't feel like I was pretending or even acting out a persona: I truly felt like the name, the identity, belonged to me.

After signing autographs and socializing with the crowd, we reconvened in the locker room. Danger pulled the bottle of champagne out of her tote bag as we stripped off our wet jerseys. "You guys stink so bad I don't even smell the puke anymore," she said. "But here—you deserve this."

After uncorking the bottle, Flux raised it up. "To victory!" she said. "And to Spark, who made it through her first Arch Rival roller derby game!"

Everyone began cheering. I couldn't stop smiling. Cruella clapped me on the back. Over the ruckus, Loki shouted, "Spark! I told you! No fourteen all week!"

When I tried to pass the bottle to Violet, who was sitting beside me, she insisted I take another swig.

"Remember that time you asked me to teach you how to stop?" she asked. "It was the first time we met. You couldn't stop to save your life."

I felt my face reddening. "Yeah," I said. "Did you see me out there? I still can't stop to save my life."

"Dude," she said. "It's like a metaphor for derby. You can't stop *playing*. You're not a stopper. You don't stop. Even when you break your hand. You know what you are? You're a go-er." I looked down, pleased but embarrassed, and put up my hand for her to stop, but she kept going. "You go to the most practices out of anybody. You go to all the cross-training. You just don't stop, don't stop, don't stop."

When I looked up again, everyone could see I was beaming. I couldn't help it. I felt so valued, so loved, so seen.

16/
BREAK

The Stunts didn't have any games scheduled in March, but we did have to bear witness to the Smashinistas absolutely destroying the M80s. On the sidelines, we cheered for the M80s, both because they were down and because nobody on our team liked the way the Smashies played. When it was our time to play the Smashies the first week in April, Lumber Jerk and Grave Danger warned us that there would be a lot of "funny business" going on: big, unnecessary hits, fake wipeouts, ploys to make it look like we should be penalized. They were right. Playing the Smashinistas was incredibly frustrating; I was so grateful my first game had been against the relatively friendly M80s instead.

We lost the game, but not as badly as the M80s had, which meant that it would be the Stunts versus the Smashinistas in the championship at the end of April. The closer it got, the more I ramped up my training schedule. I was still skating three to four times per week, plus two days of off-skates training. Taryn regularly reminded me that I only needed to log five practices a month, but I always responded with "I won't get better with only five practices a month."

Most nights when I returned home from the Skatium, I still had several hours of work to get done. In addition to my writing workshop, which involved reading about a dozen full-length books and critiquing my peers' work, I was also taking a class about place and a class called Flash Fiction. Most of the time, I struggled to stay awake in class. When our discussions failed to hold my attention, I kept my eyes open by tracing the path of individual raindrops down the long windows.

A few times during Flash Fiction, I slipped into a quick slumber. My chin hit my chest and I awoke with a start, embarrassed, but convinced no one had noticed—until my professor asked for a word after class one day. The walk from the classroom to his office was brief, but I spent it preparing my apology.

He closed the door but didn't sit down.

"This is a small program," he started. "And I've heard— I mean, I was just wondering—" Each word seemed to require an immense amount of effort on his part; my professor was like the boy who had asked me to the senior prom.

Finally I couldn't take it anymore and blurted out, "I'm sorry I fell asleep." He seemed taken aback, and I felt heat rising to my face.

"Wait," he said. "What? I just—I hear you play roller derby. And I was wondering—I mean—do people, like, come to watch? I have a kid. I mean, I have a little girl. Esmé. She's nine. Would it be appropriate? For a nine-year-old?"

I laughed in relief, and he cracked a crooked smile. That evening, I sent him the link to purchase tickets for our local championship. *We'll be in the front row,* he wrote back. And he was, with his daughter, who was wearing a button-down shirt and a tie.

During warm-up, Nox asked me who I was waving to. "I didn't think you had family here," she said.

When I told her the man was my professor and that he had brought his daughter, she held her chest and said, "That is the cutest thing I've ever seen!"

Unfortunately, my professor and his daughter didn't see me at my best. In fact, of the three games I had played up to that point, the championship game was the worst. Not only did we lose badly to the Smashinistas, I also got four penalties and spent more time in the penalty box than I did skating. No one seemed pleased by their individual performance except Bricktator, who single-handedly scored almost two thirds of our points. Even she, though, wasn't immune to the frustration associated with playing the Smashies.

"They *really* piss me off," she said at halftime. "Which is good for us, because I play better when I'm enraged."

I'm not sure an audience member would have picked up on the ways the Smashinistas were getting under our skin. None of their tactics were new; they weren't even unexpected. In the locker room before the game, Danger had reminded us that we would probably encounter packs composed entirely of All Stars and rarely C-level skaters. Draggie—their star blocker—would be on the track almost nonstop. But even though we'd been warned, our response to the Smashies' shady techniques was sloppy. We ended up losing by fifty points.

Afterward, I skated up to my professor and Esmé, trying to hide my disappointment.

"You just did more athletics in an hour than I've done in my entire life," he said.

Esmé handed me a drawing she had made during the

game. It was a cartoon of a team of women holding out their fists.

"That's you," she said. "The one with the crazy hair."

I beamed. Esmé, whose tie had gone slightly askew after the excitement of the game, looked up at me with a nervousness she was trying to hide. *I see you,* she seemed to say as she held up the picture. *Do you see me?* "I can't tell what I like better," I said. "Your drawing or your tie. Both are awesome. And I guess I do have pretty crazy hair right now, don't I?" Before the game, I had clipped in purple extensions, and the work I had done to de-frizz it with a flat iron had been completely undone by my sweating. Esme grinned up at me.

"Speaking of hair," my professor said. "Do you know anything about dyeing it? Esmé has been begging me for hot-pink hair. You just seem like someone who would know."

"I do!" I exclaimed, feeling a surge of pride. Most of my friends on the team dyed their hair wild colors and I knew exactly how to do it. In that moment, there was no award or recognition on the planet that could have made me feel more respected and valued than being asked this question, by my professor, about his beautiful child—and I was thrilled that I was able to say yes. "Hot pink is an excellent choice," I said to Esme. "You are going to look amazing."

THE MONTH OF the local championship game wasn't difficult only for me. At the beginning of April, Taryn texted me that she'd decided to take a leave of absence from roller derby to "get her life together." "Everything feels like it's falling apart," she wrote. "I'm not sure what to do." I wasn't sure how to respond except by reiterating that I was here for her in any capacity she needed. "Let's get ice cream, my treat," I suggested. Or—"Can I shop for you? Give me a list and I'll get everything you need."

What Taryn needed, it turned out, was time alone—time to soul-search, time to pick up the pieces of the life she'd created with Jacob's dad that were smashed when they broke up. I noticed on social media that she was already seeing someone new: a small man with gray hair who was in a cover band. She posted selfies while she waited for him at band practice, and mid-kiss shots, and pictures of his pre-rock-concert ensemble. She didn't talk to me about him, though, and, following her lead, I didn't ask. I babysat for her whenever I could.

By the end of April, a week after the local championship, Taryn was lamenting how much she missed derby. Officially she wasn't scheduled to come back until May, but I persuaded her to come back one day early. I missed partnering with her for drills. I missed the way she stuck her tongue out at me from across the track, the way she rolled her eyes and pretended to gag when somebody said, "Let's do some endurance!" It seemed like the best thing for both of us.

The last day of April provided a brief reprieve from torrential rainfall. According to the local news, the flooding was historic. Roads, bridges, and buildings were destroyed, several highways shut down. Our neighborhood bore visible signs of the storm when I woke up for Sunday practice. Trash cans had been carried down the street and deposited at the end of the block. Branches littered the sidewalk. Our neighbor stood with both hands on his head, surveying the damage in his yard.

Before I left for practice, I received a text from Taryn: "So, how flooded do you think the Skatium is going to be today?" I immediately understood the subtext of her message; she was suggesting we skip. It would be so simple. There would be no excessive sweating, no sore bellies or burning thighs. If we ditched practice, we could go to Stacked and split a goat-cheese burger and a basket of sweet potato fries. It was a tempting proposition, but I was itching to skate. Now that local season was over, travel season would be starting in mid-May, and because I had already passed mins, I was automatically on the C team. I was ecstatic about the prospect of journeying all over the Midwest with the C team: Taryn and Snotface and Nanny—who, since she had passed mins but skipped the draft, would be playing her first game against a neighboring city.

"Hopefully it won't be too bad," I texted back.

I imagined Taryn letting out an exasperated sigh before sending her response. "Fine," she wrote. "But I'm gonna be a little late."

Rummaging in my dresser, I found one of my last clean shirts: a tight purple tank with an image of two ferocious women and the phrase DERBY OR DIE printed on the front. I'd gotten it from the clothing exchange we'd had back in November; almost everything I wore, or enjoyed wearing, was from that exchange.

Right as I was leaving, Kelly decided to come with me. It was a happy surprise; now that she was employed, she had less time to accompany me to practices just to watch from the sidelines. She explained she didn't feel much like rock climbing today and would rather have a casual Sunday morning. "Plus I'll get to say hi to Taryn," she said.

We drove the familiar, winding route along River des

Peres; never had the drainage channel more lived up to its name. The flooding had caused the channel, which was usually slow and meandering, to swell and pulse with rushing water.

When we arrived at the Skatium, Kelly sat in her usual spot on the sidelines. I was the first on the track. Other skaters arrived and sleepily plopped down on the cement lining the rink to gear up. Flux skated over to the DJ booth, where cords of varying degrees of thickness were dangling out of the open window. She plugged her phone into one of them and started a fast song I didn't recognize.

"We're warming up now!" she yelled. "Get your gear on and let's go!"

My pace quickened to the beat of the song. I skated on one foot for a lap, then alternated feet. I could feel Kelly watching me, a stack of crossword puzzles resting untouched in her lap. As I continued warming up, I was vaguely aware of Nanny, Slob, and several others filing onto the track. They set their water bottles down, adjusted their mouth guards, and joined me. Taryn was still absent. Every time I heard the heavy Skatium door slam shut, I checked to see if it was her. How late was late? I wondered. Would she miss all of warm-up? The first water break? The first set of footwork drills?

I tried to distract myself from thoughts about Taryn by watching some of the new players. Since my Fresh Meat class had run its twelve-week course, another class had started back up again. There was something about no longer being the newest, greenest skater that gave me an added sense of belonging that I hadn't expected. I watched them try to alternate between forward and backward skating and was reminded of how difficult the motion had been for me to master. I had been terrified to shift my weight from one leg to the other—terrified of turning around and my feet not following. It was very satisfying to be able to look back and realize all that was over. Now, I could transition in *three* different ways. I favored the transitions where I picked up my back wheels and pivoted onto my front; the move impressed the rookies, and a few had even asked me to teach them. Nothing made me feel more like I belonged than being asked to help—and being capable of helping—train some of our new skaters.

Because so many skaters were still stretching on the sidelines, I had room to skate faster than I usually did—a rare opportunity that I loved to take advantage of, and part of the reason I'd made sure to come early. I enjoyed the sense of freedom and exhilaration that came with skating at speed— and once everyone was on the track, especially with the Fresh Meat skaters, things were a little tight. I spun from front to back without even needing to check over my shoulder to make sure my path was clear. I was spinning but moving forward, bounding from the inside of the track to the outside. My transitions were so quick there wasn't even time to take a stride or a breath. My motions felt fluid, natural. It was second nature. I thrilled at how far I'd come in such a short time.

And then it happened. Mid-twist, the wheels on my left skate locked with the wheels on my right, and there was nothing I could do to catch myself. Back in Fresh Meat training, we had been taught falling strategies. "This will happen a lot," Flux had told us. "Fall forward. The pads will be there to protect you." But there was no way to fall forward while spinning: there was just gravity. There was my own weight, every pound, stacked on top of my left leg, forcing it to fold.

I know that the music blaring from the DJ booth did not go mute the second I began to fall—but in my memory everything is dead silent. It is also impossible that the crunch of my bones splintering under the weight of my body repeated, like an echo, for several minutes after I hit the ground, but that's how I experienced it. Nanny, Slob, and Flux all skated by me. Nanny later told me she expected me to be back up on my feet by her next pass around. I'd always gotten up fast, she said; I usually snapped back quickly, like a rubber band. She knew something was wrong when I didn't move. So did Kelly, who leapt over the Skatium rails and landed squarely on the track.

The next thing I knew, Nanny, Slob, and Flux were standing in front of me, Kelly crouched down at my eye level. "My leg is broken," I said. The sureness of my tone took me by surprise. It was unusual for me to speak with such certainty, particularly in matters of my body. I didn't feel anything yet—but I knew that was temporary. If anything, what I felt was the inevitability of pain that would arrive any minute.

"Should I call an ambulance?" Flux asked. She seemed even taller from my vantage point on the ground.

"No," I said. "Too expensive." Even with health insurance, my mother always told me ambulances cost hundreds of dollars and should be avoided at all costs.

Slob crouched down beside me, blue hair brushing my shoulder. Her face was tight with concern, which surprised me. We had never been so close before in a non-skating context; I only really knew her through occasional pairing up at practice and high fives after games.

"Should we try to take your skate off?" she asked. When I didn't answer, she addressed the group. "Should we take her skate off?"

Someone standing behind me responded with a firm no. Then, softer, "Last time we did that we found out that it'd been the only thing holding their leg together."

The pain still felt eerily distant, like the first time I pressed my ear to the railroad tracks and heard the low rumble of a train too far off to see. My mother always had me listen for trains before we walked on the tracks, and for months we never encountered one. But one day I knelt, pressing my head to the cold metal, and felt a ringing in my temple. It wasn't a sound so much as a sensation: a low rattling, a deep humming that spread all the way to my fingertips.

Like that train, I could feel the pain barreling closer, gaining speed. I held it in my throat like the crickets I'd once consumed on a dare, felt it festering in my abdomen and running down my inner thighs like piss. When it arrived, the pain sounded nothing like the hollow ringing of that train, though. It had its own soundtrack: first, a series of snapping pencils. Then, something bigger, like trees.

As if I'd summoned her by sheer will, I suddenly saw Taryn hurrying toward me from across the track, her sneakers still on. She must have just arrived. I searched her expression for a hint about how to feel. It didn't occur to me until much later how emblematic this was of my conditioning: how dependent I'd become on my mother to tell me how exactly I should feel, physically and emotionally. How, even in her absence, I could only understand my own experiences through another's eyes. I fundamentally did not trust my own sensations or emotions.

Taryn looked stricken. A flash of unbearable fear and pain surged through my body as I looked at her face, eliminating any lingering sense of calm brought on by the adrenaline. I felt a tightness building in my chest and wished everyone else would disappear so that I could howl like the children I sometimes heard on my runs through the park. One misstep—falling sideways off the swings or tripping over their own feet—and they would wail for their moms. That was what I wanted. Not just the freedom to give in to this primal need to yell. I wanted a mom to yell to.

Kelly seemed to read a shift in my facial expression, and she turned to the group. "She needs help." This seemed to spur the group into action.

"I'm calling Manny," Flux said. There was a murmur of consent among the group. Though I had only briefly interacted with him, I was vaguely aware that Manny Pedi played on the men's team and was EMT-certified. He would know what to do. She pulled out her phone and stepped away.

I could feel everyone watching me for indications of pain, but it seemed important that I keep my eyes empty and unfocused. No one needed to know the reality of what I was experiencing, which was that it felt like the bones in my leg had been filled with ice. With each passing minute, the ice seemed to expand, threatening to explode the shell that contained it. Even if I'd been willing to articulate this, I knew I wouldn't be able to speak without throwing up. It was easier to focus on being still. Besides, giving in to hysterics or panic would only add to my humiliation. Shame churned in my stomach, bubbled in my limbs, rivaling the pain in my leg. Even though I knew that breaking bones in derby was common—expected, even—this wasn't right. It shouldn't have happened this way, during warm-up. It was supposed to happen during a bout. A contact drill with another skater. A scrimmage. Not this way—doing a variation of a skill we had been taught on our second day of practice.

"Manny is coming," Flux said, coming back into view. She paused, searching my face. Then, in a softer voice: "Do you want us to pretend you're not here until he arrives? I mean, should I just keep going with practice on the other side of the track?"

Gratefully, I nodded.

IT TOOK ABOUT twenty-five minutes for Manny to arrive. Twenty-five minutes that I spent sitting on the floor of the Skatium, my teammates giving me a wide berth while they practiced around me, Taryn and Kelly sitting quietly by my side, while I fervently wished that I were wearing goggles. When Cam was in her freshman year of high school, she admitted that she sometimes cried while she was swimming. It had been years since I'd seen her cry. But she said it matter-of-factly, as though she were commenting on the weather. When her goggles filled up, she told me, she simply dumped her tears in the gutter and kept going. I didn't tell her that I used to do the same thing. Maybe with my eyes covered, I thought, I could have asked for an ambulance. Maybe that small bit of privacy would've given me the courage to say what I couldn't admit to Flux: *Please don't just keep skating while I look on from the ground. Please don't ignore me—not now.* Maybe goggles would have meant I wouldn't have had to work so hard to remain stone-faced while I was cracking on the inside.

When Manny finally entered the building, his husband, Marco Rollo, was trailing behind. Taryn thanked Manny for coming and he replied, "We were already in the car, headed to IKEA. It was no problem at all."

Marco's expression, however, suggested the opposite. "I broke *both* the bones in my leg last season. I've seen legs dangling at a right angle. Hers seems like it could just be a sprain."

I lifted my gaze to stare at him, hoping to communicate my loathing for him through my narrowed eyes. For the first time, I realized there was one significant disadvantage of my tendency to downplay my pain: rather than coming across as tough, I could still be perceived as weak. So why was I working so hard to bottle it all up if the result would be the same?

Manny told his husband to go find some cardboard, and as we waited for Marco to return, he carefully unfastened my knee pad. When he asked me to show him where it hurt, I pointed vaguely up and down my shin. When he lifted my leg to take my skate off, I yelped in agony.

"It's okay. It's okay. It's okay," Manny soothed. "I've done this so many times. Here we go. It's off now. It's off."

Manny let me rest and gently patted my other foot as Marco returned with a flattened pizza box. He then extended two fingers and ran them along my injured leg. "Can you feel me touching you?"

Though I saw the pads of his fingers brushing my skin, I felt nothing.

"Press harder," I forced out. My voice sounded gravelly, panicked. He did not press harder. Or if he did, I didn't feel it. Manny exchanged a look with Marco that scared me more than the lack of sensation; then he started to move more quickly. He took the pizza box from Marco and folded it in half lengthwise, then slid it under my leg.

"Moving you is going to be the worst part of your day," he said. When I didn't respond, he gently shook my shoulders. "Are you okay? I need a verbal confirmation." I tried moving my lips but they felt like they were frozen shut. Manny watched me struggle and then turned to Kelly and Taryn.

"She's starting to go into shock. Go get something to cover her up. Tell Slob to get Spark's car and crank the heat."

Magilla Guerilla, who had been the announcer for local championships the week before, rolled a rickety office chair onto the track.

Manny pointed to each skater in turn. "I need you to help lift her up into the chair. And I need you to hold her leg upright." He turned to me, still running a hand up and down my numb leg. "You're going to have to push with your good leg, okay?"

Magilla's arms brushed my torso, and I felt pressure under my armpits. "Ready when you are," he said.

The trip from the rink into the back seat of my car was not an out-of-body experience in the way I've heard it described, but while I remember the excruciating journey as if it were a silent film, Kelly later described the sounds I made as barbaric and rabid. She said she had to fight not to cover her ears.

Once Magilla had hauled me into the back seat, Slob slid into the driver's seat. Through the window, I saw Manny motion for Kelly. They turned their backs to me as Manny whispered something. As soon as Kelly got into the passenger seat, Slob shifted into drive. I heard Taryn's car start; she was going to follow us to the hospital.

Turning out of the Skatium, Slob asked Kelly, "What did Manny tell you?"

"He said to request morphine before they try to move her again."

Less than a minute in, I could tell that this ride was going to be excruciating. Kelly unbuckled her seat belt and turned around so that she could cradle my leg. Every few seconds, the seat belt alarm sounded and Slob would alternate between yelling, "This isn't a time for seat belts!" and "Shut the fuck up, car!" The sunlight on her hair made it impossible to discern whether it was blue or purple, and the alarm became the surreal soundtrack to which we drove to the hospital.

I could tell that it was hot in the car, but I still shivered under the layers of coats and sweaters Magilla had piled on me. Over the years, I'd suffered my share of pain and injuries, but none that had sent my body into shock. In this state, my thoughts crumbled from solid entities into thousands of tiny pebbles: sediment that slipped through my fingers before I could fully grab hold.

"Heat," I said, forgetting the end of the sentence as soon as I spoke the first word.

"She wants the heat higher," Kelly said to Slob.

But I shook my head.

"Lower?"

I felt momentarily confused, unsure what I had been asking for.

Finally, another word came to me. "Off," I said.

My voice sounded distant; it didn't seem like it originated in my body. Or, my body was several bodies, each with a voice fighting for a position on center stage.

I couldn't figure out why one of my voices wanted Slob to turn the heat down. I needed the heat, needed it to be even hotter. The heat was what was keeping me conscious. Maybe even in this dire situation, a part of me wanted everybody else in the car to know that I was strong.

Slob turned down the heat, but she wouldn't turn it off. We were on the freeway now. When she hit a pothole, it felt like the bones in my leg were splitting farther apart. Then, on the exit ramp, she stalled the car. It jerked, shuddered, and came to a complete halt. "I'm sorry. I'm so sorry," Slob said, turning around as if expecting to see my leg dangling from my torso. Once she was able to restart the car, she started relaying how many minutes were left on the GPS until we'd arrive at the hospital. "Thirteen left. You're doing so good, Spark." And then, "Only twelve. You got this." She encouraged me as if I were skating, cheered for me as though I had knocked a jammer out of bounds instead of simply making it through another minute.

By the time we pulled into the hospital parking lot, Slob had given up any pretense of obeying the traffic signs. Someone whaled on their horn as she blew through a stop sign, flashers on, and she gestured wildly to me in the back seat. She brought us to a stop under the giant ST. ANTHONY'S EMERGENCY sign and jogged through the sliding doors, reemerging moments later with a small man in scrubs who was pushing an empty wheelchair. Kelly got out and opened my door as he approached.

"Do you have any morphine?" she asked. "One of our teammates is an EMT and he told us not to move her again without it."

He shook his head, saying that I would need to wait to be assessed. I pushed away the unpleasant thought that this wouldn't be the case if I'd just asked for an ambulance.

Even as I pointed to my poorly splinted leg, the mound

of flesh covering the protruding bone, I knew it was futile. "Sorry ma'am," he said as all three of them awkwardly maneuvered me into the wheelchair. "We can't be playing around with opioids until we get a chance to examine you." Then, sharper, as Kelly and Slob tried to protest: "Ma'am, we can't just hand out narcotics to people off the street." I realized I wanted the narcotics less for the pain and more for the validation of my injury. *But Manny knew I needed them,* I reminded myself. *This isn't psychosomatic. I'm not overreacting. I am really hurt.* Wasn't I?

The wheelchair didn't have a footrest, and the nurse didn't wait for someone to hold my leg up before he started rolling me into the hospital. I was forced to hold it myself, squeezing my eyes shut against the pain. *I am really hurt,* I repeated in my head. *This pain is real.*

The transfer from the wheelchair to the gurney was excruciating. The man supported my back and Kelly held my hand as I tried to gently raise myself onto the bed. A few moments later, Taryn found me in the examination room where I was waiting to be seen; Slob had gone back to the Skatium to let everyone know I'd made it safely to the ER. Kelly stroked my hair. I felt as grateful for her steadying presence as I did for her quiet manner. Thank God she had just happened to come to practice today. And thank God she wasn't the kind of person to fall into hysterics. Her strokes were slow and soft on my head, and as the pain continued to crescendo, I tried to focus on matching my breathing with her hand.

Fifteen minutes passed. None of us spoke. Desperate for something to distract me from my leg, I reached toward Taryn's wrist. I could see the little tattoo of a pancake being flipped on it, and I wanted her to tell me the story again:

how the tattoo reminded her of her parents and their restaurant. I wanted her to tell me how she and her brother used to sneak tubes of chocolate sauce into the restaurant storage rooms and squeeze the contents into their open mouths. Taryn, however, thought I was grabbing for her hand, so she took mine and held it tight.

By the time a nurse entered my room to do my intake, it had been over an hour since my accident, and the pain was no longer separate from me. It felt as integral to my body as my heart: a series of fiery currents being pumped through my bloodstream. I was freezing cold, gritting my teeth to keep them from chattering. Who had my mouth guard? Why didn't I remember taking it out? It seemed like such an important question, but when I turned my head to ask Kelly, I couldn't unclench my jaw.

The nurse began to ask questions—my date of birth, allergies, family history—but they hung in the air, unanswered. Talking required more effort than I had. It felt like I was collapsing into myself—distant from the hospital bed, from my outstretched leg that was stuffed into its cardboard bun like some kind of oversized hot dog. Kelly stepped in and gave the answers she knew, but when the nurse asked about the nature of my injury, Kelly didn't respond.

"Roller derby," Taryn jumped in. "We play roller derby."

At this, the nurse cheered up noticeably. "No way!" she said. "I played in St. Charles for a little while. Couldn't even make it through Fresh Meat, though. It was a lot harder than I was expecting. And dangerous too!" Her smile looked like it belonged to a different planet than the one I was on. "And how would you rate your pain right now, on a scale from one to ten?"

After a long pause, in which I hoped in vain that someone would answer for me, I forced myself to speak. "I've never been able to answer that," I said honestly. "Isn't ten basically burning alive? How am I supposed to know what that feels like?"

The nurse nodded. "We don't have too many burn patients come in here, but I've had my fair share of patients with minor sprains and cuts who rate their pain at eleven. Then I say to them, 'What if I kicked it?'" No one laughed. Finally, she said, "I'm going to put down an eight."

THE DOCTOR CAME in shortly afterward, ordering painkillers and sending me for scans. The morphine acted quickly; I could almost trace its path through my veins. I felt my body relaxing, my heart slow. It even felt almost bearable to be wheeled down on a gurney to radiology. When I got back to the exam room, my pain felt present, yet distant, and all I wanted was to stay still, like this, forever. Not long after, though, the doctor returned with my X-rays. Kelly and Taryn saw them before I did, the display screen casting a refrigerator-like glow on their faces.

"Well, fuck," was all Taryn said.

The X-rays revealed a long, winding spiral fracture on my tibia near the ankle, the doctor said—noting that it was the longest spiral break he had ever seen—and a complete displacement of my fibula near the knee. The doctor pointed to the center of the white bone, where a long horizontal column of murky blackness indicated where my tibia had split open. Several hairline fractures extended along the top and bottom of the main break like tributaries.

The fibula break was worse. The translucent ends of the bone were separated by a darkness that looked insurmountable. How would the two ends of that bone ever drift close enough to fuse back together? The doctor explained that the break was close to the peroneal nerve bundle near the back of my knee, which was possibly why my entire leg was numb.

"She'll need to see a neurologist," the doctor said to Kelly. "And she definitely needs surgery, probably early tomorrow morning when our head surgeon arrives. It won't be clear whether she's sliced through the nerves until she's on the operating table. Picture a bag of sand. Once the nerves spill out, there's almost no way we'll be able to put them all back in the bag again." He said it was too soon to tell whether I would ever regain feeling in my leg. Whether I would be able to walk or run normally. It was impossible not to groggily run through what was at stake: no derby meant no structure, no exercise routine, no chosen family. If I couldn't play, where did that leave me? Now that I knew what it felt like to belong, could I bear to be without it? My pre-derby days had been so sad and lonely. No amount of exercise, distraction, or love from Kelly could fix the loneliness that had plagued me for as long as I could remember. No strategy to find community had worked as well as joining the roller derby team. There was nowhere in the world I fit in this well, no people who better understood me. Did one wrong move, one split-second fall, mean I was on my own again?

Yet there was a completely separate train of thought running through my head as I panicked over the potential loss of derby: I couldn't stop thinking about what the doctor had said about my break being the longest he'd ever seen. As he talked on, going over Kelly's questions about recovery, I stared at the X-rays, tracing the fractures, admiring the breaks. I remembered my mother, standing at the end of Cam's hospital bed, holding the hat. I could picture exactly how her face looked when they confirmed that it was the weirdest injury they'd ever seen—the little smile, the smugness, the pride. Pride. Even in my dazed state, I realized *that* was what I felt. My mouth was even turned upward in the same small, satisfied smile.

But it wasn't just pride I felt. It was the sweet, specific relief that comes from getting validation of an experience you doubt, validation you fear may not come. These X-rays gave me a credible reason for being in pain. Unlike when my childhood doctors had suggested my foot pain was psychosomatic, I had concrete evidence this time. *Anyone* would be in pain with this kind of break. *The longest break I've ever seen*—the doctor's voice played on a loop in my head. It was what I'd always craved: a simple, undeniable proof of pain. No degree of emotional turmoil had ever provided that clarity.

But at what price? It was in this bittersweet, confusing collision of emotions—my desperation at the thought of losing derby and the simultaneous solace I found in the visual confirmation of my injury—that I finally gave in to tears.

We were brought up to a private room; I'd need to stay overnight and await the surgeon's arrival the next day. Once I was settled in, Taryn stepped out into the hall to respond to our teammates' inquiries and to give Kelly and me some privacy.

Kelly and I sat in silence to begin with. It was the first time we'd been alone since we had driven to the Skatium earlier that morning. She rubbed my arm while I cried silently.

"Does it still hurt?" she asked.

I shook my head.

"I think—" Kelly stopped, cleared her throat, then started

again. "I think we should let your family know you'll be going in for surgery tomorrow. Just—out of courtesy."

I realized three things in that moment: that I'd been avoiding the idea of calling my family and Kelly was right to suggest it, that this surgery was truly serious, and that Kelly was scared. She had never called either of my parents before. I thought briefly that I perhaps should be the one to call, but the medicine was making me feel disoriented and exhausted. I wasn't sure I could sustain a phone conversation, especially with my mother. But now that Kelly had brought it up, I felt the old, familiar mixture of apprehension and hope. Would my mother be worried? I thought wildly of the lists I used to make of things that proved she loved me. *She was inconsolable when she found out I was going in for emergency surgery,* I imagined adding.

"Put her on speaker," I said.

"I don't think that's a good idea," Kelly said, sounding strained. She squeezed my hand and stood up. "I'm going to go down to the cafeteria. Somewhere I'll be out of the way."

As she left, Taryn came back in and started showing me all the messages she had gotten from our teammates: fifty skaters who were blowing up Taryn's phone asking about me. It was the kind of support I'd dreamed of as a child, and that I'd hardly been able to imagine when I first moved in with Kelly in Ohio, when I showed up at the Skatium the first time, even when I was drafted to the Stunts. I wanted so badly to bask in the outpouring of care from this beautiful, messy community that had become so important to me. This community that had seen me go from old college sweatshirts to a wardrobe of beloved derby hand-me-downs; from awkward, shy nobody to a trusted friend and even, to the newbies, a mentor; from a clumsy skater who didn't know the

rules to a valued team member. From Gabe to Joan of Spark.
But instead, as Taryn chattered on about what my teammates
had said, all I could think about was the phone call happening somewhere in the cafeteria. Nothing had changed, I
thought with a pang of despair. Even now, when I finally had
the loving support I'd always wanted, I was still the same
little girl sitting stiffly in a red wagon, gazing ahead at my
mother's back as if she were my Holy Grail.

After a few minutes, a couple of nurses came in to assess
my pain level and make sure I was comfortable in the bed
they'd set up for me. Shortly after they left, Kelly returned.

"That did not go particularly well," she said, speaking
slowly, as if she were choosing her words carefully.

"Who did you talk to?" I asked. Kelly's eyes met mine for
a moment, then dropped to the floor. She knew what I was
really asking.

"Your mom is—disappointed," she said. I heard a sharp
intake of breath from Taryn's direction. "She said—" Kelly
glanced at me again. I held her gaze, willing her to go on.
"She said she knew something like this would happen if you
joined the roller derby team."

My heart sank and my eyes filled with tears of anger.
Why did I still feel surprised? In the pause that followed, an
alternative script played in the back of my head: what I
wished my mom had said. *Oh my god, is she all right? What can
I do? I'll do anything.*

Kelly hurried to fill the silence. "I don't think she realizes
how bad it is. But she said you're tough and she knows you'll
be fine."

I didn't respond. I wanted to tell Kelly how grateful I was
that she'd had the courage to make such an uncomfortable
call on my behalf, but my voice seemed to have disappeared.

I reached for her hand and tried to smile at her, hoping to convey wordlessly what I couldn't seem to speak aloud. Kelly and Taryn started talking through some logistics—how long surgery would be, that they'd both stay, what kinds of things they'd need to prep to get me home—and I was glad for the opportunity to be alone with my spiraling, dark thoughts. More than anything, I felt ashamed that I was still so affected by my mother. Why was a brief phone conversation, one I wasn't even part of, enough to eradicate the power and independence I'd worked hard to cultivate as I built a life far away from her? I felt stupid and small, easily imagining the disapproval and scorn in her tone.

Yet, masochistically, I had still sought it out. Part of me wanted, needed, to hear what she had to say—the part of me that clung to the hope that she'd someday love and accept me without reserve or conditions. I thought about how she offered me the grape when I had crawled out of bed after my foot operations, sat in the sun with me to help heal my wounds, knelt at the foot of my bed during that first, torturous night and wiped the sweat from my forehead. I thought about the mother who woke me up in the dead of night to chase fireflies in the backyard, the mother who had gone to bat for me at school whenever there was a conflict, the mother who once told me I was the strongest girl in the world. It would be easier, perhaps, if she'd never been kind. If I'd never had a glimpse of the mothering I craved. I wished pointlessly for the dull, faraway throbbing in my leg to come back in full force, so that my misery could feel manifested, tangibly, in my body.

Before long, the doctor and three nurses returned. He'd decided to sedate me in order to remove the pizza box duct-taped to my leg; the morphine wouldn't be strong enough for that level of disruption. Kelly and Taryn stood on either side of my bed while we waited for the needle that would knock me out completely: a sharp poke that would finally bring a darkness even blacker than the inside of my own eyelids. Kelly stroked my hair as the nurses tinkered with my IV and talked about me as if I wasn't there. In a way, I wasn't.

The last thing I saw before everything went black was Taryn snapping pictures of my X-rays and sending them off to my teammates. I didn't want their pity, except I did. I didn't want to be seen, except I did. I didn't want my mother, except I did.

PART III

17

LITTLE MOVEMENTS

Time didn't behave normally that night. Inside the room I'd been brought to while knocked out, it was never fully dark or quiet, so I couldn't distinguish between day and night. Hospital staff entered my room once an hour, sometimes twice, each time turning on the overhead lights. It was the kind of persistent disruption that would have made staying asleep impossible, but the pain and resultant vomiting kept me from any real rest all on their own. Yet I found the regularity, the predictability, to be soothing in a way. The whiteboard across from my bed displayed the next scheduled interruption down to the minute. I knew exactly how to call for help if I needed more painkillers in between, which I often did.

I spent the night alone. Kelly and Taryn had had to leave once visiting hours were over, before I woke up. I called Kelly near midnight when I felt a little more alert, and she told me that she'd gotten home from the hospital to find that Lady had been digging through one of my bags and unearthed a baggie full of ibuprofen. It wasn't clear how much she had consumed, and Kelly had spent the next few hours on the phone with the vet. Eventually she had succeeded in making Lady vomit, but the vet still advised watching her closely over the course of the next twenty-four hours. I felt horrible about the day of unending stress Kelly had been through and insisted she stay with Lady rather than trying to come back and spend the night with me. I was being taken care of, and I hoped Kelly could get some much-needed rest if she was able to sleep in our own bed.

Alone in my hospital room, I focused on the soothing drip of the IV and the rain hitting my window. Even though I knew Lady needed Kelly more than I did, I still felt lonely and scared. My body was also starting to itch. It started in the small of my back, and I could feel it spreading. When I finally couldn't bear it any longer and pressed the red button at my bedside, a nurse flipped me over and found a rash had spread over my entire back: I was allergic to the painkillers.

"We'll switch you to something else, hon," she promised. "No worries. While I'm here, though, do you have to go potty?"

I cringed at the word *potty*. I hadn't been asked that question since I was three years old. I did have to pee, though, so I nodded, and she retrieved the bedpan. The nurse grabbed the hem of my hospital gown and pulled it up to my navel, but when she tried to slide the bedpan under my butt, my leg was inadvertently wrenched to the left. Every time she tried to shift the bedpan under me, my leg shifted painfully.

"There you go, hon, there you go. Easy does it," she said. I felt humiliated and infantile, yet clung to her soft words of encouragement as if they were a life raft. The stream of urine was hot against my leg.

In the morning, I awoke to the surgeon opening the door to my room. The first thing he said was "I want you to hear that there's a chance you'll never walk normally again." There was no greeting. He spoke matter-of-factly; his eyes were dead. "I won't know until I get in there and see the extent of the damage. After the surgery, a neurologist will visit you here to do an assessment."

I looked at him blankly. Kelly was at work—she had very few vacation days, being so new at her job, and we'd agreed over text during the night that she should save them for when I was discharged—and Taryn, who had promised to work from the hospital, hadn't yet arrived. I knew I should be asking questions, but I felt so out of it I had no idea what to say. Instead, I was making a mental list of everything this meant I could lose: Derby. Running with Lady in the early morning through our neighborhood. Walking across campus to class with Tory. Getting around independently inside our home. Would I have to purchase a cane like the one I had in elementary school? Would I need a wheelchair or other assistive devices? Would that mean the layout of our house would need to change or we would need to move? There were so many skills I lacked that I would need to build, so many goodbyes I would need to say to the way I had previously lived.

"The nurses will come to prep you for surgery in a few hours," the surgeon said, then walked out.

Taryn texted me that she was running late—something had come up with one of her kids—and I felt more alone than ever until Kelly unexpectedly walked in. Her boss had let her have the day off so that she could see me before I went in for surgery. I began to cry as soon as I saw her, and

I told her what the surgeon had said. She listened quietly, brushing my hair from my sticky forehead while I spoke. Before she could respond, several nurses came in to wheel me into the preparation room.

"You can walk with us, honey," one of the nurses said to Kelly as they made to push my bed toward the door.

Kelly held my hand all the way down the hall. As we waited outside the room for the operating room to be sterilized, she started to tear up. I'd never seen her cry in public before. "You're going to be okay," she kept repeating. We hugged tightly, her curly hair spilling over my shoulder.

I don't remember being in the operating room at all, or anyone counting down. What I found out later was that the surgeon made a four-inch vertical incision on my knee through which they hammered a metal rod into my tibia. They stabilized the rod with several screws, including four at my ankle. The doctor hadn't seen any nerve damage behind my knee where the fibula had cracked apart, but we would need a neurologist to be sure.

When my eyelids flickered open after the procedure, Kelly was leaning over me, assuring me that it had gone as well as it could've. "The surgeon was very pleased," she said, two or three times. I tried to return her shaky smile, feeling like I was living the whole thing through the haze of a dream.

That night, Kelly simply didn't go home when visiting hours were over, and somehow, no one insisted that she leave. Tory and her husband, Jason, offered to spend the nights at our place and care for Lady for as long as we needed. I told Kelly there was room on the hospital bed for her to sleep beside me, but she was too worried about jostling my leg by accident. I craved the warmth of her body pressed against mine, the familiar curve of her back, the smell of her neck where she sprayed perfume into the air and walked through it every morning.

At the beginning of my third day in the hospital, Kelly was gone by the time I woke up, but Taryn was in the chair next to me, typing away on her laptop. Outside, it was still raining—the downpour that had started a few days ago had returned in earnest—and in the neighboring room I could hear the news channels saying that there was no end in sight to the flooding that had started the day before I broke my leg. I worried about Kelly driving back home and then to work. I had no idea where the hospital was in relation to my familiar St. Louis landmarks.

More coherent now and in constant discomfort, I spent the day playing Yahtzee with Taryn when she wasn't half-heartedly tending to work matters from her computer on my bedside table. We anxiously awaited the arrival of the neurologist: the only man who could determine my fate. By the time the neurologist entered my room later that afternoon for my first consult, Taryn had gone to pick up Jacob from school and Klara from grad school had taken her place. Sweet, mathematically-minded Kelly had set up a schedule of companions across my network of friends, and Klara offered to arrange a meal train for the two weeks following my discharge. It was surreal to realize I had so many people willing to support me—a *network* of friends. The neurologist mistook Klara for my mother at first, but I quickly corrected him. Sometimes Klara was self-conscious about being an older graduate student, and I hoped that hadn't made her feel uncomfortable.

"Do you have something for me to take notes?" Klara

asked instead, pushing up her big glasses in worry. "We need to make sure we catch every word."

I hadn't even thought about taking notes. I had been lucid only off and on the past couple of days, and hadn't absorbed anything the nurses or doctors had said to me. I was grateful for Klara, as prepared to make meaning in my patient room as she was in our writing workshop.

While the neurologist finished typing up some notes on the medical computer, I shuffled through the bag of clothes and personal items Kelly had brought with her a couple days ago, found a notebook, and handed it to Klara, who dutifully dated the page and began scribbling. Then, catching my eye, she mouthed, "Name tag."

Name tag? I glanced over at the neurologist's scrubs and saw it: Dr. Richard Head, MD, Neurologist at St. Anthony's Hospital. For the first time since I'd fallen, I felt an urge to laugh. He would have had an easy time picking a derby name; though it was hard to picture this serious-looking gray-haired gentleman in skates. Later, in Klara's notes, I would find the name written in capital letters, underlined three times: DICK HEAD.

"We have one goal for today," Dr. Head said, not unkindly. "Which is to get your big toe to move. If you can move any of your toes, it will mean the nerves in your leg are working."

I nodded. The athlete in me was coming out; this was like a weight lifting challenge.

Dr. Head lifted the covers off my feet and pulled the hospital sock off my injured foot. Underneath, my leg was wrapped in gauze, toes barely peeking out.

"Concentrate," he said. I strained with effort and looked

down at my toes, which remained perfectly still and, on top
of that, looked nothing like the toes I remembered. My flesh
was blue and puffy. Even the sparkly purple nail polish didn't
look like it belonged to me.

"I'm focusing," I said. And I was—but it was like the connection between my brain and my body was gone. I might as
well have been trying to telekinetically move the bottle of
ice water on my bedside table.

I stared at my toes, urging them to move, pleading with
them to move, but nothing happened. Panic rose within me.
Dr. Head gave me another thirty seconds or so before gently
asking me to take a break.

"Okay," he started, then paused as if trying to figure out
how to phrase whatever he was planning to say next.

But I hadn't stopped trying—of course I hadn't—and just
as Dr. Head started to speak again, my big toe twitched.
Klara gasped and pointed. "I saw it!" she shouted. "Did you
see it?" Dr. Head turned back to my feet, and I focused all
my energy on my big toe. After a moment that felt like years,
it moved again.

"Oh, now that's fantastic!" he exclaimed, visibly relieved.
"No nerve damage! This means that, with the proper exercise and in time, you should be able to walk and run normally!" He beamed at us.

Relief flooded through my body, beginning at my scalp
and traveling all the way to my toes. It felt electric, immediate. The minute Dr. Head left the room, I texted Kelly a
short clip of my toes wiggling. "This means I'm going to be
okay," I wrote. Klara squeezed me, and we squealed together
like little girls.

.   .   .

BY THE AFTERNOON of my third day, I was struggling with my lack of independence. I needed help with everything, including pissing into a bedpan, which would have been embarrassing if it didn't hurt my leg so much I simply had no energy left to feel embarrassed. I didn't need the pans for anything besides pee—one of the side effects of oxycodone is constipation—which I was extremely grateful for every time a nurse had to slide one under my ass.

People in scrubs darted in and out of my room constantly. They rearranged my pillows, refilled my water bottle, tinkered with my oxygen tubes and adjusted the fluids being pumped into my arm through an IV. The nurses were so good at anticipating what I needed before I even realized I needed it. Still, though, the lack of self-sufficiency was starting to grate on me; after being taught for years to never depend on anyone, I couldn't help feeling shame in my neediness.

None of them, however, broached the subject of my hair, which stuck to my scalp, matted down by sweat and grease. If only I had had a hair tie—or a hair bob, as my mother calls them—to pull it back into a ponytail. The oxygen tubes plastered my hair to my cheeks, and no matter how often I pushed it back, it clung to the sides of my neck like gills. I'd been told I could probably go home after five or so days, but no one really gave me any more clarity on that. The hospital physical therapists said I needed to be able to crutch up and down stairs for them to be comfortable releasing me, since I would encounter stairs at home.

Even more than my desperation to leave, though, was my longing for someone to take me to the shower and give me some shampoo. There was still a big sign on my door that said FALL RISK: I wasn't allowed to even attempt to shower, so the nurses bathed me with little sponges. I felt like I was at the whim of other people to do whatever they wanted: poke, prod, examine. In reality, this was purely an exaggerated version of a feeling that persisted in my everyday life—that I was one to be acted upon, rather than the one acting. Roller derby was the only arena I'd found in which I felt I had any agency.

WHEN TARYN ARRIVED at the hospital mid-morning, she asked if there was anything I needed. Kelly had been in and out quickly before work and all I could think about was my hair, but before I could stop myself, I said no. Every part of me was screaming to ask her to help me, but I simply couldn't vocalize the request; it was just too deeply ingrained in me to not be an inconvenience, and I was all too aware that she was already going out of her way to be here with me so often.

Taryn set up her workstation in front of the window and proceeded to get started on her day. Though I knew that she worked in health insurance, the specifics of Taryn's job were lost on me. Still, I loved listening to her conference calls, the gentle clicking of the keyboard, the ease with which she transitioned from her regular voice to her professional one. When speaking to her colleagues, Taryn enunciated every syllable. There was no hesitation, no hint of self-doubt. She spoke with the air of someone who knew she was good at her job, and I made mental notes so I could emulate it. I also liked Taryn's professional voice because it made the way she spoke to me feel even more special and familiar. Once she had ended a call, she would turn to me and say something like "They'd be so fucked without me." We'd laugh; it felt good to be in on a secret, to see another side of the woman I'd grown so close to.

Then, a miracle: as Taryn was washing her hands in the hospital sink later that afternoon, she noticed that the hand soap on the sink doubled as shampoo. "Check this out!" she said, holding up the bottle. "Do you want me to wash your hair when I'm done with work?"

Because she had offered—because it was her suggestion—it was easy to say yes. I could even tell myself it was more polite than to decline. Somehow, Taryn helped me off the hospital cot and into the wheelchair, managing to do the work of two nurses. Once I was sitting, she rolled me over and lowered my head into the sink.

"I'm sorry you have to touch it," I said. "It's really gross."

"Babe," she said. "Your hair isn't even close to the grossest things I have to touch. When you're a mom, you just do what you gotta do."

She turned on the water and squeezed the shampoo into her hands. I watched her eyes narrow in concentration and her toothy smile vanish as she started lathering it into my hair.

"It's weird doing this on someone else," she said. "My boys have always had really short hair so it only took two seconds." I felt myself blushing, which I always did when Taryn compared me to her kids. She made the connection so effortlessly, so naturally.

I closed my eyes while she worked, relishing her touch as she tugged at my hair to make sure the shampoo got all the way to the ends. Having her hands in my hair felt remarkably normal. I had always been self-conscious when I went to get my hair cut; I worried it was too thin, too dry, or too dam- aged from all the lemon juice I used to lighten it in the sum-

mer. None of those concerns crossed my mind with Taryn.
I felt safe. Loved. Held.

After she turned off the water and draped a towel over my
shoulders, I heard myself ask, "When I get out of the hospital, do you think you could help me put some color in my
hair?" I had wanted pink tips for years, and yet I'd never had
the nerve to make the move. Something had always stopped
me: self-consciousness, worry about fitting into the "normal" or professional world. That was my mother's voice, I
realized, always convincing me that I didn't really want what
I thought I wanted or need what I knew I needed.

"Only if you let me dye your whole head blue," Taryn
said, laughing. Then, "I thought you'd never ask."

IT WASN'T LONG after Taryn left for the night that Kelly
arrived, looking stressed. "Your mother called while I was on
my way over here from work," she said before she'd even
unzipped her jacket. "She said she's flying to St. Louis tomorrow and bringing your sister with her."

It was like all the air in the room was sucked out. I felt
shock, but not without a pinch of pleasure. A decision that
dramatic must indicate some amount of concern and invest-
ment from their end. It felt like another iteration of the proof
of injury I saw in my X-rays. *If this weren't a big deal, they
wouldn't come.* Then why did I suddenly feel like I couldn't
breathe? This was what I wanted, wasn't it?

My thoughts started racing. For some reason the first
thing that came to mind was *Why Cam?* My contact with her
had been minimal since I left home. We didn't know what to
say to each other. Everything felt loaded—my guilt and her
bitterness at being left on her own there. My anger and her

denial around the way she continued to batter her body through swimming. And what about my dad? I knew he couldn't easily get off work, but the thought of seeing my mother and sister without him was almost unfathomable. I missed him, I realized. Did I miss my mom and Cam? I couldn't tell—it was all so mixed up.

Thankfully, while I was trying to figure out what to say, Kelly had other news: the hot water in our apartment had gone out. Tory and her husband had informed us, since they'd been staying at our apartment with Lady every night since my surgery—and, hoping for lukewarm, Kelly had stopped by to try to take a shower before work. The water was ice cold.

"Everything is insane right now," Kelly said, pulling her jacket off and falling heavily into the nearby chair. "Any day you'll be getting out of here. I saw one of your doctors on the way in, and he said it might even be tomorrow. How do you feel about them being here? I felt I couldn't say no." *And they didn't exactly ask.* Neither of us needed to say that part out loud.

"I wouldn't have been able to say no either," I assured her. I guess that could have gone without saying, too.

"Does *any* part of you want them here?" Kelly asked.

I appreciated what she was implying: that she understood, and wouldn't judge me, if the answer was yes. She always tried to let me make my own decisions when it came to my family. She had held me when I cried and listened when I made excuses for their behavior. And she came from such a different family situation herself; she would definitely want her mom there if our positions were reversed.

I thought about it hard. Maybe she would be sweet and caring, as I knew she could be. Maybe I'd be able to feel that specific, primal comfort I craved so badly. Maybe I was romanticizing the whole idea and it would be a disaster. But maybe not. I'd had a lot of practice taking the good with the bad. Right now, even a small amount of good from my family felt worth it. Truthfully, I'd known since Kelly had said they were coming that I wouldn't ask them to change their minds.

I nodded, and Kelly, smiling lovingly, nodded back.

THAT EVENING, I started making a list for Tory: all the changes I wanted her to make to our apartment so that nothing would upset my mother. I would have much preferred Kelly be the one to do it, but she wouldn't have time the following day to stop at home before picking up my mother and sister from the airport. It would have to be Tory. I hated to ask her for even more than she'd already done for me, but this was an emergency. Besides, I trusted Tory immensely: sharing writing was vulnerable, and we'd been through a rigorous year together. I'd listened to many stories about the dysfunction in her family during our walks to school, and I'd told her some of my own without ever feeling judged. We felt a kinship with one another. I now knew for certain I was being released the following afternoon, but it was unclear how much time I would have between getting released and being home—my mom and sister might even arrive at the apartment before I did. There was far too much I didn't want her to see. There was no chance of it being a tension-free visit, and the least I could do was make sure I wouldn't be walking into any obvious traps. I was exhausted and my leg was aching, but the panic about having her in St. Louis fueled me.

I started with the one that sounded the least strange. *No*

AC, I wrote. *Windows open instead.* I was raised to never use air-conditioning, even on the hottest of summer days, because my mom claimed it was a sign of weakness. She said she wanted to really *feel* the summer, and I knew she would be offended if she learned that I kept the apartment the same temperature year-round, regardless of the weather. It wasn't a battle I needed to fight, plus it was an easy fix.

There was no getting around the fact that the rest of my list was way more intense. *No pictures of Kelly and me in the open, especially the frame that says "Dykes to Watch Out For,"* I wrote, my anxiety overriding my embarrassment. *Feel free to stash it in a bag under our bed.* It was bad enough my mom knew Kelly and I lived together—if she had to see pictures of us in love, she might think we were flaunting it. At the very best, it would be awkward. At the worst, it would cause a blowup. Neither sounded desirable to me.

Absolutely no writing or schoolwork out. My mother didn't approve of grad school, and she certainly didn't know that I'd ever written about our family. This one was my worst-case scenario.

Other than that, use your discretion, I wrote, thinking of the dildo that sometimes lay out in the open on one of our nightstands. As humiliating as it would be for Tory to encounter it while mom-proofing our apartment, I would much rather have her be the one to find it.

AS KELLY HAD guessed, I was released from the hospital just a few hours before my mother and sister were scheduled to land in St. Louis. The nurses told me that ordinarily they would've kept me longer—until I had proven I could crutch up the stairs and use the bathroom by myself—but the flooding was complicating everything. They didn't want me to get stranded like the news was forecasting and like several patients before me had. Footage showed that several large bridges were closing, the swells of the Mississippi underneath threatening to seep over the edges. I worried about the weather impacting my mother's flight, but when I checked online it looked like everything was still operating as scheduled.

Klara volunteered to bring me home, since Kelly was working. It was pouring rain when she brought her car around to the side of the hospital where I was waiting in a wheelchair, my entire leg swaddled in bandages. To my surprise, the doctors said there would be no cast required at any stage of my healing process because the metal rod inside my bone functioned even better than a cast. I would just need to be careful not to jostle the metal or put any pressure on the bone until it fully healed, or I could split the whole thing down the middle. I was given enough painkillers to last me a month, before transitioning to the fat bottle of anti-inflammatories in my bag. As for the rest of my recovery, my doctors advised me to be gentle with myself and to take it day by day until they saw me in a little over a week.

The windshield wipers were going at full speed as Klara drove. I sat in the back so that I could turn sideways and leave my leg extended, but I tried to keep my head facing forward so I wouldn't get sick. When we finally made it back to the apartment, the rain hadn't let up. Klara parked as close as she could to the building and, from the safety of the car, I counted the nine stairs that were required to get to the door.

Neither of us had an umbrella, but Klara put her hand on my lower back to steady me as I crutched toward the door. The first step I attempted, my crutches slipped and my stomach dropped. That was when the man living above us in the duplex, James, came flying out and insisted he could carry me inside.

"No, you can't," I said. I didn't even thank him. My face was beet red. I was sure I weighed far too much, even for this burly, muscular man. I also didn't want to be carried: it was a humiliation I simply couldn't endure. I hadn't been carried since my dad had to take me from the car to my house post–foot operations. So I sat down on the steps and scooted my way up them one at a time. Water soaked through my pants and as Klara and James looked on from above me, I started to cry. The pain was excruciating, the embarrassment profound. I felt no different than the day when I was eleven, fresh out of surgery, scooting my way to the back door from my bed to sit in the sun with my parents.

It took quite a while for me to make it to the top, but once I did, I gave Klara the key and she unlocked the door. James made me promise to call him if I needed anything. I thanked him, but I had no intention of taking him up on that, even if I was desperate. When we got inside, Klara held up a towel and said we should take off my pants. It felt like I'd peed myself. Everything was soaked, and I wanted nothing more than to get out of my clothes, but I also didn't want Klara to see me naked, which would take away the last of my dignity.

"It doesn't matter," she said, as though reading my thoughts. "Just let me help."

Once the towel was wrapped around me, I allowed myself to collapse onto the couch. Lady immediately jumped up and licked my face, tail wagging excitedly. From the vantage point of the couch, I could see that Tory had followed all my instructions. The windows were open, the writing that had been sprawled over the coffee table had been swept up and stored out of sight, the photo of Kelly and me kissing that normally hung from the fridge with a magnet had been taken down. By the looks of it, Tory had done more than I asked for, washing the dishes, sweeping, and even dusting the blinds. I felt overwhelmed with gratitude.

"It looks different in here," Klara commented. "Maybe I just haven't been over in a while." I nodded, not prepared to tell her all the work Tory had done to ensure that.

"I brought you some suppositories," Klara continued, holding out a little green jar. "I just figured you might need them." She had been there the previous day when the doctors were discussing my unresponsive digestive system and had offered to send me home with a full bottle of magnesium citrate—the substance people down before colonoscopies to clear out their systems. I hadn't consumed the magnesium citrate yet, but the doctors said I needed to do so soon; four days with no bowel movement showed that the oxycodone was wreaking havoc on my digestive system. Ordinarily, they wouldn't have let me leave the hospital in that state, but the flooding was a greater threat. It was more important I get home.

I forced myself to thank Klara even though I was quite embarrassed. "You didn't have to do that," I said. She responded that she just wanted to help.

An awkward silence fell and Klara jostled her purse in her lap. "I'm supposed to be back at school in half an hour," she said eventually.

"Of course, go," I said. As unsteady as I felt, I leapt at the chance to be alone. It had been days since I had been truly alone. I had everything I needed here anyway.

Klara hugged me tightly before leaving and patted the top

of my head. "You're doing good," she said. Then, she was gone.

In her absence, my longed-for solitude felt heavier than I'd expected. The wind blowing through the windows caused the curtains to dance, and the jackets on the coatrack by the door rustled in the breeze. Rainwater soaked the top of the couch. Every time the thunder rumbled in the distance, Lady pushed her body closer into me, looking for safety. It felt like there was something I should be doing to prepare for my mother, who would be arriving in less than an hour, but everything was done. There was nothing left to do but wait.

18

BAGGAGE

The first thing my mother did when she saw me was inform me that I stank. She's gifted with what she likes to
call a "supersonic sniffer."

"Actually, Kelly, I didn't want to say anything on the ride
over, but you stink pretty bad too," she said, turning to face
my girlfriend.

I felt a surge of protectiveness toward Kelly. Our landlord
had been dragging his feet on replacing our hot water heater
for a few days, so Kelly couldn't shower. I hadn't been able to
shower in the hospital because of the fall risk, so neither of
us had been clean in days. It wasn't Kelly's fault. And I could
already see that the twenty-minute drive from the airport
with Mom and Cam was wearing on her. What else had my
mom said to her before they arrived?

Kelly didn't respond, and my mom crossed her arms over
her chest. She was wearing her favorite light blue track pants,
the ones she'd had for years, and a white V-neck T-shirt that
exposed her naturally tan chest. I felt unexpectedly nostalgic
to see her in clothes I recognized. Very suddenly, I realized
she dressed like me: comfort over style. When I was growing

up, her hair was always permed, but now her dark locks were thin and short: grayer than I remembered, which was slightly jarring to me. In my mind, she always wore makeup, but today her face was bare. Her lips, usually coated in light pink pigment, were pursed. Her eyes, squinted. It looked like being in our apartment was physically paining her.

My sister, with her broad shoulders and long limbs, dwarfed my mother. She was wearing athletic clothes too—leggings and a swimming hoodie—and a pair of massive pink Crocs over her size eleven feet.

She hadn't said a word since they'd arrived a few moments ago. Was she mad at me, I wondered? Resentful? I only spoke with Cam once or twice a month, and mostly by text, but I knew things couldn't be easy for her at home. I remembered the pressure of senior year, the final grades before college, the last swim season, conference championships and then states. And I also remembered the loneliness, all the hoping it would get better once I was finally away from home. Was Cam looking forward to leaving our hometown as much as I had? Or was she bitter that once again my physical injuries and hospitalization were imposing on her life, as they had when she was just a little kid?

My mother set her bags down on the small table we'd set up for jigsaw puzzles, then collapsed into the recliner. Kelly, still standing, offered to give the two of them a tour of our apartment. What would she think, I wondered, of our hardwood floors, the framed anatomical drawings from my senior figure-drawing class that hung on the walls? The photo of my bare back and arms outstretched in a snowy forest that had won me best of show at the art exhibition in college, the watercolors Kelly had done of trees when I persuaded her to take a community art class with me? Mom had seen most of this artwork before, at shows and contests, but it seemed different in my apartment, the first place I lived as an adult that she had ever visited. I had even purchased my first houseplant—a small succulent—and I thought it made the space feel homey. I was proud of the apartment. Kelly and I had been there for almost a year and we'd worked hard to make it a home, our first together.

"I don't need a tour," my mom said, shoving Lady down as she tried to jump up and lick her face. And then, pointing to my cactus: "That thing will be dead in a week."

"No it won't," I sputtered, slightly offended.

Cam, who had been trying to peer down our hallway, quickly glanced at our mother and then looked down, saying, "I'm good too." I knew Cam would do whatever Mom said. I should have known, by the way I was already feeling—intimidated and slightly scared—that all weekend I would follow suit.

Kelly locked eyes with me as if to say, *Now what?* In Kelly's family, so much emphasis was put on decorum and manners—her mother would've never turned down a tour even if she had no interest in seeing the apartment. Kelly's family always did what was normal, polite. This caused a fair share of other problems, like avoiding confrontations, but it was the only way Kelly knew how to behave.

After a few minutes of standing in the middle of the room without knowing what to do, Kelly approached the table where my mom had thrown her luggage and paused.

"What is that?" she asked, pointing.

"Oh!" Mom exclaimed. She jumped up from the chair, snatched a small bag out of her luggage, and tossed it to me. "I brought that for you. Everybody's raving about it at Weight Watchers."

"What is it?" I asked.

"It's a new pancake mix packed with protein. Way healthier than that crap you eat." After a tense pause, Mom asked, hesitantly, "You still eat pancakes, right?"

She pulled out a piece of cardboard from the bottom of her bag; it was the original packaging for the pancake mix. After she molded it back into three dimensions, she plucked the pancake mix out of my lap, plopped it back into the box, and brushed her hands together as if to say, *Perfect*.

"I love pancakes," I said, hoping to turn around the awkwardness of the past few minutes. "Thank you." I *did* love pancakes, but more than that, I appreciated that my mom brought me a box all the way from Michigan because I knew it was her way of saying she thought about me—that she cared about me.

"I hope you like it, because it was a bitch to get through security," my mother said. "But I wasn't about to pay to check a bag just so I could bring you pancake powder. I mean, I love you, but not that much."

"Well—" I started. "What happened?"

"Like I said, it was a complete bitch," she continued. "A bunch of lights went off and everybody in line was staring at me. One of those people—what are they called? Agents? One of the security agents had to pull me aside and pat me down. She got a little handsy too. But it turned out okay because I told her I hadn't flown on an airplane in ten years. I think she took pity on me. That's the truth, you know. I haven't left the state of Michigan in ten freaking years."

I couldn't stop my eyes from widening. *Ten years?* I had no idea it had been that long.

"How was the flight?" Kelly asked, trying again to steer

the conversation back to the normalcy with which she was familiar.

"Expensive as shit," my mom replied. "Each ticket was nearly five hundred dollars. Plus, the last-minute hotel was two hundred dollars a night. Never thought I'd pay that much for a hotel room in my life." She went on to say that at least it included free breakfast and a dinner buffet, insisting she wouldn't pay for a single meal while in town—she'd squirrel away extra food at breakfast and make sure to be back at the hotel by dinner. Nothing about the plan surprised me; that was how I still operated at hotel buffets myself. She continued, "It really is just such inconvenient timing, but that's how you girls always do things."

For the first time, I tried to catch Cam's eye and saw her looking at me with a slightly conspiratorial smile, which I returned. Something in me relaxed just a little.

"Just think"—my mother swung around to Cam—"you would've been at your senior prom if you didn't have to come here."

I rounded on Cam. "*You* were going to *prom?*" It sounded more accusatory than I intended.

"No way," she said, taking a seat at the kitchen table. "Way too expensive. I could buy two new swimsuits for how much the ticket cost, let alone the dress and flowers and bullshit."

I didn't blame her—I hadn't gone to prom either. I barely knew the boy who asked me, and I couldn't imagine spending that kind of money on one night.

"She had other plans for the night of prom!" my mother interjected. "She was going to have a bonfire with her friends." It sounded like an accusation.

"I'm sorry for keeping you from your senior prom bonfire," I told my sister. And then, turning to my mother, I simply said, "I'm sorry."

I was apologizing for the expensive flights, for the bad timing, and for not offering to let them to stay in our apartment. I was apologizing for the way I asked my sister if she was going to prom. For my stench. For my cactus. For the handsy security agent who mistook the bag of pancake powder for cocaine. For breaking my leg. For being an inconvenience. For everything about this that was my fault.

MY MOM WANTED to go to the hotel as soon as possible, but I asked her if we could wait; Taryn had texted me saying she was coming by to drop off some food. Surprisingly, Tory showed up before Taryn did, with an extra-large pizza she had secured in a big plastic bag on the back of her bike.

"Came right from class," she said after I'd introduced her to my mom and Cam, rain dripping from her coat. "We had a celebration because it was the last day. There was a whole extra pie, and I asked if I could bring it back to you on my way home." I felt my face grow hot. Everyone knew about my accident, she said, and wanted to do anything they could to help me recover. "Our advisors are even planning to come to your house for the thesis meeting you missed."

"That's so nice of them!" I said. "Considering how hard it will be to get anywhere."

"I made sure of it," she said, throwing her long brown braid behind her back. There was sweat on her forehead and temples. "Oh, I also brought you a book. Not sure if it's any good, but I figure you'll have plenty of time for reading this summer." She handed me a small book I hadn't heard of and stood up. "Mind if I pee?"

When Tory left to use the bathroom, my mom turned to me and said, "Why does that woman have such a stick up her ass?"

"What are you talking about?" I said. I was so surprised I wasn't sure I'd heard her correctly.

"She does seem pretty stuffy," Cam said, leaning back in her chair.

"Stuffy?" I whispered, praying that Tory couldn't hear us from the bathroom.

"She thinks she's better than us," my mom said, not lowering her voice. "I can tell."

"No she doesn't," I said. I tried to remember what I had noticed about Tory the first time I met her: only that she was very thin and toned from running and that her hair was long. She wore what many other grad students wore: plaid flannel, leggings, leather shoes. I had no idea where they were drawing these conclusions from, especially as every aspect of her visit showed her generosity.

Tory squeezed me tightly before she left, and within two minutes, Taryn had arrived. It was enough time for me to worry about what my mother would think of Taryn if she found Tory so off-putting. Tory dressed and acted quite traditionally—what would my mother think of someone who didn't? I cursed myself for failing to suggest Taryn not wear her high-top Converse sneakers. I would've requested a shirt with long sleeves to cover her tattoos and maybe a hat or a bandana to conceal her vibrant hair. "It's for your own protection," I would've said. "Gives her less ammunition." I couldn't have admitted, either out loud or to myself, that it would have been for *my* protection.

When she arrived at our apartment, Taryn was wearing an old T-shirt from an Earth Day festival with the word VOL-UNTEER on the back. The sleeves were hacked off; little threads dangled from the armholes. Her hair was an elaborate tangle of red and orange and yellow, and her sandals exposed the turtle tattoos on the tops of both feet. I loved Taryn's hair and tattoos—I'd admired them since we first met and had been thrilled at the hospital when she'd agreed to dye my hair, too. Now, though, I saw her through my mother's eyes. I saw someone who was different enough to be a threat.

Taryn brought more than she could carry in one trip. She came with a crockpot full of pulled pork, buns, condiments, and a fresh salad complete with sweet Vidalia onion dressing. For dessert, homemade brownies. Kelly offered to help her bring food in, but my mother and sister stayed where they were, watching Taryn suspiciously. Each time Taryn walked past my mother with an armload of food Taryn nodded hello, and by the time she finally sat down on the couch with me, my mom had scooted all the way to the edge of her chair, as far from Taryn as she could get without actually standing up and moving.

"This is Taryn," I told my mom and sister. I tried to make my voice confident and level.

"Are you—a school friend?" my mother asked.

"God, no," Taryn said. "No, we play roller derby together. Well, not always together. Sometimes against each other. I'm on the M80s and she's on the Stunts, so we had to play each other a few times last season. But we practice together. And we'll play on the same travel team next summer, the Fleur-de-Linquents."

Mom squinted. I watched my sister scan Taryn up and down.

"Taryn stayed at the hospital with me," I told Mom. "She works remotely, so she was able to bring her work there."

"And what do you do for a living?" my mom asked.

"I'm a business analyst for a health insurance company," Taryn replied.

I don't know what my mother was expecting Taryn to say, but it certainly wasn't that. The information nearly knocked her over; her eyes widened and she gripped both arms of the chair. I laughed uncomfortably as my mother began pelting Taryn with questions—things that Kelly and I had actually been wondering ever since the accident occurred. When would my bills start coming? How would I know if the insurance—my mother's insurance, since I was still on her plan—had kicked in? Who should I contact if there was a problem? For my mom, it was like knowing that Taryn worked in healthcare gave her a superpower, one that her outward appearance didn't match but also couldn't detract from.

Taryn switched to her work voice. She fielded all my mother's questions, using phrases like "processing the claim" and "out-of-pocket maximum" and "explanation of benefits." In response to the question about who to contact if I had a question about a health insurance issue, she said, "I'm not going anywhere." Nudging me, she said, "This one's stuck to me for life."

When my mom was through grilling Taryn, Taryn started asking gentle questions about my mom's life. "Where did you fly from?" she wanted to know. "Is your husband working?" I sat in awe of the conversation, realizing that all my worries had been completely unfounded. My mother and Taryn were getting on like old friends.

After about fifteen minutes, Taryn said, "Well, I better let you get to it before the food gets cold. Hope you like it." I crutched into the kitchen after her: one last check to make sure we had everything we needed. In the semi-privacy of the kitchen, I thanked her profusely. I wished I had time to thank her for more than just the food and the visit; I wanted to thank her for being nice to my mother, for treating her with kindness and respect despite some unflattering stories I had shared. My mom loved to pick a fight. I'd heard countless teachers and coaches, waiters and customer service reps recoil from her—or submit to her, as I often did.

It didn't escape my notice that Taryn didn't make herself an easy target—intentionally or not, she had widened the pigeonholes my mother so frequently forced people into. Whatever Taryn had—confidence, or the ability to be unapologetically herself—I wanted it. It was everything that had appealed to me about roller derby in the first place.

I crutched Taryn to the door and closed it behind her. Then, turning back to the room, I saw my mother fold her arms. "Are you better than her?" she asked.

"Better than who?" I said, though I knew perfectly well who she was talking about.

"Are you a better skater than that woman who was just here?"

"It's not like that," I said. "She's my— I'm not competing with her."

"Sure you are," she said. "She said you play on different teams. And even if you didn't, you'd still be competing with her."

"You don't know what you're talking about," I said, but my voice sounded unsure.

"I bet you are," she said, taking the last swig of a bottle of Diet Coke. I felt myself swell with pride, much as I hated myself for it. No matter what I told myself, some part of me still desperately wanted her approval.

Once my mother found out we didn't have any hot water, she decided that I would go with them to the hotel for the night. I would've preferred to sleep in my own bed, even if that meant not showering, but I felt completely powerless to disagree. When she was five hundred miles away, it was easier to buy myself time—rarely did I say no outright—but now, facing her in my living room, it felt impossible. Kelly raised her eyebrows at me, asking if I was sure, and all I could do was nod. After nearly a week of driving to and from the hospital every day, I rationalized to myself, Kelly might be relieved to have a night alone.

My discharge instructions were extensive, but, as Kelly explained to my mother, the foundation was to continue with the opioids, avoid putting any pressure or weight on the leg, take magnesium citrate to wake up my digestive system, and stay hydrated. I was barely listening; I felt more exhausted by the minute. Thankfully, everything was printed out in a little packet that Kelly gave to my mother along with my many bottles of medication.

Standing, my mother said, "Let's get you back to the hotel. You need to shower soon or I'm going to keel over and die."

WHEN WE ARRIVED at the hotel, Cam insisted on running up the eleven flights of stairs while my mother and I took the elevator.

"I'm going to get fat here," Cam whined. "Four days with no swimming? I'm gonna be fucked when I get back."

It didn't take much to send me spiraling into my old patterns of thinking: hearing a teammate talk about training for a half marathon, or when one of my grad school friends speculated about how many calories were in a milkshake she had ordered. I still binged and occasionally purged on bad days; I was far from out of the woods. I wasn't under the delusion that recovery would be easy; in fact, I was sure it would be a lifelong process. I still held on to the belief that a few days without exercise would be the end of me—and a not-so-subtle fear of gaining weight. But I wanted to respond to Cam with a big sister's wisdom, to warn her away from the choices I'd made, to come up with the perfect words to set her permanently on a healthier track than mine. Instead, I stayed silent. Who would I really be talking to, I wondered—her or myself? And how could I offer her something I didn't even have?

When we got to the room, my mom led me straight to the bathroom to shower, yelling to Cam to come in and help when we heard her arrive a moment later. I realized with dread that this meant they were planning to be there as I took off my clothing. Painstakingly, and with their help, I began to strip, layer by layer, until I sat on the toilet lid before them, naked and exposed.

Although it had only been four days since the accident, seeing myself in the bathroom mirror was an altogether dissociative experience. My stomach was covered with what the nurses called hematomas: a side effect of the blood-thinning shots they had given me post-surgery. These bruises weren't like the ones from roller derby that speckled my inner arms and the meaty part of my ass. They were larger than my palms and dark as plums. Against the paleness of my white stomach, they were like three universes, swirling and expansive. The residue from the tape that held my IV in place still stained both my arms and my right hand. My skin was yellow. My earlobes were also bare for the first time since I was a child; the three sets of earrings I'd been wearing the day of the accident had been removed by a nurse when I was unconscious and returned to Kelly in a urine cup.

For years, I'd avoided situations in which my mother would see me fully naked, though at swim meets, clad only in my suit, it had been impossible to avoid her gaze. I chanced a look in her direction; she was staring silently at my body. Where was she looking in particular? Was she upset to see the bruises and cuts from derby in addition to the ones I'd gotten in the hospital? Or was she thinking about my weight?

Cam, at least, pretended not to look. I felt ashamed of whatever she was trying not to see. I used to be a model of athletic prowess to my sister. She had a photo of me shooting a bow and arrow on her bulletin board at home. She wanted to be as fast and strong as I was. Now, she was off to a big college on a substantial swimming scholarship. On the rare occasion she texted me, it usually had to do with Mom's latest tirade or swimming training. It was starting to sink in that I didn't know her anymore. I'd been out of the house for five years now, and she'd gone from an awkward thirteen-year-old to a prestigious, college-bound athlete. She wasn't my baby sister anymore. So much distance had grown between us since I'd left home. One of the hardest things about protecting myself from my mother was that it meant I was also choosing to cut myself off from Cam.

Together, my mom and Cam taped a garbage bag around my bandaged leg to protect it from the water. Then my mom retreated, closing the bathroom door behind her, and I heard the TV click on. In her absence, I realized that Cam and I were alone together for the first time in years. As she gripped my hand and helped me slide from the toilet seat to the shower stool, I was half-delirious from the shooting pain up my leg, and half consumed by a heaviness: some combination of grief, shame, guilt, and confusion I couldn't fully identify. If I wasn't Cam's big sister, someone she could look up to anymore, who was I? I knew how hard her leaving for college was going to be on Mom, and I could only imagine the weight of that on Cam. I wanted to tell her it was okay to live her own life. That she didn't have to skip her senior prom bonfire to fly to St. Louis. That she shouldn't spend her weekends driving back home so that Mom wouldn't be lonely. That she, like me, could get out. But then I looked down at my hairy leg in the too-white hotel tub and thought maybe what she was seeing of my escape didn't look so good.

"*How's it going in there?*" my mother shouted.

"We're fine!" Cam answered, turning on the water. Then, turning to me, she said, "Do you need help with anything else?"

"No," I said, firmly.

"*Make sure to shave her good leg!*" my mom called. "*It'll make her feel better.*"

With a resigned nod, Cam said, "Well, you heard her. Stick it out here, and I guess I'll shave it."

"I'll do it myself," I said. I wanted to show her that even though my leg was broken, I wasn't useless. My sister looked relieved. She plucked a pink razor from her toiletries bag and handed it to me—one final offering before joining our mother in the other room.

When she was gone, I made the water hotter. Once I had half-heartedly soaped and rinsed my body, I tried massaging my lower stomach, which was packed hard with four days' worth of food, but after a while, that got too tiring. It was easier just to sit there with my eyes closed, broken leg hanging out of the tub.

Right as I was about to turn off the water, I realized I had forgotten to shave. The hair on my good leg was long enough that it prickled under my palm. I wet the razor and took a couple swipes, starting down at my ankle and extending all the way up my thigh.

After several attempts, I put the razor down. Like massaging my stomach, it was exhausting and I couldn't finish. I touched my injured leg and felt nothing: it was still numb on the entire left side. I could feel my own fingertips if I pressed on the right side of my knee, but otherwise—it was the kind of numb the dentist induced to fill a cavity. I turned off the water and stared at the mess I'd made on my body—big strips of hair I'd missed—wishing I didn't care whether or not my mom noticed, but knowing that I did.

19/
ONE OF US

In the hotel with my mother and Cam, time stretched out before me, an endless landscape. There was no schedule of nurses entering my hospital room. There was no conceivable end, no emergency intercom to press if I started feeling too much pain. The first night in the hotel was the most brutal. In the darkness and silence, there was nothing to distract me from my body—the tightness of my stomach, the pain in my leg, the nausea that made it feel like my bed was being carried downstream. I experienced night as if I were in the Salvador Dalí painting *The Persistence of Memory,* in which regular objects only vaguely resemble themselves and the clocks, either malleable or half-melted, are draped over branches like bedsheets.

In the fogginess between consciousness and sleep, I became convinced that my body was attacking the foreign objects in my leg. When I closed my eyes, I could see the silver rod pushing the bone marrow out of my tibia like lava in a science fair volcano. The rod extended knee to ankle, threatening to shut down my whole system. I saw the new screws that pierced my leg bone in three different places and the old screws and two plates that had been hammered into my feet when I was eleven. I couldn't sleep lest my body turn on itself. If I looked away, bubbles like the ones that collected around the rim of a soda can would start eating away at the metal. And once the hardware was gone—the rod, the screws, the plates in my feet—my bones would dissolve into sand.

As I tried to get comfortable in the unfamiliar bed, these visions played on a constant loop. They were so bad I had to get out of bed. I couldn't find my crutches in the darkness, not that I trusted myself to use them at night anyway, and I couldn't crawl because of the long incision on my knee. I fumbled for underwear and then started making my way across the hotel room by scooting along on my ass. Like a toddler learning to walk, I used the toilet bowl to pull myself up.

The fluorescent lights of the bathroom helped somewhat with the nausea. I could focus on one thing—the cheap pink razor I had tried using to shave my good leg or the droplets of water still clinging to the shower curtain. But the longer I stared, the heavier my leg felt, until the pain of sitting upright overtook the dizziness.

"Mom," I croaked. One word, practically a whisper. That was all it took. Then she was there in the doorframe, in her saggy purple underwear and ratty, oversized T-shirt, holding both my crutches with one hand.

As kids, my sister and I used to joke about our mother being a light sleeper. Most nights she went to bed before my dad, and we would lie awake until he decided to turn in, too. We'd shush each other, anxiously awaiting what we knew was coming: a fit of hysterical screaming. It would pierce the quiet, rattle the floorboards. Sometimes the scream was short: breathy and brief. Other times, it would take two fits of yelling for her to realize the man standing over her bed was only my dad, and that all he wanted was a place under the covers. Cam and I laughed and teased her about it at the breakfast table in the morning. If she didn't outright deny it, she'd simply shrug and we'd collapse into giggles. She looked embarrassed, but she never said anything else on the matter and neither did my dad, stoic with his coffee and newspaper.

As I grew up, however, these near-nightly occurrences set my teeth on edge. Her screams raised the possibility that she had been hurt in ways I'd prefer not to have to think about. Why else did it take her so long to realize that she was safe— that the silhouette of the man standing above her was always my father's? What had happened to her, and when? Who was involved? Was the reason she screamed at night the same reason she mothered the way that she did—or could it explain some of her behavior? Was she embarrassed to be so affected by things that happened so long ago? Was she ashamed that we all knew exactly what her fear sounded like?

My mother squinted in the light of the bathroom and moved a few steps closer to me. "What is it?" she asked. "What's wrong?"

All I could manage was "I feel terrible."

"You're not going to throw up," she said. "I can tell."

Within a few seconds of my mom making that statement, I turned to the toilet and began retching. My belly, hardened with four days' worth of food, couldn't tolerate anything more. I was so constipated that there was nowhere else for the food to go but right back out my mouth.

When I was done, neither of us said anything, silent in the awkwardness and embarrassment that I'd done what she said I wouldn't. I felt like I'd let her down. As a kid, I'd rely on my mother to tell me that I was not hungry, not scared, not embarrassed. Most of the time I would believe her.

I made to stand up and felt a wave of dizziness. "Can you help me not to fall?" I asked.

My mother stepped closer to where I was sitting on the ground and reached her arms out. The medicine was making me feel fuzzy; I couldn't keep track of my limbs, my position, my balance.

"Lean on me," she said. "I'm like a freaking oak tree these days. Did you notice I gained ten pounds since the last time you saw me?"

I motioned for her to come closer. She handed me the crutches and, after a few seconds, nodded at me reassuringly. "You're strong," she said. "You can do this. I saw the muscles in your back yesterday when you were crutching down those stairs at your apartment." I felt a swell of pride as I imagined her admiring my back muscles from behind, waiting for the right moment to say something. But what else had she been noticing about my body that I would hear about later?

I hoisted myself up from the toilet and pushed my way through the doorframe. Mom led the way back to my bed, and once I was settled again she lay down in the other bed beside my sleeping sister.

The red digits on the hotel clock displayed the time: it was just past two in the morning. After a few minutes, I was surprised to hear my mother's voice again.

"There isn't a lot of fast food here," she said.

"What?"

"Here, in St. Louis. There's not a lot of fast food. It's something I noticed driving from the hotel to your apartment to the hotel."

I wasn't sure what to make of this statement. Was my

mother just complaining? Or was she talking because she didn't want me to feel alone as I tried to fall asleep?

"Yeah, maybe," I said. There was so much of St. Louis she hadn't seen—areas nearby that were riddled with fast-food chains, but I didn't want to contradict her.

"Where do you get your Diet Cokes?" There was something almost vulnerable in her voice, like it was something she'd been embarrassed that she needed to ask.

"At the grocery store," I said. "I get cans."

She considered that for a moment, long enough that I thought she might have fallen asleep.

"It's hard, isn't it?" she asked after a while.

"What's hard?"

"Moving somewhere without knowing anybody. But you seem to have built an interesting community here. And they seem to all care about you—both the academic, strait-laced types and the rough roller derby girls."

I understood this to be a genuine olive branch my mother was extending: a way to connect our experiences of living far from home with very little support. Part of me yearned to tell her everything—that it had been hard, how lonely I'd felt at first, and how proud I was of my life and friends. But I also felt wary and afraid. Gestures of kindness and normalcy from her had long felt suspicious to me. Believing in her momentary generosity—letting my guard down—made the inevitable barbs or judgments hurt even worse. As tempting as it was to walk through the door she was trying to open for me, I couldn't shake the sense of danger. I had only just started the process of rebuilding my sense of self outside of her image, and it felt incredibly fragile. Or would this time be different? Was this the start of a newer, kinder dynamic between the two of us?

My protective shell won out: I said nothing.

Another few minutes ticked by on the hotel clock. "What was that one woman's name again?" my mother asked, eventually. "That woman was clearly really smart. She knew a lot about health insurance."

"Taryn," I said. "Yes, she is smart. And she's been a very good friend to me."

I felt myself wanting to pivot away from talking about Taryn lest my mother compare us again, or comment on her weight or unusual appearance. That was just something my mom did: pick people apart behind their backs. While I was growing up, whenever my dad's sister came to visit, everything seemed fine until she left, at which point my mother would run through a seemingly unending list of her supposedly unfortunate physical attributes or personality characteristics. I'd heard her do the same thing with me after I went to bed, when she stayed up in the living room talking to my father. She'd break down everything I was wearing, everything I had eaten, everything I had said, and judge me ruthlessly. That was what my shell protected me from. That was what made me so nervous, even in situations like this where the olive branch dangled between us, neither of us fully grabbing hold.

"I'm glad," my mom said. The comment was so delayed I didn't even remember what she was glad about. In the quiet that followed, we both fell asleep.

THE NEXT DAY, we didn't leave the hotel. I wasn't well enough. I spent the morning with my head in the toilet bowl, unable to keep anything down. It had been five days since I'd fallen and since I'd had a bowel movement, and over the course of the day the pain in my belly got so bad it was worse than the pain in my leg.

All morning, I sat slumped in the bathroom, listening to the whine of the hotel door as Cam and my mom went to the hotel's buffet and to the hotel gym. I imagined what was happening on screen as the drone of the TV kept me company.

Sometime in the afternoon I transitioned to bed, picking up the magnesium citrate from my nightstand and downing as much as I could swallow. It was disgusting, warm, syrupy, and with an aftertaste that turned my stomach. From where I was lying, I could hear the ding of the elevator, which hurt my head. Several times I was woken up by my mother, with a little cup of water and a handful of pills; I had no idea what I was taking anymore. The nausea by itself would have been debilitating; coupled with the stomach cramping, it was unbearable. Every time I tried to shift myself into a less painful position, my leg protested. It ached all the time, but the upright position that stopped my head from spinning made it hurt more.

Kelly came to the hotel straight from work. When my sister let her in, I was in bed but only half asleep. My mind was foggy, and my thoughts slipped by too loosely to grab hold. I was dehydrated, loopy, exhausted, and felt like a disgusting child. I desperately wanted to be home, in my own bed, away from my mother's heavy presence. It didn't occur to me that I had any choice in the matter.

"Is this what you gave her for dinner?" I heard Kelly say. I poked my head out from under the covers and saw that she was pointing at the paper plate of breaded chicken and fettuccini alfredo sitting under the hotel lamp. I vaguely remembered pushing the food around on the plate and trying hard to take in a few bites, feeling like a little kid at my child-hood home's dinner table. My body had simply refused.

"She needed to eat something," my mother replied. "It was free!"

"It doesn't matter if it was free," Kelly said. She sounded angry. "You don't give a severely constipated person breaded chicken and fettuccini alfredo."

Her face tight, Kelly started tearing around the room, pushing aside dirty clothes and garbage.

"Where's the magnesium citrate?" she asked.

"Excuse me?" my mother said.

"Magnesium citrate. The doctors told her she needed to drink it." My mother and sister exchanged a glance, shrugged their shoulders. Kelly redirected her annoyance toward me, demanding, "Well?"

My head was cloudy; I didn't remember seeing the bottle since we were back at our apartment. "I don't know," I sputtered.

"Oh, Jesus," my mom said. "She already drank half of it! Clearly it didn't work or she wouldn't still be this sick. Be-sides," she added defensively, "Cam got her some other med-icine at the drugstore on the way here. She's been taking that."

Kelly picked up the box of pills my mom had gestured to.

"Oh, God," Kelly said. "This is a stimulant laxative. Do you know what that means?" My mother and sister were both silent. "It *means,*" Kelly continued, "that it works by stimulating her intestinal muscles. You shouldn't have given her this kind. It's what's causing all the contracting and pain."

My mom looked appalled. "There are different kinds of laxatives?" my mother asked. She sounded confused—and there was something else there, too. Her cheeks reddened slightly, and I realized with some surprise that she was embarrassed. Even through my opioid-induced fog, my heart swelled with the knowledge that she had tried to help me, that she had wanted to get this right.

Kelly turned to me. "You're all a bunch of classic noncompliers," she said, a harshness in her voice I had never heard before. This was the angriest I had ever seen her, and it scared me. Was she mad at me, or the situation and how powerless she felt in it? "We had specific orders. Doctor's orders. You were supposed to drink that stuff yesterday. Why didn't you finish it? You might need an enema. And you *definitely* need to go back to the hospital."

She stared at me as though she expected an answer, but I could barely track the conversation. Had there been a question? As the silence grew, anxiety and fear pushed at the edges of my consciousness. Even in my hazy state, I could sense the stakes of what was being said. It was like some kind of test: who would I choose—my mother or Kelly?

After a long pause, I said, "I just want to go to sleep."

That's when Kelly left. She didn't slam the door, but she didn't exactly stop it from slamming, either. I like to think that if I had been able to, I would've run after her, but the truth is, the difficulty I was having separating myself from my mother was far stronger than my allegiance to Kelly. When we had been hundreds of miles apart, it had been easy to feel as if my relationship with my mom was evolving. I thought my fear of her was shrinking, that placating her was becoming less important to me. But the truth was, our geographic separation was just one piece of an elaborate machine designed to give the mere illusion that I was moving forward. My fear of my mother was like the belt on the treadmill she used to work out when I was growing up; whenever I pushed the fear away, it circled back around. In her presence, I was a kid again.

Once Kelly was gone, my mom came over and sat down on my bed. She was so close she could've reached out and held my hand if she wanted.

She pointed to my leg and said, almost tenderly, "Oh, honey. You really butchered that shaving job, didn't you?" When I didn't answer, she scooted a little closer. "Why do you let her bully you like that?" she asked. "You're not like her. You're not one of those people who go running to the doctor every time they break a nail."

She paused, and with the next breath she took, I knew what she was going to say, and felt a thrilling, almost sickening split second of dread. My greatest fear and worst suspicion.

"You're still one of us."

TEST OF TOUGHNESS

The next morning, my nausea was so unbearable even my mother could no longer pretend I didn't need medical care. The day before, Kelly had supplied her with the contact information for all my doctors. "Where the hell is that note?" my mother asked, rooting around in her purse. I retreated to the bathroom; a few minutes later, I could just make out my mother's telephone voice over the splatter of my vomit hitting the toilet water.

"Yes, hi," she said. "My daughter is a patient. She was operated on last Monday. Two fractures. Metal rod. She's experiencing several complications."

There was a pause, and then, "No, no, it's not that." Then, louder: "Did you not hear me? I said it's not that." She ended the call shortly after and immediately started dialing the next number. I could hear the voice on the other end enough to piece together what was happening: the answer she received was one she refused to accept. I needed to be taken to the emergency room. There was nothing wrong with my bones, she was told, or the metal inside them. This was clearly a digestive issue; an orthopedist would be no help.

My mom ended the call again and immediately dialed the third number in the list Kelly had provided: my university's health center. I listened as she explained the situation the same way she had to the surgeon's office. Then she said, "I don't care if you don't have the medical equipment to deal with an obstructed bowel! It's not that!"

The receptionist at my school's health clinic had aligned with the orthopedist and insisted I needed to be taken to the ER. My mother requested to speak to another staff member right as I started dry heaving, and I heard nothing of their conversation. After a few minutes, she burst into the bathroom to tell me she had secured an appointment on campus in an hour.

"Why don't we just go to the emergency room?" I asked the toilet bowl.

"I'm trying to save you from that," she said. "Unless, for some reason, you deeply desire to continue puking in an overcrowded cesspool and wait for three hours for someone to stick an enema up your ass. If that doesn't sound appealing to you, be ready to go to the school clinic in an hour."

On the ride to campus, I sat in the backseat of my own car the way I had when Slob drove me to the hospital. My mother's phone rang. She looked at the screen and cast it aside as if she had touched something disgusting.

"It's her," she told Cam. "You answer it."

"No way. I don't want to answer it," Cam said.

I leaned forward in my seat and saw the caller ID: it was Kelly. She probably wanted to check in on me, see what we had decided, offer to meet us at the clinic. The call went to voicemail. It immediately started ringing again.

My mom continued speaking as if I wasn't there. "I'm not talking to her," she said. "I refuse." I said nothing.

After three tries, Kelly stopped calling. From the safety of the back seat, where my mom and sister couldn't see what I was doing, I sent her a text. "I'm okay. Going to campus clinic. Talk soon." I hoped she wouldn't be too angry that we weren't going to the ER.

When we got to campus, Cam unloaded my wheelchair and helped me slide into it. She pushed while my mother walked beside me, surveying the dormitories and cafeteria and offices through her circular sunglasses. "What do I always tell you girls?" she asked.

Cam answered: "School is the worst place on Earth."

"That's right," my mom said, nodding her head in approval. "There's nothing more painful than being forced to sit in a classroom."

A thin blond student was exiting the clinic as we were entering. She held the door open for us.

"Thank you!" my mom said. Then, pointing to me in the wheelchair, she said to the woman, "See—it could be worse!"

The woman didn't appear to know what to make of my mother's comment. When she was out of earshot I rounded on my mother.

"Why would you say that?" I asked.

"What's wrong with what I said?" she countered. "I was just being friendly."

"You don't know what she's here for. Maybe a broken leg isn't worse than whatever she's going through. Maybe she just found out she has a tumor in her boob."

My mother scoffed. "No way. She's here for birth control."

Inside, the clinic was nearly empty. The three of us were quickly brought back into an examination room where the nurses asked permission to start filtering two full bags of water into my body. I was so dehydrated that my veins kept rolling away from the needle. It took three nurses and five attempts to successfully puncture one in my left hand.

"I'm sorry that took so long," the nurse who finally managed it said.

"It doesn't bother me," I lied.

When the doctor came in, she hiked up my shirt and pressed down on my abdomen. She did her best to avoid touching the hematomas, but the pressure still caused me to writhe in pain.

"Percocet and oxycodone put your guts to sleep," she explained, "and the side effects are sometimes worse than the injury itself. Unfortunately, there's nothing we can really do. The best solution is to stop taking the drugs if you think you can handle the pain."

"Don't you think it's too early for that?" I asked. I hoped the question communicated what I couldn't say in front of my mother: that I wasn't sure at all I'd be able to handle the pain. I still vividly remembered being forced to recover from my foot operations without opioids. For weeks, I had been in agony. I felt weaker now than I had at eleven.

"Well, you can still take ibuprofen," the doctor said. "And Tylenol. Remind me how long has it been since the surgery?" I started to answer but my mother beat me to it.

"Long enough," she said. "Problem solved. This kid has a high pain tolerance, so she'll be just fine."

She didn't say it, but I got the feeling that taking me off the painkillers was a solution my mother was happy about. I was used to reading what was under the surface of my mother's statements. I'd learned from my father that reading her was crucial to pleasing her, and pleasing her was how I would get through a day without being berated or judged. Given that, I heard the subtext this way: here was an opportunity to show my toughness to her and the world.

When I was a kid and things were hard, my mother would remind me that we had moved from Denver to Anchorage when I was six months old just for the adventure. She'd continue, "I was able to drive through the Yukon in a blizzard with a baby in the back seat—we made it through all those Alaskan winters—so we can make it through this." It was one of the parables she often gave me about how to live a life. *Toughen up*, it seemed to say. *It builds character. Look what I did. You can do it too.*

Mom always spun her Alaskan adventure as a hero's journey, but I am still not sure what it had really been about for her and my dad. What were they seeking? Who was the journey for? Was she trying to escape something? To prove her own toughness? To finally leave all their comforts in the contiguous United States and have an adventure? How did it feel returning, then, when my dad could no longer survive the relentless darkness and harsh nine-month winters? Was my mom secretly relieved?

It took five hours for the bags of water to drain into my body. My mother and Cam left to go find lunch a few minutes after the process began. One of the nurses draped a blanket over me and turned off the lights. Finally alone, I burst into tears. My sobbing sucked up so much of my air that I had to gasp in between heaves. It was an angry sob, but my rage was directed at myself. I hurled questions at myself that I couldn't answer: *Why aren't you strong enough to say that you don't want to go off the painkillers? Why did you let her convince you to go to a school clinic rather than the ER? Why can't you ever say what you're thinking or what you want? Why does she have to be the one doling out the medicine? It's not her body; why does she get to barge in and make all the medical decisions? What is it that you think she can do to you now?*

The nurses didn't hear me. Or if they did, they didn't intervene. I cried until the cheap paper lining beneath me was soaked through like a dark halo around my head that tore a little every time I gasped for air.

I KNEW I had less than a day before the narcotics would be cleared from my system and I'd be forced to face the pain. The water that had been pumped into my body had eased a headache I didn't even know I had and the anti-nausea drugs helped me sleep, When I woke up the next morning, I knew I wouldn't be feeling very well for much longer.

During this short window of relief, I asked my mother to go on a drive with me. Kelly had been the one who'd given me the idea. Her parents loved visiting St. Louis. We drove them to Soulard Farmer's Market and to the Fox Theater, where Kelly ushered on Saturday nights. They liked trying new restaurants and eating at the ones we frequented. It was fun to experience our city secondhand with Kelly's parents. I knew it would be a mistake to show my mother our most sacred places—the Peacock Diner where I always ordered a big stack of chocolate chip pancakes, or the dog park where everyone knew our names. I had learned from experience that my mom felt left out and threatened when I enjoyed things that didn't involve her. But I wondered if there might be some sort of compromise—a way to show her some things in St. Louis that were less emotionally loaded, but that would make me feel like she knew something about the city where I lived beyond our hotel room.

"So what do you think?" I asked nervously. "I want you to see where I live now."

My mom picked up the hotel remote and clicked the television on. "I just don't really care about your life here," she said, laughing. "Sorry, but it's true."

My heart sank. I didn't think she would ever put it in terms as blunt as those. Why did she have to devalue everything I'd worked so hard for? And why did I feel surprised?

Still, I felt desperate to show her something in my new city that she might approve of. Her approval was how I'd learned to value . . . everything. I wanted to redeem this moment for both of us. "What about just going to a thrift shop?" I suggested, trying to sound casual. "I know a good one not too far from here." We'd gone thrifting a lot together in my hometown. She always liked going anywhere she might stumble upon a bargain.

"Okay," my mom said. "There's nothing good on right now anyway." My heart leapt. Maybe we could even have a little fun together.

On the drive over, we didn't talk much, only enough for me to guide my mother through the city streets. I was bringing her to a spot I frequented often, so often that I could visualize the aisles and knew my wheelchair would fit between the racks before we even arrived.

But as soon as she wheeled me into the store, I felt a sense of panic and dread. The store was edgy, packed with the kind of clothes people wore to music festivals and raves. There were metallic leggings, ripped purple jeans, and six-inch plastic heels exclusively in enormous sizes. We passed an entire rack of booty shorts, similar to the sparkly ones Taryn had worn in our last bout. None of the baseball caps were sports-related; instead, they said things like WHERE'S MOLLY? and QUEER. Even the earrings—my mother's second-favorite accessory, after rings—were all wrong. A large portion of them were clip-on, and the others were far too gaudy and campy for her taste.

How had it not occurred to me that my mother would feel grossly out of place in this store? How had I overlooked the fact that this store embodied my style—my new style—in my new home, and that my mother was likely to see it as a threat, a confirmation of my new separateness?

Instead of saying anything disparaging, though, my mom pushed her way through the group of teenagers trying on round sunglasses and went right for the skirts. Every so often she'd call out to me, lifting a skirt to ask if I liked it. She never used to second-guess herself, was always confident that she'd know the clothes I'd like, but things were different now. There were parts of me she didn't know, and that unsettled both of us. It was a subject neither of us broached, this separation. We took it in stride, ignoring it when it came up and refusing to really look at it head-on.

I watched her from across the store. She gently touched a Davy Crockett raccoon hat and wiped her fingers on her pants. Then, she turned back to the skirts. I could tell she was trying. Just lasting as long as she had was an anomaly, and that unnerved me. Ordinarily I would've expected her to wheel me right back out—she was clearly not comfortable here—so the fact that she was defying her usual approach made me apprehensive. The rules suddenly became slippery. It made me doubt my view of her, what she wanted from me, and not knowing what she wanted was the most dangerous position to be in. It meant risking the loss of her approval, and when she disapproved, anything could happen.

We left the store with four skirts that she'd paid for. I knew I would never wear them, but that wasn't why I wanted them. To me, they were tangible proof that she loved me. I had a sudden image of the list I'd made of her rare kindnesses, and found myself mentally adding to it: Flew to St. Louis to care for me. Came when I called her name in the bathroom. Made phone calls when I needed help with my nausea. Drove me to the university health clinic. Came to the thrift shop. Bought me four skirts. I felt suddenly overwhelmed with grief instead of the usual comfort this list brought me. There were so many pieces of evidence, even in her short visit, of her love for me. So why did I still feel so alone? Was there just too much damage? Was I too unforgiving? Couldn't I let go of the past and meet her in this moment with only openness and love? But even as I thought this, another list formed, unbidden, in my mind: Her fury when I came out. All the times she commented on my body. Invasion of my privacy. Or—being raised never knowing I had the right to privacy. Mandatory exercise with no choice to opt out. The fact that her approval hinged on whether I won or lost. All the conversations I overheard between her and my dad after they thought I was asleep: "She thinks she's the center of the goddamn universe. She's the most ungrateful child in the world." Any separateness viewed as betrayal. Constant monitoring, even after I left home for college. Reading my Facebook messages. Yes, she had my passwords. To change them was unthinkable: proof I didn't love her— that I didn't want to be close to her.

"This city has really changed," she said when we were back on the sidewalk, making our way to the car we'd parked several blocks away. "I remember visiting as a kid when my dad played baseball here. St. Louis was such a dump. Everything was run-down. It was scary to be outside."

It hadn't occurred to me that my mother had been to St. Louis before. I vaguely knew that my grandfather had once played baseball at a fairly high level, but my mom's answers to my questions about it were always cryptic. I never found out if he made it to the majors; the only photograph I had ever seen from when he was young was a black-and-white full-body shot of him in a pin-striped baseball uniform, the word CARDINALS scrawled on the chest.

It was a rare moment of personal sharing, and I wanted to seize the opportunity to ask follow-up questions, but every time I opened my mouth, my voice failed me. I worried I would push her too far, worried that my questions would further separate my experience of the city from hers.

Finally, all I said was "I love it here."

A couple blocks later, my mom rolled me up next to a bench. She sat down, turned sideways so that her pale legs could be fully outstretched, and hiked her track pants up to the knee.

"Do you remember after your foot surgeries how I brought you home and told you the sun would heal you?" she suddenly asked. "This is kind of like that, isn't it?"

"Yes," I said, feeling a spark of connection with my mother. "Kind of." I still thought about that day often. My dad gently depositing me on the bottom bunk. Crawling to the back door. My mother offering me a grape.

I had sat down on the porch beside her, still dizzy from the lingering anesthesia. Sitting upright caused my fresh incisions to pulse painfully, but I didn't dare move away from my mother. I was sitting so close I could feel her warmth, which almost felt like being touched. It was such a rarity: being close to my mother, being touched by her.

Almost twelve years later, once again we were sitting together in the sun. After everything we'd been through, apparently her love was still all I craved.

"You know, I still believe that," Mom continued. "The sun is so powerful."

"Mom, why didn't you get me a wheelchair after my surgeries back then?" I blurted out. "Do you remember how you pulled me everywhere in that red wagon?"

I'm not sure why I asked the question in that moment. What did I think would happen? I wasn't trying to interrogate my mother, though I realize now how accusatory my questions must have sounded. I wasn't trying to blame her. I wasn't trying to shatter the moment. I felt emboldened to ask a question I never would have asked before, and I think it stemmed from the feeling of intimacy that started when she shared about her father, and carried on, our bodies so close together.

"I remember the wagon," my mom said, then paused. I waited, hoping she had more to say. I wanted to hear, in her own words, why I hadn't been given a wheelchair. Would she cite the expense? Claim the chair had been unnecessary? Explain that I was too good for a wheelchair—that a wheelchair was for weak kids without resourceful parents? I was suddenly desperate for an answer, to hear her try to justify this memory that haunted me. I felt somehow that something about the wagon would explain everything to me, as if all my years of confusion and hurt and distrust hung in the balance on this random bench on a random city block in St. Louis.

Finally, she spoke again. "Nobody told me to get you a wheelchair."

"But didn't you think that since I was having operations on both feet—" I started without thinking, encouraged by her confession.

"No," my mother snapped. "No, I didn't. I didn't know what to do. Nobody told me."

She stood up, legs of the track pants falling back down to her ankles, and started pushing me again. I knew without even being able to see her face that I had crossed a line by implying she had made a mistake, but I didn't know how to fix the situation. It was so rare that my mother revealed any kind of weakness. She usually avoided such humiliations by refusing to recant opinions or offer apologies. To admit that she had not known what to do—that she might have needed help or advice—was something I had never heard her do before.

Her honesty seemed to have broken the intimacy between us, rather than increase it. She pushed my wheelchair with a new force now, and my body jerked painfully up and down as we sped along the uneven sidewalk. I felt suddenly, horribly afraid, but all I could think to do was talk. "Over there's a really good frozen yogurt shop," I said, trying to sound calm. "And that store has cute little touristy knick-knacks."

I didn't look back at her, but my mother didn't slow down, and I doubted she was looking at the places I was pointing out. It wasn't even clear where she was taking me: we were heading farther and farther away from the car.

"You're going to have to learn how to push this thing yourself," she said, finally.

"Why?" I asked.

"Because you're not always going to have somebody pushing it for you. You should start practicing now."

I couldn't tell what she was really saying. Was she literally reminding me that her visit was almost over? Or was she speaking in metaphor, saying, *You're not always going to have me?*

She stopped the chair and walked around to face me. The bag of skirts in my lap threatened to topple over, and movement—even in my arms—jostled the broken bones in my leg. Still, I took the wheels and began to push myself down the street. I pretended it didn't hurt, and that it wasn't exhausting, until I could no longer hide how difficult it was to catch my breath.

"Can you take over again?" I asked.

She sighed as if I were confirming her worst suspicions, but she came around behind me and started pushing again, back in the direction of the car. I caught my breath as she walked, feeling myself start to calm down. *Maybe this means she's forgiven me for my questions earlier,* I thought. *Maybe we're okay.*

After a few minutes, we approached a busy crossing. A few people were gathered, waiting for the light to turn. I fingered the thrift shop bag, thinking of the skirts she'd bought me. Maybe I'd wear one tomorrow as a form of apology, as a way to show her we were still connected, that it was still important to me to please her.

"I could let go right now and you'd roll right into traffic and probably get killed," Mom said matter-of-factly.

"I'd be able to grab the wheels," I said, annoyed. "I wouldn't get kill—"

Before I could finish my sentence, Mom had let go of the wheelchair. I frantically tried to extricate my hands from underneath the bag of skirts in my lap, but I was rolling toward traffic—the light still hadn't changed. Cars were zipping in front of me, several feet away. I can't imagine they were going faster than thirty miles per hour, but I might as well have been heading toward a freeway. I felt a swooping, sickening thrill in my stomach, like the vertigo I'd feel looking over the edge of a steep drop, while I tried in vain to grope for the wheels.

And then, suddenly, I stopped. I was being pulled back, and I knew it was my mother who had grabbed my chair because I could hear her laughing right behind my head. It must have been only a couple of seconds total that I'd been rolling unchecked—less than a foot of distance traveled—but my heart was pounding in my ears and I felt tears threatening to burst. My mother was laughing harder than I'd heard her laugh in a long time.

"See?" she said, finally. "I knew you couldn't save your-self."

21/
DEPARTURES

Later that afternoon, the opioids left my system and the pain, the real pain, set in. Each hour—each minute—felt like torture. The only relief I had was finally having a bowel movement. I didn't leave the hotel again until the following morning, when it was time to drop off my mom and sister at the airport. Kelly picked us up from the hotel and I sat in the passenger seat. Staring back at my mother in the rearview mirror was a strange reversal of my childhood memories of watching her dark eyes track me in the back seat. Cam was looking out the window, but my mom stared ahead, unseeing. She looked like a soldier, rigid and proud. When we pulled up to the terminal my mother got out of the car, opened my door, and bent down to hug me—the first time, I realized suddenly, she had touched me on the trip. I could smell her shampoo and the hotel soap on her skin. Her body felt solid and immoveable: someone I would have a hard time knocking over on the roller derby track. I hugged her back, trying to think of something to say, the right thing to say, the thing that would make it so everything would be okay. She stepped away before I could figure it out and Cam stepped in to hug me goodbye. There was enough space for another person between our bodies. She patted me quickly on the back with her fingertips, then picked up her bags.

"You're strong," my mom told me. It sounded like a threat. After a brief nod to Kelly, she slammed the door shut and turned around. As Kelly pulled away, I turned to see if they'd look back, but they were already gone.

ON THE RIDE home, my body felt like it was unfurling. I didn't realize all the tension I'd been holding in my back and legs. A headache pulsed at my temples. Kelly reached over and patted my leg, but I leaned away. Even the slight pressure seemed to radiate down my leg to my injury, but it wasn't the physical pain I was recoiling from—it was Kelly's soft acknowledgment that I needed comfort. She wasn't wrong, but I didn't want it. Watching my mother and sister go seemed like a reminder of everything our relationship lacked: easy communication, unconditional love, even basic trust. Once they began walking away, the first feeling I had was relief. There was a part of me that knew that was reasonable, but there was another part of me that hated myself for feeling that way—like it was a betrayal, or an indictment. I didn't feel I deserved Kelly's comfort. I felt heartbroken, angry, guilty, and filled with grief. The constant tension between what I felt and what I wanted to feel made me exhausted, too tired to scream or cry or talk.

After we returned home, we spent the rest of the day until dinner working hard to find some semblance of a routine. Our landlord had managed to fix the hot water in our apartment. Kelly restocked our refrigerator. I restored the AC and dug out all our framed pictures from their hiding places. Even when there was nothing else to repair or return to normal, an unsettledness still hung in our apartment. It lingered between us, hovering around us no matter which room we occupied. We spoke only about what was happening in the moment, which was fine by me. I was dreading the moment when I would have to talk about the visit. I was still holding out hope that it would never come up.

That evening, I crutched into the kitchen and started to make protein pancakes from the mix my mother had brought. I was exhausted and in pain, but making these pancakes for dinner felt like the most important and urgent thing in the world. They were proof of the reality that my mother had been here, that she'd wanted to do something nice for me. If I made them, I'd be honoring her gift. I'd be doing something nice for Kelly, who'd done so much for me. These pancakes would be the fragile bridge between the past few days and my future with Kelly. As I measured out the mix, I felt a renewed sense of calm and purpose.

As I took out the frying pan and poured water into the bowl of pancake mix, Kelly came in. She seemed to be moving slower than usual too. She opened the refrigerator and peered inside for a long while, without taking anything out. The tension mounted; the silence between us seemed to grow louder against the backdrop of the refrigerator's hum. I found myself trying to stir the mixture as quietly as possible, as if the clink of spoon against bowl would break some spell I was depending on for my own survival. I couldn't tear my eyes from the bowl, and Kelly continued to stand there, unmoving.

Finally, Kelly spoke. "Was she screening my calls?"

I knew that she was talking about my mother. "Yes," I said, simply.

"I knew it," she whispered. Then, "I just have to say—I really got a chance to see how she treated you on this trip and I hated it."

"What do you mean?" I asked. I knew, of course, what she was talking about, but it felt like something of a revelation that someone on the outside had witnessed our dynamic and had feelings about it. I readied myself to cling to every word.

"I mean, she got so upset with you for things you couldn't control—your pain, your nausea. The whole time I was thinking about my mom. You've met her—she's not a touchy-feely person. But she did everything for us when we were sick. I have this memory from a time when I couldn't keep anything down; she fed me little sips of water that I would then spit back into the cup she was holding. It was just pure unconditional love, and that was so glaringly absent with your mom." Kelly shut the refrigerator and sat down at the counter.

"Did it make you mad?" I asked, lighting the stove. I was trying hard to see the situation from Kelly's point of view, but everything I felt was so confusing and contradictory. Part of me felt protective of my mother; another part of me felt glad that Kelly was pointing out her flaws in such a direct way. It was such a relief that someone else could see so clearly what was happening, which is something I always prayed for in my adolescence.

"It made me furious," she said. "You saw me. I've never gotten into a fight with an adult like I did with your mom. I was taught to have respect for my elders. But I was just so angry. You didn't see this, but they laughed at me for having a schedule for your medicine planned out. They acted just like mean girls in middle school. You know I was bullied relentlessly. I can't just turn off the memory of that."

I cringed, imagining the vulnerabilities my mom and sister had ignited in Kelly. It honestly hadn't occurred to me that she might have been struggling just as much as I was during their visit.

"You're like a different person around her," Kelly continued. "You hide so much of who you are, and it's like you pretend you never left home. You act like a little kid."

Her statement felt like a punch to the gut, even though I knew it was true. I poured the pancake mix into three fist-sized circles on the frying pan, trying to calm down. The urgency I'd felt to make them just minutes ago now seemed silly and childish. Pancakes weren't a bridge between me and Kelly. They weren't the link between the kid who desperately wanted her mother's approval and the adult who had a full, independent life with her partner. They were just pancakes.

I turned around and looked at Kelly's earnest, concerned face. "I'm sorry I chose her," I said.

"What?" Kelly asked, pushing the hair out of her face to look at me.

"That day in the hotel. When you left. I should've gone with you."

Kelly didn't say anything for a long time. She stared at her hands, which were in her lap. When she finally responded, her tone was softer. "I get it. You're terrified. She terrifies you."

I was quiet. Was *terror* really the right word? It sounded so dramatic. But it also sounded true.

Kelly put her hands over mine and gave them a light squeeze. "I want to ask you something," she said. "When do you feel the *least* terrified?"

I felt surprised. Not by the level of insight in Kelly's question—her thoughtfulness was one of the things I loved most about her—but by the idea of *not* being terrified. In the wake of my mother's visit, the feeling of constant fear had not quite left my body. I paused for a moment, reminding myself I was safe, here with Kelly and Lady, in the home we'd made together.

I watched the pancakes cook on the pan, little bubbles rising to the surface of the batter as I thought about Kelly's question. As I scooped them onto two plates and turned off the stove, I said, "When I'm skating. It's when I feel the most powerful. How fucked is that?" I gestured to my broken leg.

"I don't think it's fucked," Kelly said. "I can see it. And it makes perfect sense. I think you just need to find a way to be Joan of Spark off the track."

I knew what Kelly meant. What else, in addition to not being terrified, would Joan of Spark bring to my life if I let her? Joy, certainly. A type of fearlessness. A willingness to look at the past, really look at it, and allow herself to grow, even if that meant growing away.

But what would I lose? Would this shift my relationships with my family? Who would I be, without my mother's voice telling me exactly who I was? Besides, as toxic as it was, there was comfort in our system, our established family dynamic. I wasn't sure I knew who to be without it—wasn't sure I could locate myself outside of it. What I knew for sure was that in her presence I couldn't risk being myself.

"Let's just eat," I said.

We sat down at the counter. The sun was setting and its glow reflected off my Frida Kahlo prayer candle and the succulent my mom said I would kill. We bit into the pancakes at the same time, and I nearly gagged.

"Are they supposed to taste like this?" Kelly asked, grimacing.

"I don't see how I could have messed them up," I said. "All I did was add water."

I spit my bite into a napkin and grabbed the cardboard box to verify I had followed all the instructions. There didn't appear to be anything I had missed.

Kelly swallowed audibly and took another bite.

"You don't have to keep eating," I said. I felt I was either on the verge of laughter or tears.

"It's not so bad if you don't think about it," Kelly said. She took a swig of water and smacked her lips together. "It's like a food-eating challenge on *Survivor*."

I grabbed her plate out from under her, stacked it on mine, and crutched my way over to empty them into the trash can. Then I was crying and laughing at once. Lady stared up at me from the floor in confusion; she didn't know whether to lick my face or fetch a squeak toy from the other room for us to play with. Kelly didn't know what to do either. After a minute, she got up from her chair and embraced me. We both sank to the floor—I let my crutches fall to the sides—and she held me there for a long time. Softly, she tucked my hair behind my ear and brought her face close, like whatever she was about to tell me was a secret.

"We should go out for food," she whispered. I laughed and wiped the tears off my cheeks. "My treat," she said.

22/
SPLITTING

I barely made it through dinner at the restaurant, the pain in my leg was so bad. The longer it lasted, the more panicked I felt. I imagined the pain approaching the island of my body like an invasive fleet of ships. The weapons I had to defend myself were terribly insufficient: ibuprofen, ice, elevation. I tried guided meditations for pain management. They instructed me to count my heartbeats and control my breathing, but that all felt like a kind of surrender. In the metaphor I had constructed of the pain, I thought I should be springing into action—taking risks, on the off-chance something worked, not counting my breaths and watching the enemy take my body prisoner.

The previous day, in a moment away from my mother and sister, I had contacted a woman from LA who specialized in long-distance Reiki. An undergrad writing professor I kept in touch with had recommended it and paid for my session; I agreed because it seemed like something Joan of Spark would do (and something my mother wouldn't). The pain was already triggering spells of dissociation. I couldn't come up with language to match my experience—I could only repeat the words *seizing* and *splitting* and *gnawing* in my mind like a refrain. I felt like I was falling down a tunnel with ridged walls, like a throat, scraping my fingernails down the edges on my descent. What unnerved me the most, however, was that the left side of my leg still felt numb. I could feel everything on the inside, yet when I ran a finger down the side of my leg: nothing.

An hour before my appointment, I retreated to the bedroom. While Kelly watched reruns of *RuPaul's Drag Race*, I scrolled through my phone, looking for anything to distract me from the pain. It was then I saw that Soup Beans had invited me to a secret group on Facebook. It was called Roller Derby Injuries: Blood, Sweat, and Tears (Gimp Crew). There were 2,450 members. As soon as I accepted the invitation, my Facebook feed was saturated with X-ray images, questions about complications during or after surgery, and heartbreaking posts about the financial strain of hospital bills. Five similar injuries had already been documented in the eight days since my accident. One woman had broken both legs at the same time; doctors estimated her recovery would take over a year.

Scrolling through these posts made me feel both unremarkable and lucky: a perfect antidote to the misery and self-pity and anger I felt in the immediate aftermath of my surgery. Everyone in the Gimp Crew was forthright about the ugliest parts of their healing process and emotional state. "Is this infected?" one woman posted, followed by a picture of a gnarly surgical incision oozing pus. Another posted a long rant, every sentence of which started with the word *fuck. Let it all out,* someone commented. *This too shall pass.*

I thought about posting something to ask whether anyone was recovering from surgery without opioids, but that prospect felt too scary. I was nervous about drawing attention to myself, as I usually was, but I also worried someone would ask me why I was forgoing the opioids. I didn't feel like being that open with 2,500 strangers.

When my phone started to ring, I answered it within seconds. The Reiki woman kept her introductions brief. She instructed me to lie on my back for the session, so I positioned my body on our bed. The red curtains hanging in our room filtered the sun's glow, which made me feel like I was on a stage. Sometimes I forgot we'd strung them up only because of our Peeping Tom.

Even on speaker phone, the healer's voice sounded melodic and clear. When she asked if I was ready to start the session, my legs began to tingle. Somewhere in LA, a cymbal chimed. She had only been working for a few minutes when I asked if we could stop.

"It's the sound," I told her. "I can't stop hearing the sound of my bones crunching. I don't know if I can be still and quiet."

The woman said to focus on the cymbals. She told me we could stop at any time. I don't know how long I lay there, listening to her work until she told me the session was over, but it was long enough that my sweat soaked the bedsheets. I stayed in the same position after she hung up, trying to sense any change or improvement, but all I felt was an intense desire not to be alone with my body.

THE NEXT MORNING, the pain felt slightly more manageable. It was a Monday, nine days after the fall. It was also my twenty-third birthday. Before she left for work, Kelly kissed my forehead and promised we would do something special for dinner, but I couldn't help feeling a twinge of sadness that I would be spending the day alone. She had been gone for a total of ten minutes when the doorbell rang. I crutched over to find Taryn smiling at me with a birthday Diet Coke in hand. Never had I been happier for a spontaneous visitor before.

We spent the morning watching footage from a recent tournament the All Stars had played in Oregon. Taryn had made the suggestion somewhat delicately. "If you want—I mean, if you're comfortable, we could watch . . ."

The footage wasn't distraction enough to make me forget about my leg entirely, but it was still comforting to see my friends again. Bricktator looked so joyful—joyful, yet focused—occasionally approaching the refs to inquire about a call, or to ask why she'd only been awarded three points instead of four. The announcers raved about her, complimenting her awareness and the way she bolstered team morale off the track.

As Taryn and I sat side by side, a silent question hung between us. I imagined the way she would ask it. *So, what's next? For you . . . and derby?* I felt unbelievably anxious about how to answer because it was so unclear for me. I didn't know if I wanted to go back to skating, and until we met with the surgeon again in a week, I wouldn't know if I even could. It might be nice, I thought, to talk about this with Taryn—my worries and apprehensions about lacing up my skates again—but she didn't ask, and I felt powerless to bring it up. Where was Joan of Spark now? I felt completely devoid of agency.

Before Taryn left, she brought the mail right to the couch, hugged me, and promised she'd be back soon. A small card with no return address was folded in with the bills and catalogs. There was only one line scrawled in the upper left corner: *From Rock Slobster and Friends.*

The card was decorated with sparkly unicorn stickers. Inside, someone had written SPARK in fancy, bubbly handwriting above the card's message: *It will all be okay.*

There were so many notes inside, so many signatures, I had to remind myself to go slowly and take them all in. More than once, I had to pluck a tissue out of a nearby box to dry my eyes.

Do all your physical therapy homework! Slob had written. Shimmy simply said, *You get to be a robot now!* In tiny, scratchy letters, Lumber Jerk had written, *You had a great local season and it was a pleasure to be your coach.*

As my eyes filled with tears, the messages and names began floating and colliding. *You're taking this like a BOSS. We're here to help. We miss you so much already.* From Dad Bod. Birdsong. JJ. *Stay strong. Heal fast. You're a badass. You're a champ. You'll be back to your sassy self soon.* From Fletch. Piranha. Ace. Ida. Gil. *All our love. We love you. Love you. We LOVE YOU.*

All I could think was *They remember me. They love me. How incredible is that?* I felt warm inside, syrupy sweet, a sensation I hadn't experienced in a long time—pure, unconditional love.

Bricktator's message, squeezed between two unicorn stickers, read, *The scary part is over. Now you'll come back even stronger.*

In the silence of my bedroom, I desperately wanted to believe her, but I didn't fully. I couldn't imagine lacing up my skates without hearing the sound of my body breaking.

. . .

I THOUGHT I would be alone the rest of the day, but my doorbell rang again a few hours before Kelly was scheduled to be home. It was Nanny McWhee. I'd never seen her anywhere besides the rink; it took a few seconds for me to recognize her standing on my porch. She looked so different without her helmet and the "big girl panties" that she fashioned like a bandana around her bald head. In two weeks, Nanny would break her leg during practice too.

After I managed to kick open the door with my good leg, Nanny made her way inside. She was carrying a box of cupcakes and set them on the kitchen counter, then collapsed in our La-Z-Boy. I felt distinctly awkward. I wondered what she saw, looking at my messy house, looking at me in my pajamas, my hair unwashed.

But before I could really start overthinking the situation, Nanny, who wasn't one for small talk, started peppering me with questions, inquiring with a kindness and genuine curiosity that immediately put me at ease. She wanted to know everything that had happened after I was taken away in the back seat of my own car. "We were all so shaken up," she said.

I didn't expect to embark on a monologue about my mother, but the next thing I knew, I had skimmed over the four days I spent in the hospital and instead started detailing what it was like to have her here. I told Nanny how it felt like an invasion to have my mother inside my house, commenting on my body and controlling my medical decisions. I told her about the fight she'd gotten into with Kelly and the way she silenced her phone when Kelly called. I even told her about the way she'd briefly let go of my wheelchair when we were at a busy intersection just to scare me.

Apart from Kelly, I had never spoken to anyone so openly about my mother before; I found I was getting out of breath because I was trying to get through so much pent-up information. In some corner of my brain, it occurred to me that I should be crying, but there was too much else to feel, too much else to experience. I felt guilty for spilling so much personal information; my home was always one that operated on "What happens at home stays at home." We were never allowed to talk about what happened within the family structure. It felt illicit and somewhat exhilarating to be sharing so much with Nanny. I didn't know what I was going for, however. Pity? Empathy? Shock?

"Honey," Nanny said when I'd talked myself out. "That all seems incredibly hard, but you made it. Can you see that? You made it through." She paused, seeming to consider something, then went on. "Can I tell you a little bit about my mother?" she asked. "She was the first Black beauty queen in her state. Dazzlingly beautiful. But she didn't want me to be beautiful. Beat my ass for wearing lipstick. To be fair, we lived on a farm raising horses and there wasn't a whole lot of time to be cute, but it was clear to me that being beautiful was important to her, so it became important to me. She always told me to use my brain, not my body. I was smart, and her perspective on men is that they're only predatory toward pretty women. Being smart was an inoculation against men's exploitation. It was also a way in which I felt I had to earn her love. That's the whole reason I got a PhD. That's why I applied for Fulbright grants and conducted research overseas. None of that came natural to me; I did those things so she would feel proud of me."

"Wow," I said. "I had no idea."

"My entire life unfolded the way it did because my mother's love was conditional. I never even asked myself, *What do you want to do?* All the time I think about where I would be—who I would be—if I hadn't been fighting for my mother's love."

I felt myself flush with recognition. There was so much truth in her words, so much I identified with. Nanny was more than twice my age and she seemed to represent everything I was headed toward.

"Did your mother ever weigh you or comment on your body?" I asked.

"Oh, darling, she was so good at commenting on my body. She'd go around in public and point to my ass in front of strangers. She was also good at telling me what I felt. 'You're not sad, you're embarrassed. You're not nervous, you're excited.' It takes years and years to reverse that kind of damage."

"What did your mother think about you being queer?" I asked. Selfishly, I hoped to hear that Nanny's mother had reacted like mine did. I was identifying with so much of her story already.

"My mother was repulsed by my gayness, told me not to tell anybody, but she also wasn't happy when I married a man. Heaven forbid he was Black. My mother spent all her time trying to convince people she was someone other than who she was. She wanted to be white, mostly. But she also lived with a woman for the first sixteen years of my life. Together they were my parents. But she curled her lip when people called them lesbians. It wasn't a sexual relationship. It could have been romantic, but it wasn't sexual, and because it wasn't sexual, they couldn't understand that it was romantic. They didn't have the language."

"Sometimes I pray that my parents would get divorced," I

confessed. I hadn't been planning on telling her this, but she had already said so much, I felt indebted. "In my head, if they got divorced, that would mean I could get to know my dad better. And my sister . . ." For the first time in the conversation, I felt myself choke up. I wanted the kind of relationship with Cam that I saw so often represented on television: one in which the older sister was fiercely protective and they were both unshakably loyal to each other. I wanted the kind of relationship where I could text without having a reason—a funny GIF, a little quip from my day that reminded me of her. That didn't feel possible with my mom around, looming like a storm over the two of us.

"I wish I could go back and tell myself to do whatever the fuck I wanted to do," Nanny said softly into the silence. "It sure as hell wouldn't have been getting a PhD. That was for my mother. We don't speak anymore. I realized that I cannot stay true to any version of myself with my mother weighing in."

I felt tingles spread up my back. The prospect of cutting off communication with my mother seemed impossibly scary. The idea of hurting her feelings, causing her pain, felt nearly intolerable to me, like the worst possible betrayal, worse than being gay. What would I have to face in the void of her absence? Without her approval—or lack thereof— how would I know I was okay? How would I know what to work toward? I had gone weeks without speaking to her in the past and, rather than freedom, mostly I remembered that it felt a lot like what I imagined withdrawal would be like for someone coming off drugs or alcohol. But that was just it, I realized. I could imagine infinite wreckage in the severing of our relationship, but its continued existence was actively in- credibly damaging to me. Each time, I approached our relationship thinking it might be different. Maybe she would act differently. Maybe I would react differently. Maybe the shreds of love she showed me could sustain me for longer periods of time. In simple terms, I was addicted to the dynamic that bonded us.

For a few minutes, the only sound was the soft creaking of the La-Z-Boy. It was a comfortable silence; every so often I would take a peek at Nanny from the couch where I was sitting. She looked so strong in her athletic apparel and baldness: totally unshakable. *If I'm like her when I'm in my fifties,* I thought, *I'll consider it a huge victory.* She had made the most of a PhD she didn't want by turning it into a professorship at a big university. She was brave and strong enough to still be playing roller derby. She was married to someone she chose, even if that didn't come with parental approval. And, most important, she was self-assured enough to live fully separate from her mother. No more invasive communication. No more emails or calls that took days to recover from. My mind returned to Kelly's suggestion about being Joan of Spark off the track. Joan of Spark was true to herself, above all else. She prioritized her own wants and needs. She stood comfortably in her own power. Maybe this year would be different—maybe I could find her within me.

RED TENT

M y first follow-up appointment with the surgeon fell on a day Kelly had to work, so I asked Klara to drive me to St. Anthony's. Several of my teammates had offered, but I gently turned them down. I needed someone who wasn't affiliated with derby—someone whose perception of my situation wasn't warped by witnessing dozens of similar injuries or having firsthand experience of them. I wasn't sure I could handle comparisons of the kind Marco had made the day I broke my leg. I didn't think I could bear hearing from someone who had seen a million similar injuries that mine "wasn't that bad," even if that wasn't their intent. I wanted this experience to be uniquely my own.

This appointment was also important because I would find out how long it would be before I could start physical therapy and weight-bearing again. It had been a week and a half since the operation, and every day I worked out as best I could with the hand weights my mom had purchased when she was in town. I obsessed about staying in shape. With my legs stretched out on the ground, I pulled myself up into crunches and lifted the weights over my head, feeling the stretch in my arms and lower back. As I lay on the hardwood floor afterward, sweaty and out of breath, leg throbbing, I'd think about asking the surgeon how heavy the metal rod was. Would it be a noticeable change on the scale, or would the bone marrow that had been drained out neutralize the weight of the metal? I might have asked if I was alone, but I knew I'd be too embarrassed to ask in front of Klara.

"You look good," Klara said, as I hoisted myself into her car. I hadn't seen her since the day she brought me home from the hospital, and I imagined that after seeing me sobbing in a thunderstorm, scooting up the front stairs on my ass, anything would have looked better. I gave her a skeptical glance. "No, I'm serious. Your color is back. Let's go get some answers."

When we arrived, we were given a room quickly. I leaned my crutches against the cot and climbed up, and not long after a nurse came in with a small basket for collecting the staples in my leg. She suggested I not watch as she removed them, but I was too fascinated to look away. The device she was using to pull the metal from my flesh looked just like the staple remover I used on my grad school essays, and each time she latched on and pulled, I just felt a twinge of pressure.

When the nurse was finally done pulling the staples, she sent me over to the radiation department for X-rays, and then I had to wait in the examination room for the surgeon. He began speaking before he had even cleared the doorway, and Klara again flung open a journal and began taking notes like she had the day we had met Dr. Head.

"The X-rays look good, but your breaks were tricky," he said. "One was high, up by the knee, and the other one was low by your ankle. That spinning motion really got you." I nodded, my eyes cast downward. "We're not going to cast it because the rod inside is protection enough, but it's important not to put too much weight on it too early or the three screws down by your ankle holding the rod in place might give out. Could split the bone right down the middle." Klara stopped writing and stared at me, horrified.

"We'll make another appointment here in about a month, and then we'll talk about physical therapy. You'll probably start weight-bearing not long after that." Another *month?!*

"Can I swim?" I asked abruptly. I had no idea I was going to ask this question until it was already out of my mouth. But as soon as it was out there, I realized how desperate I was for him to say yes. As the past two weeks of sitting and lying down and sleeping and doing nothing had dragged on, there must have been a magnetic, almost primal pull to the water growing inside me. And it wasn't necessarily a healthy pull, either. The worst times of my life were marked by obsessive exercise; and in this moment, I realized that all I wanted to do was swim so hard that it'd be impossible for me to think about anything else—to *feel* anything other than the water.

"You can swim as soon as the incisions are healed," the doctor said, running a pudgy finger along the longest one. "Don't get in the water until there are no more scabs. It should take maybe another two weeks. Don't rush it though, otherwise you're risking an infection that could spread to the metal, and—trust me—that is not a risk you want to take."

"And when do you think the feeling will come back in my leg?" I asked. It was a strange sensation: being in excruciating pain but having no feeling on the left side of my leg. Lately Kelly and I had been playing a game where I looked away and she asked whether or not she was tapping on my leg; I never knew for sure.

"Should start waking up sooner or later," the surgeon said unhelpfully. "The good news is we expect you to make a full recovery. Based on your scans and how the leg is healing so far, you'll be able to do everything you used to be able to do. Might have some lingering pain or discomfort, but for the most part we expect that to be minimal."

Klara beamed at me from across the room where she was taking notes. I couldn't help but smile back.

The doctor, perhaps wary of my eagerness to get back to physical activity, said, "I want to emphasize how important it is to be careful with your recovery. There will be long-term effects if you push your leg too far too soon."

I nodded gravely and promised to be careful, though truthfully I didn't have a whole lot of experience with being careful. *At least I want to* want *to be careful,* I thought. *That's something, right?*

WHEN KELLY CAME home that evening, she found me resting on our bed in the red glow of our curtains.

"How was work?" I asked.

"I just wanted to be with you," she said. "I couldn't stop thinking about the appointment."

I nodded. I felt so guilty for my uselessness. I couldn't walk Lady, couldn't help with dinner, couldn't get groceries or do laundry. Kelly was now getting up at five thirty before work just to take Lady to the dog park; she was coming home exhausted only to be faced with even more work. Her job was still new, so she was still technically on probation, and she had to perform highly to keep the job. The pressure didn't seem to be getting to her, but the long hours were. After dinner, when she joined me on the couch to watch

TV, she fell asleep almost instantly. All I could do was cover her with a blanket.

In the dim glow of the red light, my body was bare. I had stripped naked, hoping she could help me get to the shower. The only fabric on my body was the surgeon's white knee-high stocking.

"They took all the bandages off today?" she asked, from the doorway. "I know you've already seen it, but can I discover it with you?"

I scooted down the mattress toward Kelly, gently hanging my foot off the edge of the bed to make it easier for her to remove the sock. In the few hours since the appointment, the fabric had already become stained with sweat and crusted with small patches of orange fluid. She pinched it at the ankle and flung it aside as she knelt down to examine my leg. Then, she carefully lifted my leg upward to get a view from below.

"How does it look to you?" I asked.

"It looks like you've been in a war," she said, lowering my leg onto the bed.

I grasped her hands tightly and heaved myself up. The gentle curve of my calf muscle had completely flattened into a straight line down to my ankle, which was still so swollen it was indistinguishable from the rest of my leg. My foot and toes appeared to be pumped full of air.

What surprised me were the bruises. They hadn't looked like much in the glow of the medical office, but they covered my skin like continents: big green landmasses that sprawled over my calf and drifted up the sides of my leg. The scar on my foot from my childhood surgery was now barely visible; much more noticeable were the black and blue discolorations lining the arch of my foot and my ankle bone.

"What does it feel like not to have anything on it?" Kelly asked.

I considered the question and after a few seconds, smiled slightly. She demanded to know what I was thinking.

"Nothing," I said. "I was just— It's stupid."

"I want to know!" she said.

"I feel like her," I said, gesturing to the Salvador Dalí poster hanging above our bed. "She doesn't give a shit what she looks like. She's just basking in her nudity."

The woman in Dalí's painting, sprawled out and naked like me, had a body like mine: small breasts, a short torso, big thighs. The first time I saw it, I had looked at her with disgust. I liked the rest of the painting: an elephant with stilts for legs. Two tigers crawling out of a big fish's mouth. A pomegranate spilling seeds. It was just hard for me to believe anyone could see beauty in a body like that. Kelly did, though, which I came to trust the more time I spent with her. She genuinely liked her own body, and mine. She felt comfortable in her own skin, and she was more comfortable dealing with my body than I ever was, even when it was injured.

Kelly went to the bathroom to retrieve supplies for my leg. She came back with Neosporin, Q-tips, and a bottle of lotion. Before touching me, she photographed my leg from several angles, saying, "You'll want to remember this later," and instructing me to shift my body into the light. When she finished the documentation, she gently spread my toes and cleaned between them.

"Doing this doesn't gross you out?" I asked.

"Not in the slightest."

It was such a relief to hear this from Kelly, especially since the accompanying smell was putrid. I couldn't help but feel shame as she got closer. The feeling that I didn't care what I looked like was dissipating; it felt like this would be the first time my leg had been washed in a week and a half—the dirty Skatium floor, the pizza box, the hospital, the bandages, the surgery, the blood, the iodine: it was all just layers of grime on my injured leg. Why couldn't I hold on to that Dalí feeling— of ambivalence, which felt like power? In between bulimic episodes, when I felt supported by my body, or at least not betrayed by it, that feeling would temporarily surface. When I mastered something new on the track, or used my body in an effective way, shame never crossed my mind.

Through my fingers, I watched dead skin fall from my leg onto the carpet like grated cheese. After my toes, Kelly shifted her attention to the bottom of my foot. She rubbed with the pads of her fingers and then switched to her fingernails, stopping every so often to rid them of the white flakes. It felt good, and she knew it. When she finished, she spread lotion into her palms and rubbed my leg until long after the lotion had been absorbed. She didn't have to touch me for so long, but she wanted to—at least, that's what she always said when our bodies grazed each other in the kitchen while we were cooking or when she rubbed my back while we watched TV at night. She liked my warmth, just like I liked hers.

"Are you—are you thinking of going back?" Kelly asked. The question took me by surprise, and she waited only a second before continuing to speak. "I just—I'm really worried for you. I can't imagine you going back. I know I wouldn't. It would be insane."

"I don't know," I said. She looked at me skeptically and I sat up straighter in my chair. "I really don't know. It seems like something we should decide together, doesn't it?"

Kelly nodded. She looked reassured that I wanted her to be involved in the process, which seemed only fair. She, after all, was the one who would be caring for me, picking up the pieces of our lives while I couldn't.

In the following weeks, lying in the red glow of my bedroom, I was often reminded of a novel I had pilfered from the adult section of the public library when I was in middle school. It was called *The Red Tent*. The author, Anita Diamant, based her story on the whispers of violence surrounding a number of women who appear in the Book of Genesis. The novel's title referred to the phenomenon of isolating women in red tents while they menstruated. Though Diamant's plot was invented, her characters and the concept of the tent were rooted in history. Native Americans erected menstrual huts, too; the Chinese had lodges. There is even a contemporary version, the Red Tent Temple Movement, in which women have reclaimed the menstrual huts and turned them into sites of power. The movement poses several questions: "Are we keeping ourselves busy so we don't feel? What are we hiding in our busyness that may speak to our hearts when we finally take time to slow down?" The contemporary red tent has become a "woman space where we can share stories, laughter, songs, food and honor our unique cycles that we experience each month in our bleeding time."

Much of the nuance of Diamant's novel had been lost on me at thirteen, but now I could appreciate the ways in which the women in that book came to each other's service—how they honored the cleansing of their sisters.

Only women entered my sanctuary for a time. Summer vacation had started a week after my operation, and I had already turned in all my coursework the day before my injury. WashU was still paying me a stipend to write, so my only other responsibility was healing. Bricktator came with hot meals. Taryn worked from my kitchen table. Nanny came back and sat in the recliner, and we cried while talking about our mothers. Tory took Lady on long walks. Klara brought over books and read several chapters out loud to me. And Kelly—Kelly did everything, but most important, she held me. She pressed her body into mine, clinging to me until we were both asleep.

All of these women helped me remember, like the women confined to the red tents thousands of years ago, that this time of healing was both temporary and sacred. *Be gentle with yourself,* they seemed to say. I could choose to open the red curtain at golden hour. My body would repair itself, feeling would return, and one day soon, I would once again be able to carry my own weight.

24/
BABY STEPS

Memorial Day marked one month since I had fallen on the track. It was brutally hot; as I sat outside on the front porch with Lady, sweat rolled down my back and soaked the waistband of my shorts. Lady panted in the sun until she started to overheat, and then plopped down with me in the shade.

I ran a finger over my incision, which was newly smooth. If I hadn't been looking at my own finger, I wouldn't have known I was touching my leg at all. I thought about what I might be doing if I wasn't immobile. I probably would have woken up early, before the heat, and taken Lady on a run down to the storefronts. She would've dragged me over to every sprinkler we passed by so that the water could spray her in the face as she snapped at the stream. We'd be back before the sun was fully up, before Kelly had gotten up at her leisurely long-weekend pace.

I heard the front door creak open and Kelly emerged with two glasses of lemonade. She handed one to me, and then, taking a glance at my leg, said, "That's healing really nicely."

"Will you take me to the pool?" I asked. "Today is open-ing day." If I couldn't run, I wanted to swim—anything to be in motion. I held my breath as she considered it. Her face contorted with apprehension.

"Are you sure?" Kelly asked. "What did the doctor say again?"

"He said I could swim when the scabs were gone. And look—they're gone." I neglected to tell her that I had peeled the last one off earlier that morning like a small child; the bleeding had stopped and, thankfully, it was impossible to tell.

"Fine," Kelly said, clearly pained by the idea. "But I'm going in with you just in case something happens."

I was relieved to hear she'd come with me. I didn't want to go to the pool by myself; I welcomed her calm, cool de-meanor. It would also mean that we could take the wheel-chair rather than crutches, which were difficult to manage on long treks.

When we pulled into the community pool parking lot, it was packed and we struggled to find a parking spot. Finally, Kelly found a space between two minivans. My wheelchair barely fit between the vehicles, but Kelly succeeded in wedg-ing it in so that I could sit down. Then she wheeled me past the woman at the front desk. On the counter in front of her was a stack of little charts.

"What're these?" I asked.

"Lap swimming competition," she said. "The five people who log the most laps this summer get a free membership next season."

"How does it work?" I asked.

"You just write down the date and how many meters you swam. Then, on the way out, I'll initial it—or whoever's working the front desk will—and you turn in your chart at the end of the summer."

I picked up a blank chart and put it carefully in my draw-string bag. The person I had been just a few days ago in the sanctuary of my bedroom was gone. Out in the real world, my mother's voice echoed in my head: "You better find a way to be active this summer or you'll be in big trouble." Although I couldn't see Kelly's face above me, I imagined her rolling her eyes. She knew about my tendency toward competitiveness, even when it wasn't warranted, and I won-dered what she thought of this very effective way to stay competitive and avoid gaining weight while I couldn't walk.

When we got out onto the deck, the lifeguards watched me through their aviators. Teenagers gawked. A little boy tugged on his mother's sundress and said, "Mommy, look what she has to do!" I felt partially humiliated, but partially like Cinderella when she was fashionably late to the ball. All eyes were on me. Everyone's full attention. I wasn't sure whether I hated it or loved it.

We found a lounge chair for Kelly to rest in. Despite the heat, she didn't feel like swimming—didn't have the same urgent need I did to be in the water. Meanwhile, as we crossed the fifty feet from the front desk to the lounge chair, I had already begun formulating a plan for how to win the summer swimming competition. I'd need to train every day and swim a minimum of two or three miles, I figured. Con-sistency was what won contests like this. Besides, the physical goal of winning the lap swimming competition would only be in service of the real goal—keeping the weight off. I had no real intention for meeting any emotional goal, but if I could rebuild some sense of the agency that I had lost with my leg break and during my mother's visit, that would only be a bonus.

Kelly offered to help me get to the pool, but I insisted on doing it myself. If I was going to win the lap swimming competition, I would have to spend my days here while she was at work. I needed to know how to get to the water once I parked my wheelchair or crutches in the grass.

Lots of people were watching me as I clumsily lowered myself from the chair to the ground. Some didn't even bother to hide their stares; others glanced surreptitiously over newspapers or around the children they were slathering with sunscreen. I decided I liked the attention. It made me feel like I was proving everyone wrong somehow.

That was true, at least, until it came time to get from the grassy area on the sidelines to the pool. The grass was soggy, and I could feel it sticking to the part of my butt that my suit left exposed. I found if I held my injured leg straight up in the air, I was able to scoot to the poolside like a dog wiping its ass. I wished there was a more graceful way for me to enter the pool, because this method was awkward and embarrassing, but at least I was doing it on my own.

I thought back to the comment my college teammate had made after my first half marathon. "You'll run till you fuck up your knees or get bored; then you'll do triathlons or something," she'd told me. "Then, after a while, you'll realize you belong in the water." I had snapped at her that day and told her she didn't know what she was talking about—that I was done with swimming forever. But she was right. It had taken just under two years, but here I was—literally crawling back to the pool.

The journey from chair to pool was at most a few feet,

but each time I lifted my butt off the ground, I only moved forward a few inches. And the emotional distance I was traveling was much further. I was eleven all over again, fresh out of surgery, determined to make it from my bed to the back porch. I was again at the mercy of able-bodied people to push me, carry me, or pull me from one place to another. Yet when I considered how lucky I was to have people making sacrifices for me, my anger quickly turned into guilt. Kelly and Taryn and Tory and Klara were constantly reminding me that my suffering was temporary. *Temporary.* Another crucial component to be grateful for.

A boy of about twelve or thirteen did a double take when he saw my method of approaching the water. He stopped abruptly, nudged his two buddies, and said, "I can't wait to see this."

"Can't wait to see what?" I asked. All three boys stared at me, incredulous, as though I had spoken to them through a television screen. Kelly lowered her sunglasses and asked me with her eyes why I had chosen to engage. Something about these kids had ticked me off—maybe the way they looked at me like I wasn't capable of speaking back.

"Can people like you swim?" the boy asked.

"She's got goggles and everything," his buddy said. "Maybe she's going to the Olympics."

"That's ridiculous," I snapped, and then immediately regretted my tone. The boy who had voiced the possibility looked sheepish. They all suddenly seemed younger. Softer, I explained, "It's just a broken leg. It doesn't look like the broken bones you've probably seen before because there's no cast."

"Oh. Why is there no cast? Was it a real pain? Did you

have to call an ambulance? Why is your skin all black like that?"

"I didn't call an ambulance, but I should have," I said. I didn't feel like answering his other questions or going deeper into my reasons for not calling an ambulance, which I was still trying to figure out for myself. I armed myself with the possibility that he would repeat the questions I hadn't answered or ask different ones, but the boys seemed satisfied with my response. Soon it became clear that they intended to watch me until I got in the water. Each of them struck a wide stance, arms crossed.

I took my time at the side of the pool, hoping the boys would lose interest in me. But if anything, dawdling just heightened their curiosity. As I stretched my cap over my hair and adjusted my goggle straps, I felt their gaze on me. Slowly, I lowered my injured leg into the water.

"What does it feel like?" one of the boys asked.

I smiled wide. "It feels pretty good, actually." My right leg could feel the cool, refreshing water against my skin, and my injured leg bobbed to the surface. It was a strange sensation: the numbness immersed in water I couldn't completely feel. For once, I wasn't thinking about how much it hurt. I wasn't even thinking about these boys and their gaze—it suddenly seemed inconsequential.

The boy started to ask another question, but I didn't hear it because I had already tipped myself into the water. I had never entered a pool in quite this way. Sometimes I dove headfirst, even though it was shallow, even though signs on the pool deck warned me of the danger. When I did life-guard training at sixteen, we practiced backboarding for spinal injuries; I was seasoned at playing the victim. But I dove into shallow water anyway, thinking nothing like that would ever happen to me, and sometimes hoping, perversely, that it would.

Pushing off the wall with one leg only got me a few feet. The tight streamline I had been taught as a kid disintegrated; instead of squeezing my ears, my elbows pointed outward and my hands missed each other above my head. I couldn't get my bad leg to straighten. When I reached the wall, I had to bounce on my strong leg to orient myself in the correct direction.

Yet, despite my obvious rustiness, swimming quickly felt natural again. My injured leg was useless, and I dragged it behind, but I was able to kick with one leg to keep the back half of my body afloat. It took a couple hundred yards to work the stiffness out of my joints and for my breathing to match the rhythm of my stroke. Only when I sensed another swimmer getting too close did I feel my body tense. The possibility of getting kicked, or entangled with a child, scared me enough to stop swimming and go limp. I bobbed in the fetal position until the threat was gone. Then I lumbered on, stretching my body over the surface of the water, feeling the heat on my arms until I plunged them back into the cold.

THE NEXT DAY, I returned to the pool by myself. It was hot but overcast; Kelly stood in our driveway as I climbed into the driver's seat of the car. The doctor had given me the green light for driving since it was my left leg that was injured—as long as I didn't attempt to drive my own car, a stick shift, which required both feet.

"How's it feel?" Kelly asked, leaning in to the window.

"I feel very independent right now," I said.

"Just go slow and be careful," she warned. "You have your crutches, right?"

I pointed to the back seat, where Soup Beans's bedazzled crutches were waiting for me. All the equipment she had given me post-op was glittery—covered in sparkle tape or rhinestones or both.

The woman at the front desk recognized me. "How you doin', baby?" she asked. The day before, she had signed the first entry of my lap swimming card—1,500 meters, or just shy of a mile.

"Looking forward to getting in the water," I said.

"What's your deal?" she suddenly asked me. The card buttoned to her shirt said her name was Yolanda.

"What do you mean?" I asked. I could feel my face getting hot, the pressure of the glitter crutches pinching my underarms.

"Why can't you walk?" Yolanda's face was inquisitive, but kind, and I had known the question was coming. It was actually rather refreshing to be asked point-blank rather than gossiped about behind cupped hands. I felt a wave of gratitude toward Yolanda, but not enough trust that I wanted to tell her the whole story.

"Bad accident," I said. She nodded again, eyebrow raised. She knew I wasn't telling her the full truth. I just didn't want to contribute to the impression everyone had about roller derby being unnecessarily brutal and violent. Some people, like my mother, had thought my injury was just a matter of time. I was also feeling private and didn't want to give away my whole story to a near stranger.

"Well," Yolanda said, brushing a piece of hair off her forehead, "how many laps are you swimming today, missy?" I straightened; this was a conversation I was much more interested in.

"Two miles," I said. "Double what I did yesterday."

I felt a pinprick of fear in my lower back. Now that I'd verbally committed to two miles, I knew I wouldn't be able to face Yolanda again unless I had accomplished my goal. Even though I knew she wouldn't hold me to it, probably wouldn't even remember, I couldn't bear the idea of asking her to sign my sheet if I had failed.

Out on the deck, I had a better view of the pool, which I hadn't realized yesterday was shaped like a big oval. Some lanes looked to be longer than others; the ones closer to the middle of the oval were the longest, and the ones with round edges tended to be shorter. I hobbled to the middle of the pool and put my bag down on a chair overlooking the longest lane. I didn't want to be accused of cheating in the lap swimming competition by choosing the short lanes.

I collapsed onto the wet grass and reached up to the chair for my cap and goggles. As I readied myself, useless leg stretched out on the ground in front of me, I started to ask myself if forcing myself to swim in the longest lane—or even swim at all—was just a punishment. There was nothing in the competition rules that said I had to swim in the longest lane, just like there was nothing telling me I had to swim two miles today if I couldn't or didn't feel like it. But there were two warring voices in my head. One sounded like my mother and my sister. I thought back to what Cam had said when she took eleven flights of stairs to get to our room: *I'm going to get fat here. Four days with no swimming?* Then, what my mother said to me before leaving St. Louis: "You better find some way to work out while your leg is broken or else it's going to be bad." I knew exactly what she meant: that I would gain weight if I wasn't careful.

The other voice, though, was gentler. "You don't have to be doing this," it said. It was quieter than the voice of my mother or sister, but it was there.

In the water, I tried to tease out the different voices and what they were telling me. What I knew was that I felt strong—already better than yesterday. My arms pulled me across the pool; the burning in my biceps was a nice reminder that I was getting even stronger. The sun would heat my face each time I turned my head to take a breath, and I closed my eyes for a brief moment so that I could commit that feeling to memory. I wanted somewhere to go at night when the pain in my leg throbbed and surged up my body— somewhere sacred to escape when everything hurt too much to bear. Swimming, I remembered, felt more natural to me than walking. It had cradled me and supported my healing at eleven, when the screws and wedges were new additions to my feet; it buoyed my body at all the weights it had ever been. It had been a constant presence the summer after coming out, when my home was no longer safe—a constant presence since I was nine years old, twice a day sometimes, and even though the activity had become ruled by my drive to win, the water just remained what it was—still, steady, all-encompassing.

When the sun started to slip below the trees, I was only a mile and a half into my workout, but everything in my body was telling me to stop. My muscles were exhausted. The water seemed colder. My leg was throbbing. Defeated, I pulled myself out of the pool and scooted on my butt back to the chair where I had put my things. I dried off my hand and wrote how many meters I swam in the chart. Shame was already starting to seep in before I even saw Yolanda. When I got to her desk, she was on the phone. I passed her my chart and she initialed without even checking my distance. Crutching to the car, I thought how liberating that was: the prospect that people might not be expecting me to fail.

AT THE END of June, after I'd been swimming for about four weeks, I received two passes in the mail for the Worldwide Roller Derby Convention in Las Vegas at the end of July. It had been so long since I had ordered them—way before my accident, before even the local season champs. I had pictured myself taking part in many of RollerCon's open scrimmages, which all had fun themes like Beach Bums vs. Forest Dwellers and Hulk vs. Ant-Man. Kelly's spectator pass would allow her to attend off-skates classes with me— Nutrition, and History of Roller Derby, and Personal Defense. When I booked the tickets, I was sure it would be an amazing five days in Vegas. Now, I wasn't so sure.

No one in my derby circle had explicitly asked me if I was going to skate again once my leg healed, but the conundrum was always at the forefront of my mind. Some days, I woke up from dreams of skating on forest trails and felt no hesitation about putting on skates again. Other days, I awoke from nightmares about lying broken on the side of the track, immobile and voiceless. Most days I felt terrified to imagine being in skates again, petrified at the prospect of doing the maneuver that had been my downfall: a forward-to-backward transition. Any time I imagined spinning, all I saw were legs twisting until they snapped the way mine had.

"We don't have to decide right now," Kelly told me. We were driving to the physical therapist's office together for my first appointment. "We have a month, after all. You can think about RollerCon and decide later what you want to do." I nodded in response, grateful for her wisdom.

"Maybe I'll be able to walk by then," I said. Kelly looked at me out of the corner of her eye. At my last doctor's appointment, the surgeon had finally given me the all clear to start physical therapy and weight-bearing. It would be a slow process of learning how to walk again, he warned.

My physical therapist was a WashU doctor: a bald long-distance runner with a serious disposition who wanted to help me get walking as quickly as possible. He massaged my leg and foot and analyzed the X-rays I showed him. Talking hurriedly, he described the plan he had fleshed out to get me walking again.

"Do you have access to water?" he asked me. I didn't know what he was talking about until he clarified. "A pool. Do you have access to a pool?"

I nodded, confused.

"Great," he said, sounding excited. "That's going to make things a lot simpler. I'll work with you on walking technique. For homework, you'll do a series of exercises and stretches with rubber bands. But you'll also go to the pool to work on walking . . . we'll start with neck height. You can take your first step in neck-high water. Does that make sense? Go slow and see how it feels."

In the pool that afternoon, I stood like a flamingo in water that threatened to seep into my mouth. It took a lot of internal coaxing for me to put my injured leg down so that the bottom of my foot skimmed the pool floor; a tingle shot up my spine. It was the first time my foot had felt the ground in eight weeks.

Gradually, I shifted my weight so that more of my leg was

holding me up. I expected a loud cracking noise—something sickening like the day I had damaged it—but nothing happened. My broken leg could withstand the weight of my body in water—even when I picked up my good leg. The longer I held my foot up, the sorer my broken leg got, so I put it down quickly, but nothing could take away the thrill. I had just been standing on two feet. Suddenly, the lap swimming competition seemed insignificant. Now I had more important things to worry about.

The next day, instead of putting on my cap and goggles when I got to the pool, I shaded my eyes and scoured the pool deck for Tory. When I'd told her about standing in the pool, she said she wanted to be there for my first step. Finally, I saw her, in a polka dot tankini and a big sun hat. She looked like a model from the 1950s—missing only was the baby at her hip. She and her partner had just started trying, and she was excited.

"This is exactly what it's going to be like when your baby takes her first step," I joked, setting my crutches down by her chair. Tory laughed, and we both got into the water. It was neck-high, as the physical therapist had instructed, and I was quickly able to transition to a two-footed stance. In high school, the swim team liked to draw attention to my "Peter Pan" stance, which involved wide feet and hands on my hips. It was my natural way of standing when we were being given directions, which they all found hilarious—a picture of confidence. Now, in the water, it came back to me easily.

"Let's see it," Tory said. "Use me if you need to hold on to something."

I reached out for her bony shoulder and for just a second, put all my weight on my bad leg. Quickly, I swung my right leg to the front and took a step.

"You did it!" Tory cried, her eyes radiant. "You're walking! How does it feel?"

"I want to walk all the way across the pool," I replied.

Tory's eyes darted to the far end of the pool and she asked, "Are you sure? That's quite a distance for your first day." But I was already making my way forward.

In the dead center of the pool, the longest lane available, we started the trek. Each step advanced me only a few inches; I swung my good leg forward quickly to catch myself. The limp was pronounced, but I didn't care as long as I was moving forward. In the open-swimming area neighboring my lane, a gaggle of gray-haired women were halfway through a water aerobics class. Their gazes were fixed on their instructor, who stood poolside with a pool noodle and mimed the motions she wanted them to perform.

"Do you think we'll be here when we're old ladies, meeting up for water walking exercise?" Tory asked. I turned to face her, admiring again her youthful beauty.

"I would love that," I said. Then, out of nowhere, I blurted out, "My mom thought you had a stick up your ass."

Tory lowered her sunglasses and looked at me with confusion.

"I only saw your mother for five minutes," she said. "And I was giving you a pizza."

"I know, I know," I said, apologetically. Why in the world had I felt compelled to tell her this?

"It's actually a corncob," Tory said, after a beat.

"What?"

"It's a corncob up my ass. Get it? Cause I'm from Iowa. Far more cobs than there are sticks."

She broke out into a toothy grin and I felt immense relief wash over me. Once it was clear what her reaction was, a wave of clarity hit me about why I had told her this story in the first place. It was a confession, like the ones I had suffered through as a child. I couldn't stomach her kindness knowing what my mother had said about her—I just felt too guilty. Now, all I felt was gratitude and love. What had I done to deserve such good friends—both on the track and off?

I took another step and felt the pressure in my broken leg.

"Can we pause for a minute?" I asked Tory.

"Sure," she said. "You're doing great. You'll be skating again in no time."

BY JULY, I had a new routine: water walk for twenty minutes, followed by a swim. I tried to keep my focus on the walking, allowing myself to skip swimming if I didn't feel like it. It was unnatural to me—leaving the column in my lap swimming chart empty some days. This wasn't how I was conditioned, after all. Still, it felt like some sort of internal wisdom was directing me away from my old way of being and toward the importance of learning to walk again. After a week walking in neck-high water, I graduated to chest-high, where I could feel the painful pressure on my ankle and leg even more acutely. But gradually, it wore off, and I advanced to navel-high, then hip-high. The lifeguards had grown invested in my process, particularly one named Dajon, a sixteen-year-old football player who knew about the Skatium just from living in South City.

"I'd never mess with any of you roller derby gals," he said, seriously. "That shit looks way harder than football."

Talking to Dajon while I practiced walking was a nice distraction from the pain in my leg, and he seemed to get a kick out of my stories about roller derby and all the roller derby names. When he learned mine, he started calling me Miss Joan of Spark. I had never been Joan of Spark anywhere other than the track before, let alone the swimming pool. It felt like the time in elementary school I had seen my teacher at the grocery store. The knowledge that she existed outside the realm I knew her in felt uncomfortable at first, and then kind of magical, like I was in on a universal secret. Joan of Spark didn't just exist on the track; she could go anywhere.

As Dajon told me about his dreams of playing for Mizzou—the University of Missouri—I thought about my own sixteen-year-old self, who was as far from Joan of Spark as I could imagine. College coaches had just started calling my house every week to talk to me about swimming, but I had no clue what any of it meant; I was confused about boys and my ambivalence toward them; I felt pressure from my mother to stay close to her, but she was also pushing me away by telling me I was sloppy and disgusting. In addition to my library job, I had been a lifeguard like Dajon, and the pressure to save struggling swimmers weighed heavily on my shoulders.

One hot July day, I was walking in the shallow end, looking down at my feet, when the alarms went off. Dajon was stationed across the pool by the diving boards, so I had been entertaining myself by watching the way the light split across the pool floor as I practiced my steps. I knew right away: someone was in trouble. I looked up and saw Dajon on his lifeguarding stand, readying to dive. He gathered the cord for the buoy around his chest and leapt from his perch into the water. When he resurfaced, his arm was around a little girl, sputtering and kicking. I felt a wave of relief pass over my body. He had done it. He got her.

Watching Dajon's save, it was impossible not to think of

my own: it was my second year lifeguarding, and a little boy had gone down the slide and not come up. Little bubbles broke the surface of the water where he had gone under. I hesitated, unsure if I should go in or not. I was afraid of looking stupid; if the boy was just holding his breath under water, I might be jumping in for no reason. But as the seconds ticked by, fear washed over my body and I knew what I had to do.

I leapt from the top of the lifeguarding stand, forgetting to issue the two long blasts of my whistle. I landed feet-first a few feet from where the child had gone under, and I relinquished my buoy so that I could slip under after him. He was hovering just a few feet under the water, paralyzed with fear, it seemed, but as soon as I wrapped my arm around him and heaved him up, he started thrashing. *He won't need resuscitation,* I realized. *Thank god.*

The boy calmed when he saw his mother, who was waiting poolside to pull him up by both his hands. She didn't thank me, didn't even look at me, just draped him in a towel and whisked him away. It was all over in a matter of minutes, and then the pool went back to normal. Music played. Children laughed. It might have been easy to pretend it never happened except for the fact that I was soaking wet.

Right away, I feigned nonchalance. Even though my heart was racing. Even though I had allowed myself to wonder what would have happened if I hadn't jumped. The pool manager needed me to fill out an incident report, which helped make the save seem real. He asked if I wanted to talk about it, but I said no. I didn't want to risk feeling anything that could weaken me. In swimming especially, the less feeling, the better. We were taught to push through without feeling the pain in our bodies so that we could win races.

Being strong meant being stoic, especially in my family. But watching Dajon save the little girl, I started to cry. It was as if I had experienced a voice-over in the film of my own life that said, *It happened, and it was hard. You don't have to pretend not to feel anymore.* I was still crying when he made his way back to the lifeguard stand near me, sopping wet, and sat down.

"Miss Joan of Spark, what's this all about? Am I going to have to save you too?" I cracked a smile and shook my head. I remembered what my mother said when she pulled my wheelchair to safety: "I knew you couldn't save yourself." I had felt so much shame associated with those words, so much truth. I'd been waiting for years for somebody to save me. My third-grade teacher. A coach. My dad. It felt like I'd been rolling into traffic all my life. What would it look like to grab the wheels myself?

Maybe it looked like exactly what I was doing: taking baby steps in the shallow end of a public pool filled with laughing children. Walking with control, with resistance, steadfastly forward. Listening to my body to know when to stop. Trading the laps competition in favor of a healthier, more reasonable goal. Letting go of what no longer served me to make room for Joan of Spark.

25/
THE WORLDWIDE ROLLER DERBY CONVENTION

By the time Kelly and I flew to Las Vegas for the Worldwide Roller Derby Convention the last week of July, I was able to walk short distances without crutches. Flex my ankle. Balance on my broken leg for five seconds. The physical therapists attributed my quick recovery to my age and athleticism, but I knew the real reason was all the time I'd spent in the pool.

Contrary to what I had anticipated, I did not feel much disappointment about having to abstain from skating at the convention. It was actually a relief. Soup Beans had warned me back when I'd first bought my tickets that joining scrimmages with players you'd just met for the first time was dangerous: you could never be sure how they'd move or fall or hit. Some people were hazards, she told me, because they came from small leagues and overestimated their skill level. "As difficult as it is starting in a world-class league like Arch Rival, you'll be grateful for it later," she'd said. "Especially when you realize you're a much better skater than you think." Now, I had the perfect excuse to watch from the safety of the stands— and privately consider whether or not I still wanted to play.

In preparation for the five-day event, my physical therapists wrapped my leg in athletic tape to combat swelling. Soup Beans, who arrived a half day before us, put me at ease, assuring me that everything I needed would be inside the convention center. Even so, the distance from our room on the fourteenth floor to the event center might not have been more than a few hundred yards, but once we'd settled in to our room and headed over for the first time, Kelly and I agreed it felt like miles. I'd chosen to leave my crutches at home; I was embarrassed to show up at a derby convention visibly injured. I knew I'd be able to get around if I braced my leg and took frequent breaks. My limp slowed us down, and so did the lights and sounds competing for our attention. I had hoped the convention center would insulate us from the chaos of Las Vegas, but it seemed designed to do the exact opposite. The elevators were loud; instead of music, there were advertisements for Cirque Du Soleil and a Michael Jackson impersonator that played on a constant loop. One ad for a burlesque show started with a woman's voice, sultry and playful, hissing, "Sex . . . sex . . . sex." Once we were out of the elevator, slot machines, whirring and chiming, paved our way to the registration lines.

As Kelly and I made our way toward the tracks and passed players in the hallways, it felt like we had stepped directly into the RollerCon promotional materials. Leprechauns vs. Trolls, the first bout of the convention, had just finished up, and Kinky vs. Vanilla was about to get started. One woman had affixed a pale dildo to the front of her shorts; it jiggled as she stretched and did jumping jacks. Hate You #2 was pulling on socks over her fishnets; one said FUCK and the other said OFF. One lady spread her arms wide like Jesus while another sprayed her whole body with glitter from an aerosol can.

At first, I could hardly believe what I was seeing. It was everything I had ever dreamed of when I decided to join the world of roller derby. So much of the sport's culture, I had learned, was about fighting to become recognized as legitimate, which involved as much conventionalizing as possible. In this realm at RollerCon, individual athletes were fighting for the opposite: the power to stand out. There was a collective breaking away as skaters reclaimed the sport. The more unique their costumes, the more expressive their performance.

We passed one skater waiting in line for the bathroom wearing all of their protective gear on top of a plaid onesie. The butt flap hung open, displaying underpants that said I LIKE TO BE WHIPPED. A tall person with purple hair was passing out pages from a new derby-themed coloring book—the one I selected at random displayed the legendary Scald Eagle with her characteristic face paint, pumping her fists in the air. Distracted by my new acquisition, I almost walked straight into a skater on an electric scooter. Their jersey was the same deep purple as their cast, which was covered in names such as Piña Collider and Mental Block.

The crowd pushed Kelly and me straight into Vendor Village, which turned out to be a labyrinth of tents and stalls. Once we were inside the retail village, it wasn't easy to find our way out again, and even when we finally saw the exit, I found I wasn't ready to leave yet. There was too much to see—too much I wanted to buy. Most vendors sold athletic apparel, from sweat-wicking jerseys to glittery booty shorts. Custom armbands were drawing a huge crowd; skaters were growing tired of writing their numbers on their arms with permanent marker. One sign boasted DERBY-PROOF LIPSTICK: LASTS UP TO EIGHTEEN HOURS! and I stopped to take a coupon.

Knowing there was no way I could afford most of the stuff made it easier to yearn for it. I could dream about how amazing I'd look wearing a shimmering sports bra and matching booty shorts without having to consider the reality: that I still didn't know if I wanted to skate again.

In Bruised Boutique—an entire room devoted to selling roller skates—we ran into Tutz and her husband, Bled Zeppelin. I tried waving to the couple, but they were busy fitting someone with new skates. As sponsored athletes, they were flown to RollerCon to play in high-level scrimmages and to help sell Roller Derby Elite merchandise. Tutz was vying for a spot on Team USA, so it didn't surprise me that she would take advantage of the opportunity to play with other elite athletes from all over the world. Twelve countries besides the United States were represented at RollerCon, including New Zealand, Korea, and the UK. Members of Team USA would be playing in various bouts over the next five days, so there would be plenty of opportunities for Tutz to showcase her talent. I'd marked down all of the scrimmages she was playing in and couldn't wait to cheer her on.

I sat on a folding chair across from Bruised Boutique to rest for a bit. We watched a young queer couple examine a pair of Riedell skates. They were holding hands.

"Have you thought about getting new skates?" Kelly asked, her eyes on the couple. Her voice was measured, careful—there was no accusation in her tone, but no encouragement, either. My heart started to beat a little faster. Between assuming I would definitely return to derby, or trying to avoid the topic so as not to stress me out, people had stopped asking directly about my plans. This was the closest anyone had come to outright asking me if I wanted to keep playing.

I glanced at Kelly out of the corner of my eye. She was still looking fixedly at Bruised Boutique, but I saw that her leg was doing a nervous bounce. I felt a rush of affection for my brave, generous partner. I loved Kelly for having the courage to raise such a loaded question. I loved her for trusting me enough to decide on my own—for not trying to persuade me in one direction or the other. I loved her for coming without complaint to a giant convention in celebration of the sport that had severely injured her partner. I loved the way she loved me. My throat felt tight, as if I might burst into tears.

Kelly cleared her throat. "We could buy them here if you want."

"I'm still not sure," I mumbled. It was all I could manage, and it was true. To purchase new skates meant that I could imagine putting them on and skating around: something I still couldn't bring myself to visualize. The fear was too great; every time I pictured standing up in skates, I imagined my leg buckling and snapping under my weight. I was still re-learning how to walk properly. All I could allow myself to look forward to in the realm of athleticism was getting back in the community pool when we returned to St. Louis. When I looked at the RollerCon athletes, it was like looking at the first roller derby game I had ever been to. "How do they do that?" was the constant question on my mind. It was like my brain had been wiped clean of everything I had learned. Deep inside, though, I knew my body remembered.

Eventually Kelly succeeded in pulling me out of Vendor Village, and we made it to the main event center: a 70,000-foot square room with a 9,000-person capacity, big enough for the 7,000 people I had read were attending the convention this year. It was difficult not to stop and stare. The room fit four full-sized roller derby tracks—three flat and one banked. Two of the flat tracks were reserved for the themed, open scrimmages, and the one with the most spectator seating was designated for the highest-level and most-anticipated bouts. Vagine Regime vs. Caulksuckers was expected to draw a huge crowd. So was Magic Mike vs. Chippendales, because advanced, male-identifying skaters would be stripping during the game to collect cash for colon cancer research. The banked track would be used mostly for classes. Very few banked-track teams remained, mostly because banked tracks were expensive, rare, and dangerous, but many skaters still longed to give them a try.

Not only was I blown away by the scene itself: I was in awe of the skill and organization of those who had put together the event. Outsiders often assumed that roller derby players were messy and disorganized because our look was so different from the uniformity of baseball or football players; in fact, it was the exact opposite. Every scrimmage, every class, every social event, and every participant had a place. Derby was about inclusion, and real inclusion required organization. The organizers had essentially created a derby paradise.

Part of that paradise fantasy was fueled by the chandeliers and intricate, regal-looking carpeting, which made the scene even more magnificent. Not only did they provide a stark contrast to the St. Louis Skatium and other warehouse-like venues I'd played in, they were also a reminder that this space wasn't designed for skating. It was a host space, much like my high school parking lot had been a host space for the carnival that came to town every summer. It always amazed me how quickly all the rides and stalls appeared and then vanished; the temporariness made it magical. Except for overflowing trash cans and the occasional popped balloon, nothing was ever left behind. Like the carnivals of my childhood and the original Transcontinental Roller Derby, which had traveled between cities like a circus, RollerCon would be here today, gone tomorrow.

When Kelly and I settled down to watch Hollywood Punks vs. Valley Girls, a woman named Diamond Drill(h)er plopped down next to us. She had come to RollerCon all the way from Australia, she told us, and made a living by selling precious stones; within five minutes, we had become fast friends. Since she was rooming with Soup Beans's friend Te-Killah, I assumed they knew each other, but Diamond told us they had met on a Facebook group for roller derby rookies. "Te-Killah sent me some American candy and I sent her some from Australia," Diamond explained. "Then I asked, 'Hey! Wanna room with me in Vegas?'"

The forwardness of this interaction made me think of Drive Bi, who'd introduced Kelly to the company that would lead to her career. We hadn't known her at all, and within minutes of sitting down and talking, she was giving Kelly her contact information. It was a reminder that it wasn't just the glitz and glamour that made derby special. It was the way it brought together so many different people, united in their love of fun, their need for community, and most of all, the shared experience of feeling a little different, whether from queerness or quirkiness or both. So many of the people I'd met through derby knew what it felt like to be an outsider, to be the black sheep of their family, to be an underdog, or to not quite fit in with normative culture. In derby, we created acceptance and inclusion and safety for each other. There was an undercurrent of generosity that was immeasurably attractive to people like me.

Not long into the scrimmage, I could no longer ignore how badly I had to pee. Kelly asked if I needed help, but I assured her I could manage on my own. I hobbled to the nearest bathroom, and only once I was inside did I realize how loud it was in the main event center. My ears began ringing, and the muscles in my face started to relax after so much excessive smiling. A woman in full derby gear had commandeered a sizable portion of the counter space for her makeup. She was wearing a green vest and purple jacket, on the back of which she'd painted her numbers. The white powder she was using to dust her face haloed her whole upper body. A minute later, she began applying black makeup to her eye sockets, which produced an eerie, skeletal effect. I tried not to stare while I washed my hands, but then I noticed that she was wearing a brace on her left knee.

"Did you tear your ACL?" I asked, surprised by my own brazenness. I hated when strangers interrogated me about my injury, because nine times out of ten, the conversation ended with an offhand comment like "You're not thinking of going back, are you?" or "Guess your derby days are over!" That had always been the case in Forest Park when Kelly took me for walks in my wheelchair, but it was different when another derby player asked. People in derby came back from gruesome injuries all the time.

"Not yet," she said. "I'm trying not to push it."

"What bout are you playing in?" I asked.

The woman smiled and turned her back to me. I briefly thought she had chosen to ignore my question, but when she turned around again, she had drawn two long slashes on either side of her mouth with red lipstick.

"Harley Quinn vs. Joker," she said. "At first, I wasn't sure if I should go more Jack Nicholson or more Heath Ledger, but then I figured—who am I kidding? All I really need is the mouth, and people will know exactly who I am."

I laughed, and the woman stuck both her forearms into the sink. She lathered them with soap and scrubbed, occasionally lifting an arm to her nose and shaking her head.

"My wrist guards smell so bad they're contaminating my skin," she said. "I haven't even played yet today and my arms already smell like a stale bag of Doritos."

"That happens to me too," I said. "Sometimes it takes days to get the stench off."

As I made my way back into the event center, I couldn't stop turning over that last sentence in my mind. Something about it had sounded strange. What I had said was true: once pads get enough wear, they reek so bad that no amount of bleach can reverse the smell. It wasn't that. It didn't hit me until I got to the bleachers: I had spoken in the present tense.

Over the next couple of days, Kelly and I lost count of how many bouts we watched, letting it all wash over us in a tide. Some of the scrimmages had no prerequisites except for skill level. Any female-identifying skater with a moderate to high skill level could enter Goth vs. Glam, for example. The same was true of Crop Tops vs. Side Boob, Gorgeous Ladies of Wrestling vs. American Gladiators, and Peter Pan vs. Alice in Wonderland. Some bouts had a few more regulations. It was expected that every skater playing in West Coast vs. East Coast stayed true to their geographic place of origin. A similar rule was in place for Big Booties vs. Lil' Booties, though no exact regulations were given for distinguishing a small ass from a large one.

One of the bouts I looked forward to most was Robots vs. Zombies, which took place on the afternoon of the second day. I'd learned from the Gimp Crew Facebook group that this was the scrimmage for players who'd come back after serious injuries. Team Robot—consisting of players who had metal implanted in their bodies post-injury—wore silver costumes and metallic accessories. Some players prepared by turning their faces into cubist works of art, painting each plane a different color.

The zombies, on the other hand, had needed human or animal cadaver parts, like tendons or ligaments, to make a full recovery. A few sat on the sidelines ripping the hems off their jerseys, hacking at the cloth to make it fray or tear. One zombie announced she had brought a tube of fake blood, and the team passed it around.

Soup Beans qualified for both teams. The hardware in her leg and ankle made her a robot, and the cadaver ligaments in both knees made her a zombie. She notified the coaches months before RollerCon that they could put her on whichever team had fewer players, and she relayed this story to me with more than a hint of pride. "Robot, zombie—I'm everything," she said. "I'm thirty-seven and have been playing this sport since the dawn of time. I'm just going to keep getting doctors to put me back together so I can keep playing."

Neither Team Robot nor Team Zombie struggled to fill a full roster, though, and Soup Beans was placed on Team Robot. Right when I started derby, I would probably have assumed that recruiting twenty-four players for this bout— a minimum of twelve was required to make a team—would be a difficult task; but now, as a member of the Gimp Crew, I knew it would be easy.

Through the Gimp Crew, I also came to understand that there were two types of "robots," and that there was a rivalry between the two groups that could occasionally tip over into hostility. People like me who had broken both the tibia and the fibula, and therefore had a metal rod put in the lower leg, were considered very lucky: we got to stay in the hospital longer than those who'd "only" been kitted out with plates, and our X-rays generally looked more gruesome. We also tended to recover faster since the rod supported the tibia, the primary weight-bearing bone. These disparities annoyed the plate people, who in addition to their fibula break usually had to contend with ligament damage. They often wrote comments under our X-rays like *Lucky!* or *Must be nice to know you can skate again in four months.*

If I was one of the lucky ones and my recovery was this grueling, I was determined to cheer for everyone, and to cheer loudly. There were women on the track I recognized from the Facebook group—I had read intimate accounts of their trials and frustrations. My mother used to say sports weren't worth watching unless you cared who won, but never had that felt less true than here. I didn't look at the scoreboard once. There was so much else to be invested in. In this game, there were no winners and losers—there were only women who had gotten up again after being knocked down.

On the second-to-last night of the convention, I heard there was going to be a marriage ceremony happening on the track, and feeling almost high on the excitement and adrenaline that filled the convention center, I knew right away I wanted Kelly and me to participate. I had read about this event in the RollerCon informational materials: basically it was a fake wedding ceremony for derby wives—women who had proclaimed themselves platonic spouses who wanted to publicly declare their "love."

"It's not for us," Kelly said, after reading the description of the event.

"I don't care," I insisted. "Let's get dressed up and get married."

She cracked a smile. Kelly usually didn't like anyone looking at her. She didn't like unnecessary attention and she had already told me that if we ever got married, she would want it to be very small. Still, I could tell the idea was tantalizing. This was a way for us both to participate in RollerCon without skating. It was a way to throw ourselves into the oddity of the convention full force.

"Okay," she said, fully smiling now. "I'm in."

In preparation, we each donned a white jersey, and Diamond gave me a flowered headband and veil. "My derby wife's not here," Diamond told us. "Don't let my accessories go to waste." Solemnly, we ripped it in half; Kelly tucked the veil into her ponytail and I wore the headband like a crown.

Soup Beans caught us on the way out the hotel door. "I have something for you too!" she said, digging through her luggage. Then, she gifted us a large, rubber ring that blinked different colors when it was squeezed. Kelly barked a laugh and put it on her ring finger, admiring it with her arm outstretched.

When we arrived on the track, there was already a line of derby wives standing two by two. Two women wore WIFEY shirts over their jerseys, still sweaty from a recent game. Another wore a white bikini. Another held a bouquet of daffodils. I had never seen so many women being openly affectionate with each other before, and we gladly took our spot at the end of the line.

The announcer began saying something I couldn't make

out, and organ music played: "Here Comes the Bride." The line slowly started moving forward as we paraded onto the track. Before we even took a step, Kelly linked her arm in mine. I couldn't help wondering if this was how we would walk down the aisle at our real wedding.

As we made our way onto the track, spectators fought to high-five us. Tutz and her husband, Bled Zeppelin, stretched their long arms through the crowd, and I slapped their palms. In the center of the track, a pair of women presided over the ceremony—they'd gotten married here a decade ago. When the song ended, the taller one grabbed the bedazzled microphone and said, "We are gathered here tonight to honor the union of these skaters in the grand tradition of derby marriage." Another uproar. I could feel my face flushing from the ridiculousness of it all. I loved it: every moment.

She told us all to join hands and repeat after her. There was a moment of shuffling while couples all around us linked arms or held hands. I grabbed Kelly's hand, linking my fingers with hers.

"I take you to be my derby wife," the tall woman's voice boomed over the speakers. I looked at Kelly, whose face was flushed, too. A chorus of voices repeated the words. Kelly and I both left out the word *derby* and exchanged conspiratorial smiles. Was I actually making a vow to Kelly, right here, in this moment? It felt like it. And was this how it would feel to marry Kelly for real—this much lightness, this much love?

The tall woman continued, "I promise to ride with you in the ambulance if you ever break your arm in a bout, even if the EMTs are all ugly." Kelly emphasized the word *ambulance* and I giggled.

"I will always tell you when your pads start to smell like a goat's ass in the summer." I could no longer distinguish either of our own voices in the swell of the refrain, hundreds of people repeating these ridiculous words, words that felt all the more beautiful in the juxtaposition of silliness and togetherness. I thought suddenly of the choir I heard every Sunday in my hometown church and didn't even fight the urge to laugh. *This* was my kind of church. This was my kind of hymn.

"I vow to always take pictures up your skirt at afterparties, and to hold your hair back if you get sick on the sidewalk. I will always be your first phone call from jail, even if I was the one who got you there in the first place." Kelly and I were both laughing by this point, so hard it was difficult to speak at all.

"I will always remind you about that amazing last bout if non-skating matters start to annoy you." I loved this one in particular, thinking about how Kelly always watched my games on repeat, pausing and replaying each jam I was in. "Look at you there!" she would say. "Look at that move!"

The tall woman cleared her throat. "I promise to be your biggest fan—unless we face off. Then I promise to hit you harder than anyone else on your team, because I'd never insult you by going easy on you." It was too long for the big group to repeat back perfectly. Instead, as one, we picked our favorite phrases. "Face off," I heard. "Hit you harder," and "going easy." *I never go easy on Kelly,* I thought, my smile fading slightly. *Sometimes I wish I knew how.*

"So with the power vested in me by Ivanna S. Pankin and the RollerCon convention, I now pronounce you derby wives. You may kiss the bride." There was cheering, flashing lights, women swept off their feet by other women. Bouquets flew like graduation caps and Kelly leaned into me. I had never kissed Kelly in public before—not at derby events, not in front of friends. It had been drilled into us for so long that we could never be too careful with who was watching, but for the first time, I felt safe enough not to care. Our lips met and we lingered in the moment, arms wrapped around each other, fingers lost in the other's hair.

THE LAST MORNING, we headed to one class at Roller-Con that was particularly attractive to those of us suffering from a derby-related ailment: Care & Maintenance of the Derby Athlete. Jill Nye the Science Guy, our teacher, wore anatomic tights that illustrated all the bones, muscles, and tendons in her legs. She began by informing us that roller derby wreaked havoc on the body, and not just because of its inherent danger. The real threat, according to Jill, was not the sudden trauma of a broken ankle or cracked rib—it was the imbalance created in the body by skating only in a counterclockwise direction, something that had never even occurred to me to worry about. What we called "derby direction" she called "the left turn of death." She also stressed the importance of balancing out our movements.

Lying on the carpet with our feet planted firmly on the wall, Jill instructed us to dig our left heels in and flatten our spines as if we were turning right on a roller derby track. The exercise hurt my leg, and I stopped right as Jill was approaching me to check my form. She ran a finger along my scar—a sensation I could just barely feel—and asked, "Tib fib?"

I nodded.

"When you start skating again, it will be so important to maintain balance," she said. "Don't just skate derby direction. Don't just rely on that strong right leg to turn left all day.

You're going to have to do what's uncomfortable and trust that your body remembers."

It was good advice, but what stood out to me was that Jill had, very deliberately, it seemed to me, said, "*When* you start skating again," not, "*If* you start skating again." I thought about the people I had encountered in Forest Park who asked about my injury and just assumed I would never skate again. Was this the difference between those who played derby and those who didn't?

On the way to my next class, Mental Toughness, I passed Ballroom 1, where Pain Train was leading a tutorial called Game Face Makeup. Lemony Kicket was commanding Ballroom 2; all her students were lying down for Meditation for People Who (Think They) Hate Meditating. Shouting was coming from across the hallway in Ballroom 4, where Sensei Tom was teaching a self-defense and personal safety class.

Em Dash, an editor from New York, was leading the Mental Toughness class. There were about fifteen of us, sitting in desks facing our teacher. Thin and wiry with a tuft of bright purple hair, she leaned toward us to ask the first question: What are you most afraid of?

"Sucking," one woman answered. "Getting hurt," another said. "Letting my teammates down." "Not getting drafted."

I remained silent. I was afraid of all of those things, too, but none of them felt quite right. Some of them were things I *had* been afraid of, but wasn't anymore—not even getting hurt. I had been warned that it would happen, and it had. What *was* I most afraid of? It felt more complicated than physical pain. Something I couldn't figure out how to articulate in a quick soundbite. My mother? Failure? Gaining weight? I was afraid of a thousand things. I felt scared all the time. But what did it all come down to? Why did none of these individual things sound quite right?

It wasn't until an hour later, while watching a bout called Drag Queens vs. Drag Kings, that it dawned on me. Kelly and I were sitting with Diamond again, and just like with Robots vs. Zombies, it was impossible not to root for both sides equally. Every single player had gone all out; the drag ranged from ultra femme to over-the-top masculine, with everything in between.

One woman had fashioned a beard out of her ponytail; Scald Eagle was wearing her sister's mustache and had donned the name Rodger. Every time she broke through the pack of drag queens, she flexed her muscles in a loud mockery of masculinity. Even the referees were in drag; they wore purple ball gowns and long pink wigs under their helmets. Occasionally, one pretended to trip while making a call and showed the crowd his lacy pink underwear. It was messy and extreme and cartoonish. Everyone was fully inhabiting and totally owning their individual gender performance. There was so much power in their boldness, and it was beautiful.

I felt overcome with the kind of full-hearted joy I could only recall ever feeling before in dreams, where I was free of self-doubt and anxiety, unencumbered by the concerns of reality. I watched Scald Eagle do a 360 jump and felt my heart flutter. It was, ironically, in this moment of pure joy that I realized what I was most afraid of: that I would lose the belonging I'd just begun to feel in this world, in this sport and this team.

When I first entered the Skatium, I was, without knowing it, taking my first step into a community where I'd discovered true friendship, healthy athleticism, accepting community, and proud queerness. The fear that I would lose it all was partly connected to my injury, but truthfully, it had been present since the beginning. Even if I got back on skates, even if I proved myself to be a valuable member of the team, was there something within me—something just plain wrong about me—that would prevent me from ever really belonging? Would I wake up one day and find myself rejected? Could I really trust that the love I felt from this community was unconditional?

Scald Eagle passed four of the opposing team's blockers by scooting around them on the outside line. My palms were sweating. I felt exactly like I did on the precipice between sleeping and waking, when I could still sense the contentment of my dreamscape, but also felt it evaporating in the face of my return to reality.

The game went on, unaffected by the earthquake I felt in my core. I was dogged by the threat of conditional love, I realized. Maybe my mother and I weren't so different. Fear is a powerful motivator. It had turned me competitive to my own detriment, fostered a ruthless eating disorder, kept me small and silent and separate. What role had fear played for my mother? For the first time, I could see the fear in her bravado. Her tantrums. Her judgment—even her cruelty. I could see fear in her reluctance to leave the little sphere of my hometown. How easy it was for both of us to seek power and control in the only places we could: in food, in our bodies, in our homes.

A sense of peace washed over me. I saw Kelly cheering, the announcers shouting, the players crashing into the walls and the floor and each other, but it was as if the volume had been turned down. I, too, had clung to the place I was most comfortable: the constant state of terror in which I'd grown up. When I was little, one of our neighbors had a dog that was contained in their backyard by an invisible fence. Years passed before I realized that the "fence" was electricity that pulsed through the dog's collar—and that, after a while, the dog didn't even have to be wearing the collar to stay within bounds. This was the kind of conditioning my mother relied on . . . and that I had relied on, too. If I could avoid being out of bounds—gaining weight, not being tough, losing races, exiting the family sphere, being gay—I thought I could stay safe and loved. But I'd taken that conditioning all the way to the end, and it hadn't delivered on its promise.

Sitting there on the bleachers next to the woman I loved, who was here with me in this absurd little pocket of Las Vegas because she loved me back, I thought about how out of place my mother looked in that hip St. Louis thrift store, searching desperately for a skirt I might like. I remembered her tone when she said that she had no interest in a short tour of our apartment—or of seeing any of St. Louis at all. It wasn't so complicated after all, I realized. My mother felt the most comfortable in spaces where she felt in control, where she could elicit fear rather than feel it herself. I never thought there would be much overlap in the places we felt we belonged, but I wasn't so sure anymore. If drag is a performance of the absurdity of gender, then maybe roller derby is a theater to explore fear and being feared—exerting power and losing power. Maybe I'd just found a different avenue for having those same things. To be feared. To have power. The difference was that within the confines of the track, there were equitable rules and shared goals. The difference was that I didn't have to hurt anyone else to find what I was looking for. Including myself.

. . .

ON THAT FIFTH and final day of RollerCon, Bruised Boutique appeared pillaged. No one had bothered to make the
shelves look full; they bore all the signs of ransacking. Empty
cardboard boxes were piled like snowbanks along the room's
edges. The sparkly red skate laces were mixed in with the
purple. Volunteers took down tents by snapping and folding
their legs. Kelly and I passed a person who stuck their entire
arm into a box of half-off booty shorts to grab a pair with
black and blue sequins. "I think my ass might fit in these!"
they said.

Tutz, who was always so sprightly and energized, sat
under the Roller Derby Elite tent with her feet up while
Bled massaged her shoulders. All the sponsored skaters working in the boutique were visibly exhausted—which made me
feel guilty for waiting until the last day to try on a new pair
of skates.

As Kelly and I walked through Bruised Boutique, she
suddenly stopped and grabbed my arm.

"Are you going to skate again?" she asked. No pretense.
No beating around the bush.

It was the question that had been on my mind all weekend, and I didn't know if I was brave enough to face it yet. I
couldn't give her a firm answer. Maybe I still wasn't sure.
Maybe I had never been in doubt. Maybe getting back on
skates felt inevitable after five days of being surrounded by
people who assumed I would return because that's just what
we did. Or maybe, in twenty, forty, sixty years, I would curse
myself. I'd call myself young and stupid and point to the scars
on my body as evidence. Maybe, maybe, maybe.

In Bruised Boutique, an Australian skater with white hair
and green lips handed me a leather boot. She was striking; I
could tell Kelly thought so too by the way her gaze lingered.

When I shook my head no, she offered me another skate, this one narrower and lighter. There were no wheels—it was easier to try on skates without wheels—but it wasn't hard to skate a couple laps in my mind. I had been skating this way since my accident.

"How's it feel?" the Aussie asked once I'd put it on. "Lots of people like this boot. Why don't you try the other one too?"

Kelly gestured toward my injured leg. "She still can't feel this," she said, running a finger down the side of my kneecap and down my shin.

I slid my foot into the wheel-less roller skate. I stood up, wiggled my toes in the boots, and shifted my weight like I would if I were skating. I shook my head. "No, I feel it," I said. "For the first time. I feel everything."

ON THE ROOFTOP of the convention center, there was a pool shaped like a uterus. In the moonlight, everyone I passed looked mysterious: a skater named Papa Crisis sauntered by in a bowler hat and a tuxedo with the arms ripped off and "69" painted on the back. Someone whose fishnets stretched higher than her bellybutton, stopping only at the bottoms of her breasts. A woman in a wheelchair with feathers in her hair. I watched as she entered the pool and the feathers haloed like a headdress.

Kelly stayed back in a lounge chair, just like the first day she took me to the community pool. As I climbed into the cervix of the uterus-shaped pool, she smiled up toward the stars it was too foggy to see. *She's moon-bathing,* I thought. *I shouldn't interrupt her.* But how desperately I wanted her to feel this water, warm and syrupy, so different from the harsh, cold pool where we first met in college. Here, there were no lanes and no starting blocks, just bodies. This pool, pulsing with sound, on the rooftop of the Worldwide Roller Derby Convention, was the place where all the freaks and queers and misfits commuted to from their typical place in the margins. I felt at home.

Miss Joan of Spark, is that you? I thought to myself. I had never imagined I would find a little place of queer heaven like this—especially back when I was kissing Kelly under bridges, back when my mother was screaming, "Don't do this to me!" Maybe I wasn't afraid of not belonging to derby, to these beautiful outsiders in all their glory. Maybe I was afraid of not belonging to myself. I bounced on my good leg until I was in the water up to my waist, then turned, put my injured leg down, and began walking back toward the edge again, the water getting shallower with every step. The pool was crowded, but no one knocked into me. One step after the other.

A woman wearing only Calvin Klein boxers jumped into the pool. She was far enough away from me that I wasn't thrown off balance, but close enough that the water from her splash hit my face. When I opened my eyes again, everything was blurry, but I didn't feel afraid. I kept walking until I found the wall of the uterus pool and pulled myself out. The bass was a pulse. There was a sudden shriek of laughter somewhere near me. I reached for a towel to rub the water from my eyes—each time I blinked, I could see more clearly. Two women in Burger King crowns wading near the ovaries. A dancing figure wearing a bedazzled ape mask. Kelly, lounging in the moonlight, her hand reaching for mine. The grace at the center of the holy mess.

JOAN OF SPARK

Three years later

The morning of the day Kelly and I planned to elope, in October of 2020, I got a text message from Muckety Muck, the derby announcer. "Hiya!" it said. "Sorry for the last-minute request. We want to do a news story on the weddings at City Hall today. Can I shoot your ceremony?"

I read the message a few times, my stomach knotting up. I didn't care so much about the cameras—I'd gotten used to them in the past three years of derby bouts and team photo shoots. I found that I thrived in the limelight, and had even been in a couple of local news TV spots with the team in the last couple of years. The knotting was more about Kelly than me. I was certain she wouldn't be excited about it, and I didn't want any bit of disagreement on our big day.

I figured the best approach was casual and direct, and shouted into the bathroom, where she was taking a shower. "Kelly! Muck wants to put our wedding on the news!"

The water turned off and the curtain flung open. "Did

you say we're going to be on the news?" she asked, grabbing a towel.

"Only if you want to," I said.

A year earlier, back when I proposed to Kelly, we envisioned a Halloween wedding at Das Bevo, a German event space with an iconic spinning windmill, 150 guests in costume, a full dinner, and a spread of small, spooky wedding cakes made by my teammate CupQuake, who worked as a professional baker. We'd purchased 150 sparkly mini pumpkins at Walmart for half off the day after Halloween and puffy-painted our wedding date onto every single one, handing most of them out at derby events.

Then the coronavirus pandemic hit. Like thousands of other engaged couples, we canceled our wedding in spring 2020, writing personalized notes to everyone who was invited. Everyone was understanding and sympathetic to the situation. "Maybe next year," they said. And like thousands of other couples, we were hugely disappointed, but we didn't let ourselves dwell.

At the time, I was working as a teacher in a correctional center. I had a class of seventeen incarcerated men, some of whom were writing poetry and essays for the first time. When quarantine began and all visitors were banned from entering the prison, we switched to an online-only platform. The men wrote me from inside the walls: *Things are batshit crazy in here. Everyone has lost their goddamn minds. We miss you. When will we see you again?*

There was always a sense of urgency to their messages. Working with these men made me feel silly for lamenting a canceled wedding: the act of planning a wedding on its own, pre-coronavirus, had made me feel frivolous at times. Now my students' concerns and fears dwarfed any sadness I felt about the whole situation. Most days after teaching I got home from the prison and went straight to bed. Seeing the conditions in which the men were contained gutted me. Reading their poetry and prose about past abuse, both experienced and perpetrated, did me in altogether.

Kelly, on the other hand, still had the job Drive Bi had helped her secure: computer programming at a pharmaceutical company. Since she regularly worked from home, transitioning to a completely remote role was simple. Her biggest challenge was, and always would be, the sexism that accompanied representing such a minority within the company. One of her male coworkers signed her up for a mentorship role, saying, "We need at least one woman in there." Others called her style of communication "aggressive," when she assured me she was just being direct. Working from home posed an additional challenge, however: in our small apartment, I couldn't escape the sounds of her meetings, which droned on all day. Grading and working on my own writing were nearly impossible. We had also adopted two cats, one of which had only one eye, and the apartment was feeling even smaller.

We decided to move. By sheer luck, we found a two-story house off the interstate closer to downtown and our friends. Rent was only a few hundred dollars more than our small apartment, and with the money we'd saved by postponing the wedding, it was well within our price range. It was only about fifteen minutes away from where we had lived before, but it had a big backyard for Lady, an office with a door that shut for Kelly, and room for me to spread out downstairs. Taryn verified that the neighborhood was safe, and on a hot July day, we made the move. Later that evening,

Taryn came by with a ladder and a weed whacker. Betty White Trash, a local-season teammate, came straight from work to help us organize our furniture and plants.

The move was a new side of me: I was learning how to identify and ask for what I need and want, not settle for what was available, or more than I previously thought I deserved.

KELLY AND I felt no hurry to reschedule our wedding initially. When the *Obergefell v. Hodges* ruling had come out in 2015, I had just graduated from college. I was on my way to a nannying job in upstate New York and Kelly was starting graduate school in Ohio. We couldn't celebrate together, and it was still too early in our relationship to be thinking about marriage, but we shared in our elation. The whole country was celebrating equal love.

But when Ruth Bader Ginsburg passed away, there was a sudden wave of uncertainty about how much longer we would have the right to marry. We had endured four years of a Trump presidency and anything seemed possible. Her death seemed to represent plunging back into a time before *Obergefell v. Hodges*. Knowing how volatile and conservative the newly appointed Supreme Court justices were, we felt fearful that by the time the pandemic was over we would be stripped of the right to marry.

It was hard not to remember what my mother had said about my wedding, still a hypothetical, in the months following my coming out and the *Obergefell* ruling. She had started sobbing in church, so suddenly and profusely I had actually thought she'd somehow gotten injured.

"What is it?" I whispered.

"You were supposed to get married here," she said, gesturing to the altar. "Now you never can."

The tears stained her pale face, and I felt a wave of shame pass through my body. Mom was right, and she was wrong. Now in 2020, when I had found the woman I wanted to marry, we still couldn't marry in a Catholic church, and we didn't want to. To my mother, getting married in a church was the gold standard, but to me, churches had only ever represented sin. I could legally marry Kelly and was—in some states, though not all—protected from losing my job for being openly queer. Sometimes I wished my mother could see how happy I was, how I didn't want to get married at any altar, ever. How I never had. But mostly by now, I'd given up wishing for her to see who I really was.

We hadn't spoken in two years. A couple of months after she and Cam left St. Louis, I had tried starting a conversation about a small part of the dysfunction between us—my bulimia, and the fractured way in which I saw my own body and self as a result of the way she had spoken about me as a child. But she couldn't hear it. All she said was "You break my heart." Cam had been forced to choose sides, and she chose my mother. I understood because I would have, too; she was still so dependent, barely eighteen. My dad and I still conversed by email: short missives about work and the weather. Communicating with him was loaded, though. I mostly enjoyed his messages, but they also came with a dose of fear. There was so much potential for pain—so much we didn't say to each other. For one, I didn't tell him about the engagement.

We weren't the only people who worried about LGBTQ rights being rolled back. A couple weeks before, Kelly had encountered a Facebook post sponsored by an organization called Lot's Wife Trans & Queer Chaplaincy. *Come elope (get married) or renew your vows October 12, 13, 14, and 15 in front of City Hall. A bunch of officiants, a photographer, and witnesses will be there to celebrate your love and help you claim your legal rights. Why this time and these dates? Because this is the confirmation hearings for Amy Coney Barrett and she has explicitly indicated she would like to roll back LGBTQ rights including equal marriage and other vital protections for all of us under Roe and the Affordable Care Act. Other people are working on political solutions, Lot's Wife and this huge group of volunteers are doing our part by offering to marry folks while we still have the right to do so.*

It seemed too good to be true: a safe way to get married, just for queer folks, that spoke back to the political disasters happening in Washington.

"Maybe we should do this," Kelly had told me, showing me her screen.

"It's perfect," I agreed.

That evening, we received a text from Kelly's mother. She and Kelly's dad wanted us to know that they supported our decision to elope. They were excited for us, and it felt good to know they had our backs.

We signed up and asked Taryn to be our witness. She then told two of our other recently retired teammates, Boomeryang and R'holler Girl. Soup Beans heard about it and invited herself.

Now it was the big day, and this offer to be married on the actual news felt like just one more unexpected thing 2020 had to offer. Kelly began pulling on jeans, her hair in a towel.

"So what do you think?" I asked. "Are you okay if our wedding is on the news?"

She looked unsure. I stayed silent, remembering when

she had said that she wanted a small wedding with as few people looking at her as possible. Finally, she said, "Do you think people might see and be inspired?" I broke out into a grin. I could tell she was sensing what I was feeling: this was bigger than us.

When we arrived at the courthouse, we parked and put our masks on. It had been months since I'd worn makeup; Kelly was wearing a blazer, which she'd gotten from her freshman roommate in college, that made her feel powerful. It was unseasonably warm for October, so I went without a jacket altogether and instead wore a strappy purple tank. We looked nothing like traditional brides, but we did look like our favorite versions of ourselves. "Thank god you sent a picture this morning," Taryn had written in a text. "I was going to wear the exact same color. Everyone knows you can't wear the same color as the *bride*."

Kelly and I approached City Hall hand in hand. Kelly held our marriage license inside a white envelope, which we had obtained the week before inside City Hall. It had been a quick process; at every step I expected trouble. I didn't think it could be so easy, filing for marriage, especially same-sex marriage. It turned out that even in Missouri, it was simple. Two willing adults. A fifty-five-dollar processing fee. A couple of signatures. That was all it took.

The full impact of what we were about to do didn't register until we found the site of the weddings. There were rainbow balloons, an updated Pride flag, and a banner that said TOGETHER IS THE BEST PLACE TO BE. Streamers were draped around the railings. A crowd of people congregated there, including a queer couple standing in the middle of the steps. One person, the taller of the two, wore an elaborate pink ballgown and glimmering tiara. Their partner, a head shorter, was in a tuxedo. It appeared that the ceremony had just finished; a photographer was shooting portraits of the two of them while the witnesses chatted idly at the bottom of the steps.

"This feels right," Kelly said to me, looking at the just-married couple, the Lot's Wife staff, the decorations strung about.

"Yes," I said. "This is absolutely perfect."

Pastor Tori, the leader of Lot's Wife, met us on the sidewalk in front of City Hall with cupcakes and gift bags. They were a big person with a warm disposition, and they handed everything to us with a kind of flourish. "These are provided by my congregants," they said. "People in the community who support you and your love."

As I accepted the items Pastor Tori gave to us, I realized that I had never met a nonbinary pastor before. There was a nonbinary minister on the derby team, but I had never seen them in a religious context. I had never seen any female, queer, or trans person in any position of power in church, which is why Pastor Tori's presence was so special. It also felt somewhat surreal to be the beneficiaries of such kindness: strangers who had taken the time to bake, buy, and craft us trinkets through which we could remember our special day. I didn't know what to say to Pastor Tori except thank you.

My eyes flickered to the couple still taking photos, and Pastor Tori glanced up at them too. "They'll be done in just a minute," they said. "Then it'll be your turn."

"We have to wait for—" I started, turning around to check the sidewalk behind me. And there they all were. Taryn, in a shimmery silver top and newly dyed purple hair.

Soup Beans, in a green crop top, high-waisted floral skirt, and combat boots. R'holler and Boomer, in their typical athletic apparel. And Muckety Muck, with a gigantic camera resting on his left shoulder and one of the TV anchors I'd seen on Channel 2 following closely behind.

"My wedding party!" I finished. Underneath my mask, I was beaming. I could tell Kelly was too by the way her eyes squinted. They had started out my friends, but now they were hers too. Really, they had become family. Over the past three years we'd been to countless volunteering events, derby trips, and even a weekly *RuPaul's Drag Race* Watch Party at Soup Beans's house on Friday nights. We looked forward to it all week, especially Kelly, who was elated she finally knew someone who loved *RuPaul* as much as she did. Early in the pandemic, Soup Beans had instituted a virtual talent show, in which Tutz lip-synced "She Fucking Hates Me" by Puddle of Mudd in full drag, Taryn intrigued the audience with a series of string tricks, and Kelly showcased her yo-yo tricks live for the first time. Her performance was called "Yos and Hos" and she won third place, after Tutz, who won second, and Snotface, who had done a striptease, which involved removing over thirty shirts and ended with an accidental shot of her nipple.

I loved being virtually surrounded by derby teammates, but it did make the sting of losing roller derby so much harder. A week before all derby bouts were canceled for the foreseeable future due to Covid-19, I had made the All Stars team. Bricktator had looked me in the eye after practice, put her hands on my shoulders, and said, "You nabbed the last spot. It's time to work."

Never had I been more ready to devote myself fully to a

team before. Arch had lost the bronze medal to Victorian Roller Derby League of Australia in the semifinals of the WFTDA championship in 2019. That memory was still fresh for these skaters, and they were hungry for gold in 2020. To be drafted onto one of the best roller derby teams in the world—especially after so recently suffering such a bad injury—was an honor. And even though we stayed in touch virtually—drag makeup sessions with Tutz, virtual workouts with Ida, and small-space skating practice in my driveway with Brick—it didn't feel the same.

For the first time in my life, I had nothing I needed to be training for. Nothing to work toward. No reason to push my body to the breaking point. For the first two weeks, I didn't accept the pandemic as a reality and continued working out twice a day—runs in the morning and homemade workouts by Loki in the afternoon with Kelly. As we watched the Covid cases and deaths climb, however, I began to accept that derby would not be returning anytime soon. I stopped running and doing bodyweight exercises and gently suggested to myself that it was okay if my only exercise was walking Lady.

Some days that was easier to accept than others. There were days I still pushed myself relentlessly for no reason other than to silence the voices in my head that noticed my changing body and labeled my decisions as laziness. But most days, I let Lady stop and sniff when she wanted to instead of yanking her along as quickly as possible. I used that time to take in my new neighborhood: the houses, the trains that passed by on the hour, the cats that roamed the streets, the ferns that swayed in my neighbors' yards. Sometimes, I could shut into a little box the voices urging me to move faster and bury it in the back of my mind, instead focusing on the wind on my cheeks, the gentle pull of Lady's leash in my palm.

Pastor Tori waved to my wedding party. "Amazing! I think we're just waiting for Kim," they said.

"Who's Kim?" Kelly asked.

"Kim is Sunday," I said. "The woman who's marrying us."

Kelly's eyes widened with pleased recognition; I'd told her Sunday was marrying us, but Kelly of course didn't know her real name. Ever since she had moved to St. Louis from Denver a year earlier, we had referred to her by her derby name, Sunday School Slammer. I vaguely knew that she was a queer minister at a progressive church downtown, but I had no idea she would be involved with these pop-up weddings until I saw a status she'd written on Facebook that said she would be presiding over them. When I'd reached out to ask if she would be the one to marry us, she said she would be honored.

Sunday arrived a few minutes later. She was wearing a dark pantsuit and carrying several garment bags. She wished Kelly and me a happy wedding day and told us to pick out what we wanted her to wear. In one bag was a set of expensive-looking elaborate gold robes. In another, a simple pride scarf and minister's collar.

Kelly and I were in agreement: the pride scarf and minister's collar best suited our simple ceremony. Sunday strung it around her neck and did a last-minute check of our ceremony on her tablet. "I think we're ready to go!" she announced.

At the top of the City Hall steps, Kelly and I removed our masks. Taryn, Soup Beans, and our other derby friends stood lining the steps. Muck and the anchor set up at the bottom

with Pastor Tori. Sunday stood several steps below us, looking up at us with her copy of our ceremony open like a
hymnal. A small crowd of people had gathered—people who
I didn't know but stood in support of us. Standing at the top
of the steps, it was hard not to imagine the crowd we had
planned for this day: the rest of my derby team, grad school
friends, high school and college friends, Kelly's family.

Kelly took my hand, and we waited for the crowd to
quiet down. As the two of us stood there hand in hand, I felt
completely at peace. I felt love for the people witnessing, for
the cars passing by on the busy road, for the weather, for the
birds, for my forever partner.

Sunday started to speak, and I did my best to concentrate
on what she was saying. I wanted to be present, not drifting
back into the past or speculating about the future, but right
here in this moment like I sometimes was on walks with
Lady. Kelly's hands were sweaty in mine. I wanted to be even
closer to her, closer to our future together.

I could see Muck's camera on me as I repeated my vows
after Sunday. Then it was Kelly's turn. Her voice wavered
with nerves, but she projected the vows loudly. We exchanged rings—simple rubber things we'd been wearing for
the past year with plans on picking out metal ones once the
pandemic was over. Sunday pronounced us wife and wife
and invited us to kiss.

I touched Kelly's cheek as her face got closer to mine.
Unlike at RollerCon, I had no fears about kissing in public
this time, no story in my head about what might happen if
the wrong people saw. We kissed long and slow as people
cheered. I felt my heart swell; I could tell Kelly's was swelling
too by how tightly she squeezed my hands.

. . .

BACK HOME THAT evening, makeup scrubbed off and in our sweats, Kelly and I watched our news segment air. Tory had surprised us with a wedding cake in the shape of a heart, and both of us had a giant piece in front of us. My derby group chat was exploding in anticipation.

Suddenly, the anchor I recognized from earlier that day was on screen, explaining the concept for the pop-up weddings, describing Lot's Wife, and introducing the viewers to Kelly and me—a couple whose wedding had been thwarted by the pandemic. My face was suddenly on screen, and I was explaining that queer people were at risk of losing their right to marry, that Kelly and I wanted to secure that right while we still could. Watching us get married on TV made my heart beat fast with excitement and pride. How I longed for my ten-year-old self to see us. What would she think? I wondered. Probably that it was a little weird. But it would save her so much pain and confusion later on; it would give her something to remember and cling to.

THE FOLLOWING MORNING after breakfast, I received an email from my dad. *Saw the news segment last night,* he wrote. I expected him to express anger, or maybe hurt that I hadn't shared with him our plans to elope, but what followed instead was a question. *What exactly is "queer"?* he wrote. *That was not an endearing term when I was young. What does it mean now?* I showed Kelly the message and she looked at me, puzzled.

"Does he really not know?" she asked. It was hard for her to imagine parents so in the dark about basic LGBTQ terminology when hers had been so accepting of their three queer children.

"I guess he's trying to learn," I said. It made me feel warm, but also a little bit freaked out. I wanted him to know about the wedding, wanted him to be curious and kind and loving and supportive, but his message also felt somewhat obtrusive. I had spent the previous day surrounded by love and support, and suddenly there was my dad's name in my inbox, and all the potential to feel the bottom drop out. Staring at his name, I felt panic about what his email might say. And relief at what it did not say: *This is the last straw. I cannot accept this. It's over. I'm done.* Or worse—a description of what my mother had done when she found out, which could include any number of unpleasant behaviors. How would I explain what *queer* meant to someone who refused to or simply couldn't see my queerness for years? This was an important opportunity, I knew, and I didn't want to let it pass by. There was freedom in knowing that I belonged to myself now, not to him or my mother. I'd spent the past three years learning that I answered to myself; I only had to address his question if I wanted to, and I did.

Our house was a mess from the day before; our presents from Pastor Tori were scattered all over the table, a JUST HITCHED wreath Boomer had made us lay at the foot of the front door. I closed my computer and we got up from the kitchen table to begin cleaning. We hung the etching Taryn had done for us—our initials and yesterday's date—and Boomer's wreath. All the fake flowers in Paster Tori's gifts we placed in a vase on the front desk. The four little pride flags we had waved in pictures we displayed next to the flowers, so they would be the first thing we saw when we entered. Kelly pulled her hair back as we admired the entrance, and I thought how beautiful she was with the light from the window illuminating her neck.

I started sweeping the dog hair off the steps, then broke our comfortable, warm silence. "I'm going to tell him that *queer* is a word we reclaimed," I said. I knew it would be hard for him to understand. Where I'm from, the only thing reclaimed is the wood used to build a shed in the backyard.

"I think that's good," Kelly said. She was wiping down the mug stains from the coffee table. "Tell him things are changing."

I looked around at our house, at the fluorescent OPEN sign we'd purchased at a vintage shop, at the side table I'd découpaged that held the basket with our keys, the leg lamp with a skate as its base that Kelly had made the year before, and all the candles I had set up on the bookcase. I looked at the silver rubber ring on my finger, a placeholder for when we could visit jewelry shops again, and at my sleeping dog. I looked at our art hung in frames on the wall, at my skating awards and the pride flags.

I would tell him things were changing. And they were.

ACKNOWLEDGMENTS

Versions of these chapters have appeared in *Boulevard Magazine*, *Brevity: A Journal of Concise Literary Nonfiction*, *Hobart*, and *just femme & dandy*. Deep gratitude to the editors for believing in my potential.

Thank you to the Kimmel Harding Nelson Center for the Arts for offering the time and space to begin transforming a random series of essays about roller derby into chapters of a full-length memoir.

Thank you to my MFA advisors, Kathleen Finneran and Edward McPherson, and the special people I met at Washington University in St. Louis who had a hand in making this book possible, especially Elizabeth Brown, Daniella Linares, Gwen Niekamp, Katie Rice-Guter, Lydia Paar, Miranda Popkey, David Schuman, and Sylvia Sukop.

To my biggest advocate and mentor, Diane Seuss, who told me once, "Our stories—of our origins—are very important to many people. They embolden others. Remember that."

To my Arch Rival family: thank you for being an inspiration—for this book, and in my life. I want to especially thank Sandy Giovannetti for being my most important role model on the track and off.

Thank you to my Kalamazoo College community, especially Kathy Milliken and the swim team.

My good friends Alli Buttermore and Ariel Hoeft have been my supporters from the beginning. Thank you for cheering for me, whether that's at the end of my lane or from across the country.

My medical team and physical therapists at St. Anthony's Hospital and Washington University in St. Louis mended my bones and my faith in the kindness of strangers. Thank you.

Endless gratitude to Margaret Howard and Kathy Dobbs for being examples of the kind of fierce women I hope to become and giving me the courage to boldly tell my story to the world.

Sarah Einstein and Addie Tsai were two of the earliest readers for this manuscript; I'm so grateful for their patience and expertise.

To my dear agent, Markus Hoffmann, and Regal Hoffmann & Associates: thank you for finding me, believing in my work, and being champions of this book.

Nicky Watkinson, all the way in London, applied a keen eye to these pages; I am so grateful to have worked with her.

Thank you to M&D Media for the incredible author portrait.

Thank you, beyond measure, to Dial Press, especially Whitney Frick, Donna Cheng, Evan Camfield, Elizabeth Rendfleisch, Madison Dettlinger, Debbie Aroff, Avideh Bashirrad, Andy Ward, Cassie Gonzales, Briony Everroad, and Erin Richards for their support and professionalism.

Katy Nishimoto: when I was dreaming of an editor for this project, I didn't dare let myself imagine someone as profoundly smart and empathetic as you. You see me. You understand my vision and my capabilities. You know how and when to push me further. Thank you from the bottom of my heart.

Finally, and especially, I thank my wife, Kelly, without whom this would be a very different story.

ABOUT THE AUTHOR

GABE MONTESANTI is a queer Midwestern roller derby player. She earned her MFA in creative nonfiction from Washington University in St. Louis. Her piece "The Worldwide Roller Derby Convention" was recognized as a notable essay in *The Best American Essays*. She lives with her wife in Denton, Texas, where she teaches creative writing at the University of North Texas.